Power versus Prudence:
Why Nations Forgo Nuclear Weapons

With the end of the Cold War, nuclear non-proliferation has emerged as a central issue in international security relations. While most existing works on nuclear proliferation deal with the question of nuclear acquisition, T.V. Paul explains why some states have decided to forswear nuclear weapons even when they have the technological capability or potential capability to develop them, and why some states already in possession of nuclear arms choose to dismantle them.

In *Power versus Prudence* Paul develops a prudential-realist model, arguing that a nation's national nuclear choices depend on specific regional security contexts: the non-great power states most likely to forgo nuclear weapons are those in zones of low and moderate conflict, while nations likely to acquire such capability tend to be in zones of high conflict and engaged in protracted conflicts and enduring rivalries. He demonstrates that the choice to forbear acquiring nuclear weapons is also a function of the extent of security interdependence that states experience with other states, both allies and adversaries. He applies the comparative case study method to pairs of states with similar characteristics – Germany/Japan, Canada/Australia, Sweden/Switzerland, Argentina/Brazil – in addition to analysing the nuclear choices of South Africa, Ukraine, South Korea, India, Pakistan, and Israel. Paul concludes by questioning some of the prevailing supply side approaches to non-proliferation, offering an explication of the security variable by linking nuclear proliferation with protracted conflicts and enduring rivalries.

Power versus Prudence will be of interest to students of international relations, policy-makers, policy analysts, and the informed public concerned with the questions of nuclear weapons, non-proliferation, and disarmament.

T.V. PAUL is an associate professor in the Department of Political Science, McGill University. He has published several books and numerous articles on international security and the politics of nuclear weapons, including *Asymmetric Conflicts: War Initiation by Weaker Powers, the Absolute Weapon Revisited: Nuclear Arms and the Emerging International Order,* and *International Order and the Future of World Politics.*

FOREIGN POLICY, SECURITY, AND STRATEGIC STUDIES

Editors: Jacques Lévesque and Charles-Philippe David

The Foreign Policy, Security, and Strategic Studies Series seeks to
promote analysis of the transformation and adaptation of foreign
and security policies in the post–Cold War era. The series welcomes
manuscripts offering innovative interpretations or new theoretical
approaches to these questions,
whether dealing with specific strategic or policy issues or with the
evolving concept of security itself.

MONOGRAPHS
*Canada, Latin America, and the New Internationalism:
A Foreign Policy Analysis, 1968–1990*
Brian J.R. Stevenson

*Power versus Prudence:
Why Nations Forgo Nuclear Weapons*
T.V. Paul

COLLECTIONS
NATO *after Fifty:
Enlargement, Russia, and European Security*
Edited by Charles-Philippe David and Jacques Lévesque

Power versus Prudence

Why Nations Forgo Nuclear Weapons

T.V. Paul

The Centre for Security and Foreign Policy Studies
and
The Teleglobe+Raoul-Dandurand
Chair of Strategic and Diplomatic Studies

McGill-Queen's University Press
Montreal & Kingston · London · Ithaca

© McGill-Queen's University Press 2000

ISBN 0-7735-2086-4 (cloth)
ISBN 0-7735-2087-2 (paper)

Legal deposit fourth quarter 2000
Bibliothèque nationale du Québec

Printed in Canada on acid-free paper

This book has been published with the help of
a grant from the Humanities and Social Sciences
Federation of Canada, using funds provided by
the Social Sciences and Humanities Research
Council of Canada.

McGill-Queen's University Press acknowledges
the financial support of the Government of
Canada through the Book Publishing Industry
Development Program (BPIDP) for its publishing
activities. It also acknowledges the support of
the Canada Council for the Arts for its
publishing program.

Canadian Cataloguing in Publication Data

Paul, T.V.
Power versus prudence:
why nations forgo nuclear weapons
(Foreign policy, security and strategic studies)
Copublished with the Centre for Security
and Foreign Policy Studies and the
Teleglobe+Raoul-Dandurand Chair of Strategic
and Diplomatic Studies.
Includes bibliographical references and index.
ISBN 0-7735-2086-4 (bound) –
ISBN 0-7735-2087-2 (pbk.)
1. Nuclear weapons – Government policy.
2. Nuclear nonproliferation.
3. Security, International. I. Université
du Québec à Montréal. Centre d'études
des politiques étrangères et de sécurité.
II. Teleglobe+Raoul-Dandurand Chair of
Strategic and Diplomatic Studies. III. Title.
IV. Series.
U264.P38 2000   327.1'747   C00-900058-5

Typeset in Sabon 10/12
by Caractéra inc., Quebec City

Contents

Acknowledgments

With the demise of the Cold War, nuclear proliferation has become one of the major challenges to international order. The nuclear tests by India and Pakistan in May 1998 and the reported efforts by other states, especially North Korea, Iran, and Iraq, to acquire nuclear weapons have increased international attention paid to the subject. Statesmen and scholars, especially in the West, have been concerned about the arrival of several states with nuclear weapons since the early days of the nuclear age. This resulted in the creation of the non-proliferation regime and a number of restrictive measures designed to prevent the transfer of technology and materials to potential nuclear states. However, during the five decades since the advent of the atomic age, several technologically capable states chose to forgo their option of building deliverable nuclear weapons, while some erstwhile nuclear states gave up their acquired nuclear arms, generating a gap between popular expectations and the empirical reality regarding the nuclear choices of nation-states. The enormous attention being paid to the question of why nations acquire nuclear weapons is not complemented by efforts to shed light on why countries forgo nuclear weapons. This book attempts to provide a theoretical explanation for the puzzle of nuclear forbearance by several technologically capable states, while simultaneously explaining nuclear acquisition by some others.

I have benefited enormously from the kindness of colleagues, friends, and family members while researching and writing this book. Several colleagues read chapters or the full manuscript and provided valuable comments and criticisms. They include: Robert Art, Mark Brawley, Lawrence Broz, Marc Busch, Francis Gavin, John Hall, Richard Harknett, Albert Legault, David Mares, Baldev Raj Nayar, Phil Oxhorn, and James Wirtz.

I revised the manuscript while I was a visiting scholar at the Center for International Affairs (CFIA) and the Olin Institute for Strategic Studies, Harvard University, during 1997–98. The support extended by Jennifer Cairns, Michael Desch, Anne Emerson, Jeff Frieden, and Inga Peterson was invaluable, and the center's active intellectual life was a constant stimulus. Seminar presentations at Harvard and elsewhere allowed me to test my ideas, and I learned from remarks made by several scholars. I thank Samuel P. Huntington and the pre- and post-doctoral fellows at Olin for their criticisms and comments. I am grateful to organizer Brian Mandell and participants at CFIA's Canada Seminar, where I presented the material on Canada (in chapter 4), and organizers Michael Brown and Sean Lynn-Jones at the Belfer Centre for Science and International Affairs, where I delivered chapter 3, on Germany and Japan.

For their hosting of work-in-progress seminars and their valuable comments, I also thank Robert Art and Seyom Brown at Brandeis University; Michael Mastanduno and Alexander Wendt at Dartmouth College; Kanti Bajpai and B. Vivekanandan at the Jawaharlal Nehru University, New Delhi; Christopher Coker and Terry McNamee at the London School of Economics; James Clay Moltz and Tariq Rauf at the Monterey Institute of International Studies; Lynn Eden and Scott Sagan at Stanford University; Allan Castle, Brian Job, and Mark Zacker at the University of British Columbia; Patrick Morgan, Wayne Sandhoz, and Alec Stone at the University of California – Irvine; Benjamin J. Cohen at the University of California – Santa Barbara; Christine Ingebester and Resat Kasaba at the University of Washington.

Grants and financial support came from the Rockefeller Foundation, the now-defunct Cooperative Security Competition Program of the Canadian Department of Foreign Affairs, and McGill University's Faculty of Graduate Studies and Research. I thank the Rockefeller Foundation's Thomas Graham and Rebecca Rittgers for their support, and the chair of McGill's Political Science Department, Hudson Meadwell, for granting me timely leave to work on the book. I also thank Jacques Lévesque, editor of the security and foreign policy series, and Aurèle Parisien, editor, at McGill-Queen's University Press, for their interest and support. Several individuals assisted me during my field research trips to Argentina, Brazil, Germany, India, Japan, Korea, South Africa, Sweden, Switzerland, and Ukraine. Graduate students who provided research assistance include Christian Dinwoodie, Saira Khan, Mark Lanteigne, Matthieu Moss, Mark Peranson, and Kirsten Rafferty.

I thank my wife, Rachel, and daughters, Kavya and Leah, for their love, understanding, and patience during my several absences from home to research and write this book.

PART ONE

Theory

CHAPTER ONE

Introduction:
Theory and Nuclear Weapons Choices

This book addresses two related paradoxes in international politics: the propensity among some states not to acquire nuclear weapons even when they have the technological capability or potential capability to manufacture them, and the decision by some others to forgo nuclear weapons that they already possess. Argentina, Australia, Brazil, Canada, Germany, Italy, Japan, the Netherlands, Norway, South Korea, Spain, Sweden, Switzerland, and Taiwan are some notable examples of the first category of states that forswore their options to build deliverable nuclear weapons despite existing or potential capability. South Africa, a state that had manufactured seven nuclear weapons, Belarus, Kazakhstan, and Ukraine, three successor states of the Soviet Union, gave up the nuclear weapons that they inherited.

Explaining the dynamics of nuclear acquisition and non-acquisition has significance for foreign policy and international relations theory. In the policy realm, non-proliferation goals can be achieved only if we understand what causes states to acquire or forgo nuclear weapons. The theoretical puzzle is that since nuclear weapons carry the ultimate destructive power, states should be extremely sensitive to their possession by friends and foes alike, and yet they forgo their nuclear capabilities. States should also be unwilling to give up their sovereign right to build these weapons, given that from the perspective of deterrence theory, only a country's independent nuclear deterrent capability could guarantee that no nuclear attack on it would take place.[1]

Predictions since the 1950s assumed that atomic weapons would spread in the same way as other major weapons of past epochs. Influential scholars such as Bernard Brodie and Frederick Dunn argued that efforts to control their spread would not succeed.[2] President Dwight Eisenhower, while presenting his Atoms for Peace Proposal to the United Nations in December 1953, warned that the knowledge of nuclear technology possessed by the United States and a few other nations "will eventually be shared by others – possibly all others."[3] President John F. Kennedy, while seeking support for a proposed treaty banning nuclear tests warned that "15 or 20 or 25 nations may have theses weapons" by the 1970s.[4] U.S. policy-makers from the beginning of the atomic age assumed that more countries with technological potential would acquire nuclear weapons in due course. The efforts to establish a non-proliferation regime and various mechanisms for restrictions on nuclear supply sprang from the desire to stem the tide of expected proliferation.

Yet national preferences in this area have been paradoxical; over 186 countries have acceded to the Nuclear Non-proliferation Treaty (NPT) and accepted its rules, norms, and principles. So far, almost all have complied with the regime. Only two signatories (Iraq and North Korea) are presumed to have violated treaty obligations. The nuclear club remains confined to seven declared states (Britain, China, France, India, Pakistan, Russia, and the United States) and one undeclared state (Israel). More significantly, several technologically capable or potentially capable states have forsworn the production of nuclear weapons, which creates the puzzle that is the main focus of this study.

In this book, I argue that contexts and situations matter significantly in explaining the nuclear choices of nation-states. I contend that whether a non-great-power state acquires or goes without nuclear weapons is determined largely by the level and type of security threats that it faces and the nature of interactions or conflict with its key adversaries and allies in its immediate geo-strategic environment. However, the nuclear choices of great powers (Britain, China, France, Russia, and the United States) are determined chiefly by larger powers' relations in the international system. For an aspiring major power (such as India), both regional and global considerations could drive nuclear choices. In chapter 2, I develop the concept of security interdependence to explain the choices of states in non-weaponized strategic environments. Accordingly, a nation could do without nuclear weapons if its leadership perceives that nuclear acquisition would generate intense negative security externalities or costs for others and exacerbate its own security threats by encouraging other states to take countermeasures. These measures could include other states' acquisition of nuclear weapons, targeting of nuclear arms by existing nuclear powers (or increased hostility if they are already targeted), and deterioration of politico-economic relations with allies. While expanding the argument, I introduce a second variable, namely, the level of conflict in a region where a given state is situated, and based on that I create three analytical zones – high conflict, moderate conflict, and low conflict – in order to examine the problem systematically.

In a high-conflict environment, states engage in enduring rivalries and protracted conflicts. Regional states that face nuclear enemies or that do not have a great power protector are likely to acquire nuclear weapons in order to deter their adversaries. States in moderate- and low-conflict regions are more likely to do without nuclear weapons, which could generate high levels of negative security externalities for neighbouring and other states, especially great powers deeply involved in the security affairs of their region. A technologically capable state in a high-conflict region that forgoes nuclear weapons may have credible security guarantees provided by a great power or possess a countervailing capability in conventional and chemical and biological weapons. I also postulate mixed regions: nuclear choices may change as a state's geo-strategic environment changes. In order to provide a dynamic explanation, I draw insights from realism and liberalism, while maintaining their separate assumptions as much as possible. I argue that the explanatory power of these two paradigms for nuclear choices depends on where a nation is situated.

I hope in this book to bring into focus the prudential elements of realism, whereby interests drive national choices, but not always in the direction of maximizing power through greater acquisition of arms. I call this soft realist version "prudential realism" – nations under certain circumstances may prudently forgo military capabilities that other states see as threatening. Norms pertaining to nuclear non-proliferation may be consistent with the interests of national actors who place prudence high in their security calculations. States are security-conscious entities, but their military policies are driven by "most-probable threat" assessments, as opposed to the worst-case assessments offered by hard realism. Cautiousness and enlightened self-interests characterize states' behaviour in a matter such as nuclear weapons, possession of which could generate unanticipated negative consequences.[5] States accordingly balance their interests and capabilities so as to minimize the security challenges they pose to others and in the expectation of reciprocal benign behaviour in return. Prudential realism thus acknowledges the mutual elements of security and explains attempts by countries to avoid generating intense security dilemmas.[6] I argue that hard realist concerns regarding nuclear arming are pertinent especially in the choices of states engaged in enduring rivalries and protracted conflicts in regions of high conflict and are of little relevance for states in zones of low or moderate conflict.

THEORY AND NUCLEAR CHOICES

The processes of states' acquiring and not acquiring nuclear arms have received inadequate attention in international relations theory, although the two prominent theoretical paradigms – realism and liberalism – make strong claims about states' behaviour and their propensity to obtain arms. Many prevailing explanations for nuclear choices fit into these broad paradigms.[7] Using their precepts on national behaviour, I deduce several hypotheses and alternative explanations about how states should behave with respect to nuclear weapons. I next delineate insights from both realist and liberal versions to develop a situational explanation for the nuclear choices of nation-states, especially their decisions to forgo nuclear weapons.

Power-based Explanations

Power-based explanations for nuclear acquisition and non-acquisition derive mostly from the realist theory, especially the hard realist variety.[8] For hard realists, states acquire arms in order to protect their vital interests, including survival in an anarchic international realm. The anarchical system – one that lacks a central governing authority – makes states worry that their neighbours may engage in military actions against them if there is nothing to prevent them from doing so. States therefore perceive the need to be prepared and to deter any possible attacks by acquiring armaments. Countries in such a self-help system would not ordinarily forgo nuclear weapons, because forbearance would require conviction on the part of every country that other states do not possess or have intentions to acquire such arms.[9]

States formulate their security policies, realists argue, on the basis of worst-case assumptions and are wary of the time required for them to catch up with the technological and military capabilities of other states. The result is a constant effort by countries to increase their capability to defend themselves and deter aggression. Any effort by one state to bolster security through this method could decrease the security of another, leading to a condition of security dilemma and a mutual spiralling arms race.[10] Nuclear weapons, combined with air power and missile technology, have decreased the defender's time to respond, and so nations are more likely to acquire nuclear weapons so that they can deter surprise attacks. Self-help should be much greater in this context than in conventional defensive efforts, where one can seek the help of an ally or a great power or undertake one's own defensive measures. Hard realists contend that effective regimes in issue areas such as non-proliferation are rare, because of states' concerns about others' cheating, their own falling behind, and problems with detection.[11] Hard realism sees states as wanting superior weapons capability so as to increase their power and prestige, preserve their autonomy, and obtain wider margins of safety in dealing with the less powerful.[12]

Hard realists therefore believe that states should not ordinarily forgo their right to manufacture weapons that may deter potential adversaries and increase their own power and prestige. If they do so, it should be only because of constraints imposed by the structure of the international system. Specifically, nuclear choices should reflect the relative capabilities of states, their participation in alliances, and their role within the international system.[13] For instance, within a bipolar structure, the leading alliance partners – i.e., the two superpowers – tightly control allied states' nuclear ambitions, whereas a multipolar system allows more states to obtain nuclear weapons. Thus, during the Cold War, structural constraints prevented major states such as Japan and West Germany from acquiring nuclear weapons. With the end of the Cold War, these states are likely to rethink this policy.[14] The structural-constraint argument also assumes that alliance relationships provide some states with a nuclear "umbrella." The nuclear protection that the big-power ally extends could assure a state against nuclear attack without its acquiring a national nuclear capability. The smaller alliance partners would thus "free ride" on the nuclear protection provided by their superpower patron.[15]

A second hard realist perspective – the hegemonic stability theory – would view nuclear forbearance by states as a function of the coercive and non-coercive power of the hegemonic power – i.e., the United States. A hegemon could engage in benign policies, such as economic rewards, or coercive policies, such as economic and military sanctions, to keep subordinate states from acquiring nuclear weapons. Benign policies would constrain most alliance partners while coercion would keep non-allied and unfriendly states in line.[16] For some hard realists, u.s. hegemonic power was also essential for the creation of the non-proliferation regime. Regimes are products of existing power relationships, and they change along with the balance of bargaining power among the states that negotiate them.[17] Additionally, when the hegemonic power that helped create the non-proliferation regime declines, so does the regime, as there is no strong nation to impose regime rules and regulations.

These hard realist arguments seem reasonable and valid in several instances of nuclear forbearance. The factors that hard realists have

identified seem to affect leaders' complex calculations on acquisition
or non-acquisition of nuclear weapons. One may, however, raise questions about their full empirical "fit." To begin with, hard realists, based
on their assumption of anarchy, argue that co-operation is difficult if
not impossible in the security area. The empirical evidence – i.e., the
co-operation thus far developed in non-proliferation – challenges this
basic argument. Many states, both capable and not so capable of
producing nuclear weapons, have adhered to the regime, which takes
away part of their sovereignty in this matter. It seems that the number
of countries that acquired nuclear weapons after the original five is so
small that these cases seem more like an anomaly than the norm.
However, hard realists are right in understanding the anomaly – anarchy-
induced insecurity and desire to obtain hard power military resources
strongly influence some states – as evident in their efforts to acquire
or maintain nuclear weapons.

Let us examine the factors that hard realists use to explain nuclear
forbearance. Although there is substantial merit in alliance-based arguments, they need to be further specified and made conditional if their
validity is to be established beyond doubt. We must figure out how
alliances would forestall nuclear acquisition and how withdrawal of
alliance protection could spur independent national acquisition of
nuclear arms.

Other problems trouble the nexus of alliance and non-proliferation.
First, U.S. protection did not stop allied nations from developing conventional forces, some as part of alliance structures for burden sharing,
but most as independent national forces. What makes nuclear weapons
so different from conventional forces in the thinking of these countries?
Second, most states signing the NPT felt no hegemonic pressure similar
to what the theorists would expect.[18] Most decisions not to acquire
nuclear weapons were national in origin and antedated the active phase
of U.S. non-proliferation policy, which began after India's nuclear test
of 1974. Third, much of the pre-1974 proliferation occurred among
states belonging to alliances. Though not under direct security umbrellas, the alliance relationships of Israel and Pakistan with the United
States, and of India with the USSR, did not prevent these states from
acquiring nuclear weapons.[19] Finally, the majority of states that have
forgone nuclear acquisitions by acceding to the NPT had no security
guarantees against a nuclear attack by another state. These four dis-
crepancies suggest the need for clearer specification of the relationship
between alliances and non-proliferation.

The end of the Cold War and the dismantling of the bipolar structure
should test the realist arguments even further. Although it is premature

to make any definitive conclusions, it is not clear whether allies that were under nuclear umbrellas are rushing to acquire nuclear weapons.[20] Some hard realists have argued that the system change will erode the credibility of nuclear umbrellas and force erstwhile allies such as Germany and Japan to obtain their own nuclear forces.[21] Thus far no clear evidence points to such a change. Perhaps only dramatic alterations in their security environment can produce such a change.

Hard realism, of both classical and structural varieties, makes several postulates on national behaviour with respect to the propensity of states to engage in arms races. Hard realists alert us to the problem of relative gains and the self-help aspect of international politics. These dimensions help explain why some states choose to acquire capabilities such as nuclear weapons. Non-acquisition, however, remains the practice of most states, including some leading countries in the international system. Just as we need to explain arming behaviour, so we must address disarming behaviour and the conditions that facilitate it. Hard realist insights seem to be relevant to some cases, and chapter 2 considers their pertinence, in addition to outlining the elements of prudential realism.

Norm-based Alternatives

The key norm-based explanations for nuclear forbearance come from the liberal schools of institutionalism and interdependence.[22] To liberal institutionalists, international institutions determine or constrain state choices in specific issue areas such as nuclear proliferation, as do the norms and rules contained in regimes.[23] The interdependence school contends that the growing economic interdependence or the "reciprocal effects of mutual dependence" among states has made military conquest difficult. In the national agendas of states that are economically interdependent, military security does not constantly figure as the uppermost item. In addition, states that are economically interdependent do not use military force against each other and therefore rely more on other instruments to exercise power.[24] Some states may devote equal or more attention to economic and welfare goals, and so security considerations become lesser priorities. Hence nuclear forbearance may serve their economic objectives. Additionally, states could realize that attempts to become autarkic or to avoid becoming entangled in interdependent relationships through military aggrandizement would not succeed.[25]

Institutionalist analysis comes principally from regime theorists, especially from functionalists. To functionalists, regimes and institutions regulate state behaviour in many ways. They reduce verification costs and punish violators of norms, while their norms reduce the complexity of decisions. Regimes also provide information to national governments and help solve some major problems of collective action.[26] Liberal institutionalists see national decisions to eschew nuclear arms, especially since the early 1970s when the regime became embedded, as largely the function of constraints imposed by the nuclear non-proliferation regime and its two pillars – the NPT and the safeguards system of the International Atomic Energy Agency (IAEA). The non-proliferation regime establishes several norms, or standards of behaviour regarding acquisition and transfer of nuclear weapons and materials, and these norms would usually prohibit national acquisition of nuclear weapons. The key principle is that "members of the regime should not act in ways that facilitate nuclear proliferation."[27] The regime's norms, rules, and principles ordain that states forgo their nuclear weapons option. A state, once a party to the regime, has "assumed an international legal obligation not to manufacture nuclear weapons" and therefore could face severe repercussions, including social opprobrium, if it abrogates its commitment. It may confront diplomatic isolation or even economic, technical, military, and/or trade sanctions. Worst of all, its action could trigger a domino effect, and its neighbours might decide to acquire countervailing nuclear forces.[28]

Regime theorists contend that regimes can alter actors' interests as well as capabilities. However, they have not yet fully identified the conditions under which regimes alter an actor's interests and choices in national security. It is difficult to specify what a state's choices would be in the absence of regime rules and on issues in which those rules diverge from national interests. Why do some states readily accept regime rules and norms, while others disregard them? Why do some nations undertake legal commitments for a period in order to obtain nuclear materials and then pursue nuclear weapon programs clandestinely? Iraq and North Korea have signed the NPT, yet they have chosen to engage in such secret endeavours. Are there other variables that determine whether a given state would adhere to and continue to abide by the regime's norms and principles? If so, do the independent variables lie in factors other than the regime?

A critical question for regime theorists is at what stage in national decision-making on nuclear weapons a regime becomes the crucial determining factor. Does a nation decide to forswear nuclear weapons prior to its joining the regime or while acceding to it? If it had already made the choice before joining a regime, how much independent effect has the regime exerted on the nation's nuclear policy? A possible method of determination would be to see whether the forbearance decision or forbearance itself preceded subscription to the regime or whether it followed the event. Alternatively, one could look at national deliberations and see how much the regime figured in the decision by leaders not to acquire nuclear weapons.

Another method to ascertain the significance of the regime would be to raise the following questions in different national contexts. Does continuous adherence to the policy of non-development result from constraints imposed by the regime rules? Or has the state already made a choice not to develop nuclear weapons? Would a state break its nuclear promise, in the absence of its adherence to the regime? Until these questions are answered, the independent effect of the regime remains unclear. Yet the regime does serve a purpose; otherwise, few states would have joined in it. Once a state joins the regime and its associated treaties, it could be difficult for it to exit without a powerful reason.

The discussion so far suggests that the liberal perspectives may help us understand sustained nuclear forbearance by states. These explanations touch on the interdependence aspect of interstate interactions and the effect of regimes and norms on states' behaviour. However, these perspectives cannot fully account for why some states acquire nuclear weapons and why some states break regime rules and norms even after adhering to them. Also absent is the role of power and leadership, especially of great powers, in creating a security regime. A comprehensive understanding of nuclear choices should draw theoretical insights from realism and liberalism, while developing a new approach to explaining state choices in an international system in transition.[29] I take up this task in the next chapter, where I develop an explanation that combines power, norms, and interests. The puzzle of nuclear forbearance justifies, I believe, the combining of insights from different paradigms.[30] As I mentioned above, my analysis centres on a refined version of realism called "prudential realism."

TERMS AND DEFINITIONS

A brief discussion of the terms used in this study is essential at this point. I do not use the verb "renounce" to describe the phenomenon of nuclear forbearance because it implies giving up nuclear weapons "definitely." Instead, I use "forgo" and "forswear" interchangeably, as national decisions in this realm are contingent and context-dependent. Critics may argue that it may be prudent to "go nuclear" under certain circumstances, especially if a country's adversary possesses such weapons. In a literal sense, prudence may characterize some decisions to acquire nuclear arms. But the arming behaviour corresponds more to the dictates of hard realism than to those of soft realism, which I categorize as prudential realism.

The use of the term "nuclear proliferation" generates controversy because of the negative connotations attached to it and its excessive use by scholars and by policy makers in declared nuclear-weapons states or their allies, sometimes with political biases obvious. Although I favour the terms "nuclear acquisition" and "non-acquisition," I use "proliferation" and "non-proliferation" occasionally because of the absence of better alternatives that can capture the phenomena with all its political connotations. Some readers may ask whether possession of nuclear materials, even if intended for energy programs, constitutes proliferation. There is some merit in the argument that countries possessing fissile materials have crossed varying thresholds of nuclear acquisition and are latent proliferators. However, it still remains a puzzle as to why these countries have not chosen to develop operational nuclear weapons.

For this study, whatever the state of a country's technological competence, as long as it has not embarked on an operational weapons program and has no plans to do so in the immediate future, I treat it as a "non–nuclear weapon state." In this respect, I differ from the NPT definition of a "nuclear weapon state" as one that acquired nuclear weapons prior to 1 January 1967 and a "non-nuclear weapon state" as any other. This is a politically motivated cut-off date, and it cannot account for four states that have acquired nuclear weapons since then – India, Israel, Pakistan, and South Africa.

CASE SELECTION AND METHODOLOGY

Chapter 2 presents a theoretical model based on situational analysis to explain nuclear forbearance by technologically capable or near-capable non–great power states. Such an analysis would allow for change and variations in national policies and can provide a more comprehensive and nuanced explanation for the arming and dis-arming tendencies of nation states. I attempt to disaggregate factors that affect the choices of states in different circumstances and diverse regional contexts.

The study draws on comparative case-study and process-tracing methods, with some modifications.[31] I also use the method of conceptual homogenization and pairing, comparing in chapters 3–8 pairs of countries with similar attributes on the basis of the concept of "nuclear forbearance."[32] I pair similar types of states on the basis of their key attributes, such as size, politico-economic strategies, alliance relationships, and overall place in the international system. This method allows interstate comparisons of similar states and also inter-type comparisons of pairs of divergent states that are otherwise similar in terms of the outcome variables – i.e., nuclear forbearance and nuclear acquisition.

I draw the cases from various regions, strategic situations, and foreign-policy orientations. They include developed and developing, aligned, neutral, non-allied, and middle and small powers, as well as major economic powers. These states provide variations in case studies across countries of differing contexts, locations, and sizes and thereby increase our confidence in the theory and in the robustness of the findings. The main focus of this study, however, is not the five major nuclear powers (China, France, Russia/USSR, The United Kingdom, and the United States), but the non–great power states. The target is thus not vertical proliferation (increase in the number of weapons held by major nuclear states). The calculations of great powers tend to be global and less regional, and therefore the model may explain only partially their choices concerning nuclear weapons.

The study includes "hard" and "soft" test cases. The hard test cases are Germany and Japan, because they are major economic powers and former great powers that had engaged in protracted conflicts and enduring rivalries with the Soviet Union and enjoyed protection under the U.S. nuclear umbrella. My effort in chapter 3 is to see to what extent their nuclear choices were influenced by the considerations articulated in the theoretical framework of this study. Canada and Australia (chapter 4) are soft test cases, as they are situated in low-conflict regions yet have enjoyed security protection from the United States. Neutral states Sweden and Switzerland (chapter 5) are somewhat hard test cases, as they had no direct nuclear umbrellas yet were hostile to the Soviet Union during the Cold War era. Argentina and Brazil (chapter 6) are also somewhat "hard" test cases as they had no allies and were involved in a limited, enduring rivalry. Chapter 7 discusses three additional examples of nuclear forbearance to see whether the factors identified in this study apply to such other cases as well. These cases – South Africa, South Korea, and Ukraine – provide a supplemental test for my arguments. In chapter 8, I offer a brief discussion on India, Israel, and Pakistan, three instances of nuclear acquisition, to establish whether these cases follow the explanation provided in this study. If they do, the robustness and theoretical validity of this work increase. Chapter 9 draws out theoretical and policy implications and prognoses.

CHAPTER TWO

Explaining Nuclear Forbearance

Both realism and liberalism make strong claims regarding state behaviour in general and conflict and co-operation in particular. And both paradigms furnish insights into national nuclear choices. Yet, singularly, both fail to explain the puzzle of nuclear forbearance adequately. Hard realism tends to overpredict acquisitions of arms (including nuclear) and arms races, while liberalism errs in the opposite direction, with overly optimistic expectations for co-operation and non-proliferation. Although hard realism can account for nuclear acquisitions, there has in fact been much forbearance. Liberalism can elucidate why nuclear non-proliferation may be sustained, but it does not explain proliferation well. The difficulty lies in offering a comprehensive explanation for the choice between acquisition and forbearance, as one cannot shuffle the separate assumptions that these paradigms hold on international politics to fit the particular choice.

This chapter offers a different starting point. I explain nuclear forbearance largely through situational variables, while drawing from the insights of both paradigms without dropping their assumptions about states' behaviour. This framework also helps explain why some states do acquire nuclear weapons and why some parties to the Nuclear Non-Proliferation Treaty (NPT) ignore their obligations. The rationale for this framework is that states' choices with regard to arming vary with their external security contexts, although common patterns can be discerned across cases. The degree and type of security threats that a non–great power state faces, and the conflict dynamics of the region in which it is situated, determine these variations.

Hard realist insights are useful in explaining the nuclear choices of the most heavily involved states in regions with high levels of protracted conflict, whereas liberal perspectives may provide clues as to states' choices in an economically interdependent, low-conflict region.

The framework gives sufficient credit to regime theories, and it includes the rational and normative factors that states consider while choosing not to acquire weapons of mass destruction. The normative consider-ations may arise out of prudence and could include cognizance of power, interests, and principles. The rational basis is that the cost–benefit calculations of national leaders deriving from awareness of their country's position and the probable consequences of their actions antedate their decisions to forgo nuclear weapons. These states behave as prudential realists – i.e., they balance their interests, capabilities, and intentions to the extent of not threatening others while maximizing their own security in a benign environment. The analysis in this chapter concludes with a discussion of the nuclear revolution, the impact of learning since Hiroshima, and the taboo against use of nuclear weapons.

The key situational variables in this study are the level of conflict and co-operation and the level of politico-security interdependence in a given region. Nuclear forbearance occurs when technologically capable non-nuclearized nations, especially non–great power states, seek to avoid a security dilemma situation involving other significant states or states whose behaviour most seriously impinges on their security. This out-come results from the operation of *security interdependence* among states in a region. This concept posits that nuclear choices of techno-logically capable non–great power states depend on the degree of mutual vulnerability and the resultant anticipated sensitivity in their relation-ship with states with which they are connected most closely in the region (henceforth "significant states"), both allies and adversaries. States involved in security interdependence are aware of the consequences of unilateral action more than are states that lack such a relationship.[1]

This interdependence manifests itself in the awareness among tech-nologically capable non–great power states that their behaviour in nuclear matters is tied to the expected behaviour of other significant states with which they interact, especially neighbours, and that there are costly reciprocal effects associated with breaking away from such a relationship. They thus know about the consequences of arming and hence prudently choose to avert a negative outcome. In more formal terms, nuclear forbearance is the result of a conscious effort by tech-nologically capable states not to create an intense negative security externality for other significant actors that will be most affected.[2] These states realize that their nuclear acquisitions would be costly and that they may compel other significant states to take counter-measures, thereby decreasing their own security.[3] Decision-makers in the states that forgo nuclear arms calculate that they can achieve security by eschewing the same weapons that otherwise could provide defence or deterrence. Forbearance may allow a nation to minimize risks and thereby avoid possible losses to its security. Some states could note the possibility of costly arms races resulting from their behaviour; they are thus aware of the operation of the security dilemma as a matter of common sense and know that their acquisition of nuclear weapons would exert pressure on their significant neighbours to obtain counter-vailing capability. If others acquire such capabilities, it would mean a decline in their security and the emergence of a security dilemma, by which I mean an outcome resulting from arms races involving two or more countries.[4]

Moreover, leaders of a technologically capable non–great power state may believe that their acquisition and deployment of nuclear weapons would result in greater conflict with those neighbouring states that they will affect most prominently and the targeting of their countries by hostile nuclear powers. The responses of adversarial states could include, in extreme cases, threat of military strikes and, in ordinary circumstances, balancing behaviour – i.e., seeking the help of extra-regional powers for protection. Allies, especially major-power benefac-tors, could undertake undesirable actions such as reduction or removal of security guarantees and disruption of economic and military sup-port.[5] In the case of a non-allied state, the first consideration could be paramount, but for an allied state, the motivation could be a combi-nation of the two. Decision-makers might thus believe that even though their intention may be to deter potential attacks, actual and potential adversaries as well as allies would view nuclearization as a dangerous step.[6] When other nuclear states target their nuclear weapons on a newly nuclearized state, the latter is in fact decreasing its security, as some of its marginal gains accrued through nuclear acquisition would be nullified by its constant worry about the possibility of an attack, especially if it does not possess a second-strike capability. Thus a state's leadership could come to the conclusion that its acquisition of an indig-enous nuclear capability could diminish its security, while its non-pos-session would help maintain a benign security environment.

Security interdependence can be both symmetrical and asymmetrical. Symmetrical interdependence exists where two states are equally vul-nerable or sensitive to each other's policies; in asymmetrical interdepen-dence, one side's actions matter more to the other side than vice versa. A state is in asymmetrical interdependence in security matters if it is more vulnerable and sensitive to the anticipated behaviour/responses of other states, and consequently it desists from undertaking actions that would increase that vulnerability or sensitivity. Geo-strategic location and historical interaction with other significant neighbouring states are two key factors that determine whether or not a state is in an asym-metrical security interdependent situation.

Is security interdependence unique to nuclear weapons, or is it relevant to conventional, chemical, and biological arms as well? All forms of weaponry can cause negative security externalities, but my contention here is that nuclear weapons carry the highest level of such externalities because of their "uncontestable" nature.[7] In terms of their speed, magnitude, scale of destruction, and long-term consequences for the health of the population and the economic and political survival of the attacked state, nuclear weapons are incomparable, and that is why they are called the "absolute weapon." They carry with them deterrent and offensive qualities simultaneously, and their possession by a neighbour dramatically increases its offensive capacity to inflict devastating damage in a short period by engaging in indiscriminate attacks on civilians. Rational or moral or normative restraints may still prevent use of such weapons, but their mere presence in a neighbour's arsenal could generate high levels of uncertainty for the state that lacks such weapons. Because the impact of conventional attacks tends to be slow and incremental, and because the time available to absorb the costs of such attacks is generally longer than that for a nuclear attack, states are often less worried about proliferation of conventional weapons. There are no adequate defences against a nuclear attack, unlike the situation for most conventional weapons. Even the effects of the use of chemical and biological weapons can be limited by adequate defensive measures. However, biological weapons also cause high levels of negative security externalities as new versions of defenceless weapons emerge over time.

Why are the arguments presented in this study more pertinent to non–great power states than to great powers? I argue that balance-of-power considerations, especially vis-à-vis other major powers, determine great power nuclear choices. Thus I assume that the power position of a state in the international system matters and that its interactions with regional states or heavily involved major powers largely determine its security choices. The nuclear behaviour of a current or aspiring major power will be influenced and shaped by its interaction with other great powers. For a regional actor, its interactions with other key regional actors and with the most heavily involved major powers in the region are crucial security determinants. Thus states placed differently in the international system have diverse security concerns and interests. Great powers tend to have global interests, while the security concerns and interests of most middle and small powers focus on their regions. An aspiring great power (for example, India) also could perceive its security as being tied to the larger balance-of-power processes in the world involving other established powers.

Great powers could view nuclear capability as a deterrent against wars with other great powers, as a currency of power in the international system, and as insurance against another great power's becoming menacingly powerful as a result of the revolution in the technology of warfare. Thus, they could see nuclear weapons as providing them with structural, compellent, and deterrent power vis-à-vis other states in the international system. The great powers' structural power results from their larger global military and economic reach, which allows them to affect directly and indirectly the choices of smaller actors. Compellent power allows a state to coerce another to follow certain policies. Deterrent power – that is, the ability to prevent war involving another state with nuclear weapons – is the most valued utility of nuclear possession. Nuclear weapons could also provide insurance against a decline in power position and sudden shifts of power that might follow major changes in the economic, military, and technological capabilities of great powers.[8] Non–great powers, unless they have intense aspirations to become great powers, or are engaged in a bitter rivalry with a great power, do not face such considerations. Nuclear weapons would not confer great-power status on a small state unless it possessed other attributes necessary for the status and were recognized as such by other members of the international system.

The effects of security interdependence vary from region to region and situation to situation.

REGIONAL DYNAMICS

The nuclear choices of a potential proliferator are likely to be greatly influenced by the security environment and conflict level of its region. As Thompson characterizes it, a region consists of at least two proximate nation-states whose "pattern of relations or interactions exhibit[s] a particular degree of regularity and intensity to the extent that a change at one point in the system affects other points."[9] The level of security threat that a state perceives may be based on its regional environment, especially the specific threats arising from its adversarial interactions with one or more significant actors in the regional subsystem.[10] As a result of regularized interactions, regions form security complexes when "a group of states whose primary security concerns link together sufficiently closely that national securities cannot realistically be considered apart from one another."[11] Security-related actions by or developments within a member state can have a major effect on other members. The factors that hold together such complexes may include geography, history, economics, and culture, but geographically distant actors may also be involved.[12] Thus a great power active in a region could be part of the complex, most often by imposing, but sometimes by receiving, negative and positive security externalities. For example, the United States is an active member of the regional security complexes of East Asia and the Middle East.

The size of the region and the impact of the security environment could vary for different states. My assumption here is that states' regional considerations differ with their security environment. The security focus of a non–great power state is essentially its immediate geo-strategic surroundings; for a major power, it can include other regions of the world. For regionally involved great powers, nuclear acquisition by smaller powers could generate powerful negative security externalities. What defines a great power is largely its capacity to intervene in the affairs of a minor power without receiving physical threat to its home territory. When a smaller power acquires nuclear weapons and delivery systems such as ballistic missiles, it may be able to constrain the freedom of action of the great power and its allies in the region. Nuclear weapons, under certain circumstances, could act as a "great equalizer" in the strategic relations between small powers and great powers. The American interests in stemming nuclear proliferation spring largely from that nation's concern for negative security externalities emanating from smaller powers' nuclear capabilities.[13]

Drawing partially from the literature on complex interdependence, I create three ideal types of regions or zones for analytical purposes.[14] The zone concept does not suggest that all states in the region will be equally affected or engage in conflict vis-à-vis each other. The zone is usually dominated by the interactions among two or more of its significant states and actively involved great powers. Other states may live in peace with these actors and may be only marginally relevant to the central conflict. There are zones of high conflict, zones of moderate conflict, and zones of low conflict. The conflict level in a zone may be measured with the following indicators: severity, intensity, duration, and scope of conflicts involving key states, especially the significant dyads in the region, in terms of militarized inter-state disputes and crises. I adopt the definition provided by Gochman and Maoz on militarized inter-state disputes (MIDs). They define an MID as "a set of interactions between or among states involving threats to use military force, and actual uses of military force." These acts must be explicit, overt, non-accidental, and government sanctioned." Gochman and Maoz identify fifteen types of MIDs under the rubric of threat of force, display of force, and use of force.[15] Other measures may include membership or lack thereof in common alliances, offensive or defensive military strategies and doctrines that states hold against each other, and economic interdependence, measured in terms of trade among the regional states as a percentage of overall imports and exports.

The first type of zone is a high-threat environment characterized by protracted conflicts and enduring rivalries among two or more significant actors in the zone. The analytical constructs of protracted conflicts and enduring rivalry capture somewhat similar phenomena: a long-standing intense conflict involving two or more parties with a history of crises and, in some instances, war. These conflicts are marked by competitive relationships over one or more issues crucial to the actors. The issues may be highly emotional, such as territorial, ideological, or ethnic disputes, and may spill over to many spheres of inter-state inter-actions. Protracted conflicts are characterized by hostile interactions that extend over long periods, with sporadic outbreaks of crises and open conflicts. The intensity of these conflicts may fluctuate from time to time. They are also deep-rooted conflicts and often involve intra-societal hostility.[16] An enduring rivalry is characterized by "sustained mutually contingent hostile interaction," with parties considering the gain or loss of a stake to the rival as more important than their "own value satisfaction."[17] Analysts differ on coding an enduring rivalry. One of the most commonly accepted criteria suggests a minimum of five militarized disputes between participants during a twenty-year period.[18] Such conflicts tend to assume "zero-sum" characteristics, as parties view their opponent's gains as losses for themselves. The indicators described above are strongly present in conflicts among states. They are at least five militarized interstate disputes in a twenty-year period, with one or more possibly leading to war, lack of membership in common alliances, and very low levels of economic interaction.

In this type of zone, states follow hard realist patterns of behaviour and pursue a "security first" approach because they are extremely con-cerned about relative gains and less worried about the negative security externalities that they may impose on their enemies. Trade and eco-nomic relations are minimal as interdependent relationships could gen-erate conditions of vulnerability, which each party wants to avoid. The Middle East, South Asia, Cold War–era Europe (in relation to the East-ern bloc), and the Korean peninsula correspond to this pattern. Defence policies of states engaging in an enduring rivalry or protracted conflict rest on worst-case assumptions – i.e., they assume that their opponent would make use of military "windows of opportunity" unless deterred by strong countervailing capabilities. They will take nothing for granted, as they view the opponent's gestures at co-operation with suspicion. Mutual distrust thus typifies such relationships, and security interdependence is low.

A zone of moderate conflict is one in which states often pay approximately equal attention to security and to economic goals. States are mindful of negative security externalities emanating from their individual actions. Militarized inter-state disputes may exist, but their frequency, intensity, and scope are lower than in a high-conflict zone, and they are unlikely to have led to border wars. States may not belong to the same alliance but may be members of organizations dealing with regional security or economic co-operation. The threat environment is moderate, and although security goals may dominate the agenda during certain periods, such questions are less prominent in daily interactions. Inter-state conflicts are not protracted or enduring but episodic, while states experience moderate levels of economic interdependence. The post-1990 "Southern Cone" of Latin America, the ASEAN region of South East Asia, and post–apartheid era Southern Africa exhibit these characteristics. In these zones, states tend to adopt a less hostile approach towards each other, and much of their behaviour vis-à-vis each other would be akin to what prudential realism would predict. Although conflict may erupt over major issues, it may not involve the threat or actual use of military force.

High levels of economic interdependence characterize a zone of low conflict.[19] This is a low-threat environment, force is rarely applied in mutual relations, and economic issues dominate in normal inter-state interactions. States are extremely mindful of the negative security externalities emanating from their actions. In terms of the earlier measures of conflict, states in this zone would have had no militarized disputes and armed conflicts among the principal actors for at least twenty years and no conventional arms race vis-à-vis each other. States are unlikely to resort to force to resolve their disputes. They may agree on the inviolability of borders and adopt a benign defensive military posture vis-à-vis each other. States may be bound by pluralistic security communities or be active members in the same alliance and economic organizations.[20] States' behaviour is dictated by the postulates of prudential realism. Western Europe and North America come close to this model. Economic interdependence is the lowest in the first type of zone, and it increases as one moves towards the third, while a reverse pattern emerges with respect to conflict level and security dilemmas caused by the arming and potential arming of principal states (see Table 2.1).

Apart from these ideal types, three analytically distinct *mixed* zones can be created. The first is a variety with high/low conflict, in which states may be in active protracted conflicts with an extra-regional

Table 2.1

Region	Militarized inter-state disputes/crises	Economic interdependence	Conflict level/security dilemma
High-conflict	Yes/ frequently	Low	*High.* The region is characterized by protracted conflicts and enduring rivalries. States are extremely sensitive to relative gains. Interstate economic relations are minimal.
Moderate-conflict	Maybe/ occasionally	Moderate	*Moderate.* Economic and security issues could receive equal attention among states.
Low-conflict	No/no	High	*Low.* Economic issues dominate state interactions. Countries avoid militarily provocative acts vis-à-vis each other.

adversary but have low-conflict interdependent relationships with each other. Nuclear choices may be constrained by both the interdependence relationship and the alliance factor. Western Europe and North America (in their relationships with the Eastern bloc) during the Cold War era approximate this type of zone. A second variety is a region of high/moderate conflict, where some actors may have both intense and moderate conflicts with different states in the region. East Asia in the post–Cold War era approximates this pattern. A third variety is a zone of low/moderate conflict. Actors may maintain moderate conflicts with an extra-regional adversary but have little conflict with their neighbours – for example, Europe vis-à-vis Russia in the 1990s.

This model suggests that technologically capable states in zones of low and moderate conflict are most likely to forgo nuclear weapons, while a state in a high-conflict zone would have the greatest incentive to acquire such weapons, especially if it is engaged in a protracted conflict or enduring rivalry with an already existing or an emerging nuclear-weapon state. If a technologically capable state in a high-conflict region forswears nuclear arms, it does so largely as a function of countervailing deterrent capability, provided either by an ally or by the state's own capability, such as chemical weapons or conventional superiority, that can somewhat neutralize the nuclear capability of the adversary. An ally under a security umbrella would desist from acquiring nuclear weapons if acquisition could complicate collective efforts by the alliance partners and thereby the effectiveness of the deterrent capability itself. If the tightness of the alliance declines, if the ally loses or perceives uncertainty about the security umbrella, and if the protracted conflict continues, the ally may pursue the nuclear option. However, not all alliances produce non-nuclear policies among allied states in high-conflict zones. Credibility of the allies' commitment is critical in dissuading a technologically capable state in a zone of high conflict from "going nuclear." Factors that determine alliance credibility include active troop presence, nuclear and conventional weapons deployed on the ally's territory, integration of both states' forces, and a security treaty that stipulates automatic entry by the great power on the side of the smaller ally in the event of war. While the alliance relationships of NATO members, Japan, and South Korea contain such specifications, the great-power alliance relationships of India, Israel, and Pakistan did not include such provisions at the times when the latter states chose to acquire nuclear weapons.

In a zone of moderate conflict, technologically capable regional states would not obtain nuclear arms unless their potential and existing rivals pursued that path. Nuclear proliferation is unlikely, given that states would want to stress economic objectives, while growing economic interdependence would preclude highly sensitive activities such as nuclear acquisition. The lessening of any existing conflict would substantially boost their prospects for a region free of nuclear weapons. These states are likely to emerge economically interdependent in the long run, forming security communities along the way, as they tighten their co-operative relationships. The coming into power of democratic regimes with liberal economic objectives would also facilitate nuclear forbearance. If states pursue pro-nuclear policies, they may do so most likely because of bureaucratic politics or the organizational interests of the armed forces. Such a region is a good candidate for denuclearization and eventual achievement of a nuclear free-zone. Examples would be Latin America and South East Asia.

In an area of low conflict, states are most likely to forgo nuclear weapons, as independent national acquisition would generate intense negative security externalities for other actors. States in these zones are acutely aware of their economic and security interdependence. Independent nuclear acquisition would result in heightened alertness and readiness, with enormous attention being paid to early-warning and other command, control, and communication systems.[21] States in such a zone usually place economics as the top priority and avoid potential disruptions to such interactions. They tend to use economic and diplomatic instruments to induce co-operation from other states in their zone. Security, though important, may be maintained through low-profile strategies that do not attract adversarial responses by neighbours and trading partners.

On defence issues, national leaders in low- and moderate-conflict regions tend to act according to the dictates of prudential realism and make "most probable" assessments of their neighbours' capabilities and intentions, as opposed to worst-case assumptions.[22] Worst-case assumptions take it as given that an adversary would use a possible military opportunity and therefore that the state should be ready for all types of contingencies. "Most probable" scenarios would make assessments on the basis of the most likely contingencies if and when a conflict erupts. Often in such a region neighbours will not exploit windows of opportunity even if there is no nuclear weaponry.

In a moderate-conflict zone, states may be aware of the dangers of engaging in militarily threatening or provocative behaviour against their neighbours. A state's unilateral acquisition of nuclear arms would increase the other states' perceptions of threat and could result in their undertaking balancing measures, including inviting outside powers into the region.[23] These threat perceptions could dramatically increase when a state suddenly acquires nuclear capability on the pretext of deterrence in a zone where there are no significant intra-regional security challenges that require nuclear weapons. Other states would probably view such a capability as offensive and see a change in the state's security posture from benignness to aggressiveness as threatening. The cost of acquisition and the risk of use or threat of use are too high, and therefore for states in such a region the utility of nuclear weapons decreases in their relationship with one another.

According to the framework presented in this study, countries most likely to nuclearize and least likely to denuclearize are those in high-conflict zones experiencing protracted conflict or enduring rivalry. Low-level security considerations, like those present in zones of low and moderate conflict, are not enough to push nations to opt for nuclear arms, as nuclear weapons involve tremendous costs for a medium-sized or small state. However, security considerations in an ongoing conflict may be the biggest incentive to nuclearization. Rivals in such a region would undertake measures to deter aggression and to defend themselves if deterrence fails. States engaged in protracted conflicts and enduring rivalries, especially those inferior in conventional capability vis-à-vis their opponents, might see nuclear arms as useful for deterrence purposes. If a technologically capable state in such a zone denuclearizes, it could be because of an ally's clear-cut security guarantees, or because the protracted conflict shows signs of ending, or because the state possesses another effective deterrent, such as chemical weapons.

Zones of moderate and low conflict would provide a technologically capable small or medium-sized state fewer reasons to nuclearize. In a zone of medium-level conflict, states would be less prone to acquire nuclear weapons because of a fear that such a move would transform their region into one of high conflict, a condition that they want to avoid. Nuclear weapons would seem less of a force for increasing security in a benign strategic environment. A state's nuclear acquisition could be equivalent to sending a sudden negative signal to its neighbours with respect to its own intentions and capabilities. Nuclear forbearance is thus the result of a desire to minimize negative security externalities, as opposed to unilateral maximization of security. States in low- and moderate-conflict regions may believe that the problem of security dilemma can be ameliorated through concrete choices. As the intensity of the security dilemma varies with a state's location, reversing or mitigating the dilemma is a strategic option available to a state, especially if it is in a benign, low- or moderate-conflict security environment. The self-help system does not automatically direct a state to maximize its relative gains, because it knows that single-handed pursuit of security maximization through nuclear acquisitions could eventually result in a loss of security for itself and for other significant actors in the region. The optimal situation is that no state obtain nuclear weapons or at least that one's neighbours do not.

In an economically interdependent, low-conflict region, or in a moderate-conflict region where states are moving towards interdependence, countries could believe that nuclear acquisition might hamper their efforts to achieve economic prosperity.[24] Aversion to economic loss could thus affect a decision about acquiring nuclear weapons. The liberal claim that a national agenda is not hierarchically organized, with security as the topmost item, seems to be valid in these instances. Security considerations, though important, could be subordinated and purposely made less significant by states that are more prone to trading strategies or that value economic and welfare functions. Such states confine defence strategies mostly to tactical and political measures that "would reduce another state's temptation to strike," placing primary emphasis on trade and internal economic development. Such an emphasis could be the result of a prudential calculation among such states of "the increasing costs and decreasing benefit of purely military approaches to national advancement."[25]

The mixed regions also differ in their propensities for nuclear acquisition and forbearance. A state in a high/low-conflict zone is likely to forgo nuclear weapons if it can contain an intense conflict with an extra-regional adversary through an alliance or some other means, such as a superior conventional deterrent. Its nuclear choices may be influenced by the considerations of states in both low- and high-conflict zones. For example, West Germany's non-nuclear policy during the era of the Cold War arose from its place vis-à-vis a low-conflict zone (Western Europe) and a high-conflict zone (Eastern Europe). States in a zone of low/moderate conflict also are unlikely to pursue the nuclear option as long as their region maintains its status and slowly reduces conflict. In post–Cold War Europe, Latin America, and South East Asia states are unlikely to pursue the nuclear option. Countries in a high/moderate zone are more likely to acquire nuclear weapons, if and when their region becomes a zone of high conflict involving the principal actors. Under this characterization, technologically capable states in post–Cold War era East Asia exhibit the highest propensity for nuclear acquisition.

This model does not suggest that regions remain static in terms of conflict relationships. Changes in external or domestic circumstances could transform a region of moderate conflict into a high- or low-conflict zone. Similarly, a zone of high conflict could become a moderate zone.[26] If such a change occurs, a state's incentives and disincentives for nuclear acquisition could also alter. Shifts in conflict level result largely from the rise of issues that generate militarized conflicts and rivalries, especially protracted conflicts and enduring rivalries. In the modern international system, two such issues that generated enduring rivalries and protracted conflicts have been territorial disputes and ideological rivalries.[27]

In elevating security variables to a higher profile, this explanation invites criticism from those who emphasize other motivations for nuclear acquisition, such as prestige, domestic politics (especially bureaucratic and organizational politics), culture, and the dispositions of individual decision-makers.[28] Certainly these factors may influence nuclear choices at various points in the evolution of a country's nuclear policy. As Bradley Thayer contends, they may also explain the manner in which nuclear proliferation occurred in a state, but they are not sufficient to explain proliferation.[29] They are not, I believe, as powerful determinants as security considerations, such as enduring rivalries and protracted conflicts. For a non–great power state to undertake the crucial final step necessary for building an actual weapon, simple security threats, bureaucratic pressures, or prestige considerations are not sufficient. Domestic politics can speed up the process, but bureaucratic actors do not operate in a vacuum. A country's security environment determines whether the bureaucratic or political actor carries his or her day and succeeds in implementing a costly enterprise such as acquisition of nuclear weapons. However, not all security pressures lead to nuclear acquisition; it is indeed one type of conflict – i.e., enduring rivalry – that generates the greatest tendency to acquire nuclear arms among non–great power states. If a state pursues nuclear weapons for purposes other than deterrence against an enduring rival, it is likely to emerge as a candidate for nuclear forbearance. Argentina and Brazil (two states for which domestic politics seem to have played a significant role) did not actually make the bomb, because their rivalry did not warrant such a step.

POWER, NORMS, AND INTERESTS: PRUDENCE AND NUCLEAR CHOICES

Decisions by technologically capable states in regions of low or medium conflict to forgo nuclear weapons may also be the result of a complex set of prudential calculations involving power, norms, and interests. Theoretically, in terms of raw destructive power, nuclear weapons should increase the possessor's putative military capability, as a nuclear-armed state can destroy an opponent's population and industrial sites. But if influence is the goal, the threat of destruction of a neighbouring state may not achieve that objective. Transforming putative into actualized power seems a formidable task in a zone of low or medium conflict.[30] This is especially relevant to small or medium-sized states in such zones. They tend to realize that their attempt to develop nuclear weapons could waste resources in an effort for the "kind of a power that cannot be used easily and whose existence limits in fact their freedom of maneuver by comparison with the centers which can afford to be more dashing or adventurous."[31]

A non–great power state in an economically interdependent region could be most sensitive to prudential power calculations. In such a region, power relationships among states would take place largely through diplomatic bargaining, co-optation, persuasion, and other non-coercive means. Independent nuclear acquisition could indeed decrease a state's non-military-based power, as others might view it as threatening and initiate counter-measures. Nuclear weapons thus present several dilemmas for decision-makers and defence analysts. Definitions of "power as influence over actors and outcomes" suggest that the ability to convert resources into influence over other actors is an important dimension of a nation's power capabilities. "Power conversion is the capacity to convert potential power as measured by resource, to realized power, as measured by the changed behaviour of states."[32] Their realization of the difficulties of wielding unilateral military capability through acquisition of nuclear weapons helped push many states to accede to the NPT and the non-proliferation regime, even though these instruments allow the five declared nuclear states to maintain their nuclear monopoly while preventing non-nuclear states from pursuing such weapons.

WHAT DOES THE NON-PROLIFERATION REGIME DO?

The role of the non-proliferation regime and its chief component, the NPT, is not a determining factor in decisions on nuclear forbearance. However, it becomes more important once a state chooses a non-nuclear policy, as it provides assurances of similar behaviour by other states. Moreover, once states join it, the exit costs become high, as a technologically capable state's decision to leave the regime would elicit harsher international reaction than if it had not joined in the first place. The role and importance of institutions and regimes vary by zone of conflict, as we saw above. Thus the non-proliferation regime matters most crucially in zones of low and moderate conflict, whereas in a zone of high conflict it plays a limited role. Even when states in such a zone adhere to the regime, because of their extreme sensitivity to relative gains they are most likely to break the rules if and when they perceive that it is in their national interest to do so.

In the zones of low and moderate conflict, the non-proliferation regime may provide states with a number of assurances regarding neighbours' intentions. The regime assures them that, under ordinary circumstances, a neighbour that is party to the NPT would not acquire nuclear weapons. It thus provides "transparency" and a legal basis to nations for their non-nuclear policies. In this way the regime helps at least partly to ameliorate the security dilemma. Prudential behaviour requires that states receive and gauge information on the capabilities and intentions of others so that they can formulate their policies accordingly.[33] In a moderate-conflict zone, states may view regimes as a way to develop mutual confidence and eventually transform the region into a low-conflict zone. The regime is also an avenue for such small and medium states to exert at least limited influence in international politics, especially on this issue.[34]

Those middle and small states not engaged in protracted conflicts and enduring rivalries have a prudential self-interest in creating non-nuclear norms, as they cannot ordinarily afford costly arms races. They may believe that their acquisition of nuclear weapons would hurt the international norms and laws that give them legitimacy and protection. General adherence to regime principles and norms and observance of the NPT appear to restrain other states in the region, especially if it has low or medium levels of conflict. By acceding to the NPT, the non-proliferation regime, or a regional nuclear-free zone, a state increases its security, especially if its neighbours also sign on, as the regime provides for international inspections, by the IAEA or some other relevant agency, of the neighbours' nuclear facilities, to ensure that civilian nuclear programs are not being used to develop nuclear weapons. Regimes may also provide guarantees against rapid shifts in the power capabilities of states. [35]

Grasping the nexus between international regime and level and type of conflict is crucial in order to understand the puzzle of nuclear non-acquisition. In a zone of high conflict, parties engaged in enduring rivalries or protracted conflicts are most likely to defy the rules, principles, and norms of the regime. The behaviour of Iraq and North Korea attests to this contention. More than the regime, it was American power and diplomacy that put a temporary lid on the nuclear activities of these states. However, as long as their regions remain intensely conflict-prone, and they lack strong alliance partners, these states will retain a high propensity to acquire nuclear weapons. Only the defusion of conflict in their regions, through major rapprochements with their adversaries, could produce genuine non-nuclear policies and full adherence to the nuclear non-proliferation regime.

To several small or medium states, the awesome destructiveness of nuclear weapons has made the unilateral search for security difficult. States in low- and medium-conflict zones tend to realize that only collective action can lessen the potential burden of arming, reduce the incentives for others to acquire weapons in response to their own actions, and provide early warning against possible defections.[36] Unlike previous eras when violation of treaties did not entail the possibility of self-destruction, the nuclear age brings forth the prospect of a state's total annihilation or large-scale destruction in a nuclear war. The security predicament of the nuclear age is that no actor can simply violate the rules and norms without creating the possibility of further proliferation. States that forgo their nuclear options want to preserve their ability to defend themselves and reduce the cost of a potential war if they ever get involved in one. However, their neighbours' acquisition of nuclear weapons would make defence difficult. Realization of potential vulnerability and loss of security thus precede the choice of these states to forgo nuclear armaments. The perceived lack of defences against nuclear weapons produces a sense of vulnerability unparalleled in previous historical eras.

This is why the non-proliferation regime, despite being discriminatory, became acceptable to several small and medium states. It establishes two types of states – those who possessed nuclear weapons prior to 1967 and those who did not – and gives different types of rights and obligations to them. It does not restrict the nuclear activities of the established nuclear weapons states, while it forbids non-nuclear states from acquiring nuclear arms or undertaking other activities that would help the spread of nuclear weapons. The nuclear-weapon states have supported this regime largely because it legitimized their nuclear status and allowed continuation of their monopoly. They also want to prevent the rise of any new challengers to their dominant status.[37] The regime has been opposed by some middle-ranking states that face nuclear adversaries and that aspire to becoming major powers. For instance, India, which exploded a nuclear device in 1974, became the leading critic of the regime.[38] This opposition was further reinforced in May 1998 when New Delhi conducted five nuclear tests and declared itself a nuclear-weapon state. This opposition by a regional state that faces nuclear adversaries is exceptional. India, as a state with great-power ambitions and as a country that is engaged in enduring rivalries with two nuclear-armed states, China and Pakistan, is driven largely by both systemic and sub-systemic considerations.[39]

The qualified "no-first-use" pledges of the nuclear-weapon states and the tradition of non-use, or "nuclear taboo," have further strengthened the regime and in turn reduced the security incentive of several states to acquire nuclear weapons. Two nuclear states – the Soviet Union (in 1982) and China (in 1964), after its first nuclear explosion – unilaterally declared no first use. Britain, France, and the United States have made conditional "no first use" pledges to the effect that they would not use nuclear weapons against a signatory to the NPT or any comparable binding international agreement, except in the case of a non-nuclear state launching an attack on these states or their allies, carried out in alliance with a nuclear state.[40] India, the sixth nuclear state, has in the aftermath of its May 1998 tests unilaterally declared a policy of no first use against nuclear states and no use at all against non-nuclear states. Pakistan refused to reciprocate, arguing that India's overwhelming conventional superiority forces it to maintain a first-use policy.[41] The NPT contains implicit guarantees that a non-nuclear signatory will not be targeted or attacked with nuclear weapons. The non-proliferation regime has also been viewed as an instrument to strengthen the "nuclear taboo," or "tradition of non-use," that nuclear states have observed since the atomic bombing of Nagasaki in August 1945. The tradition forbids the use of nuclear weapons against non-nuclear states unless an extremely vital interest such as national survival is threatened. As Schelling argues, a powerful normative tradition forbids the use of nuclear weapons despite declarations or tactical advantages in their use.[42] Nuclear weapons are generally perceived to be unique; once introduced into combat, they could not be "contained, restrained, confined, limited."[43]

The "nuclear taboo" has developed largely as a function of the awesome destructive power of atomic weapons. The potential for total destruction gives these weapons an "all or nothing" characteristic that in turn makes it likely that the possessor will not use them against another state except as a last resort. This means that a nuclear state will not use its ultimate capability unless a threshold is crossed – for example, a threat to a vital interest such as the survival of the state itself. Decision-makers and the public at large in most nuclear states believe that use of nuclear weapons poses a great danger, in both psychological and physical terms, with respect to casualties and after-effects. Breaking the "taboo" could bring forth the revulsion of generations to come unless it were for a matter of vital importance – a situation that thus far has failed to materialize. Not surprisingly, nuclear states, even when they could have gained considerable tactical and strategic advantages through the use of nuclear weapons, abstained from their use. American unwillingness to use them in Korea and Vietnam to obtain military victory and the Soviets' refrain from using them to avert defeat in Afghanistan suggest the entrenchment of the taboo among the superpowers even during the peak of the Cold War period.[44] The Chinese aversion to using them against Vietnam in the 1979 war also shows that other nuclear powers have observed the taboo.

The taboo was also probably strengthened by the powers' realization that a military victory following a nuclear attack may not be materially, politically, or psychologically worth obtaining if it involves the destruction of all or most of an enemy's population and contaminates the territory with radioactive debris. Analysts have warned that "victory in the classical sense of obtaining policy objectives by constraining an opponent's will through force of arms becomes meaningless where it involves total destruction of the enemy's territory and possessions."[45] Thus the tradition of non-use has emerged largely because of "the realization that there are severe limits to what one can accomplish by actually using a nuclear weapon."[46] For instance, after-effects such as the spread of radioactive debris may pass beyond the target state's territory. Neighbouring states that may be neutral or aligned with the nuclear state could be the victims of a nuclear attack as well.

These constraints have further reduced the prospects of nuclear conflicts between a nuclear and a non-nuclear state.[47] States with nuclear weapons have been careful not to threaten nuclear attack on non-nuclear states, especially since the 1970s, a factor that helped lessen the need for countervailing nuclear capability by many medium and small states. Technologically capable states may also believe that the constraints preventing nuclear states from using these weapons are enormous, largely because of the taboo against their use; by *not* acquiring nuclear arms they are not reducing security but in fact avoiding the hostile attention of nuclear powers.

Nuclear weapons also present several burdens for medium-sized and small states, with which the superpowers attempted to grapple during the Cold War. They could make it hard for national leaders in the capital to maintain a firm grip on military operations if a war were to erupt. In addition, they may increase the possibility of the accidental nuclear war.[48] These wars could begin through an unauthorized use by either side, accidental detonations, or false alarms. Unlike in the past, when military leaders had considerable time between warning and actual mobilization, the leaders of nuclear forces need to be constantly alert because of the swiftness with which an attack can take place. Non-nuclear states in low- and moderate-conflict zones have little incentive to get into high alert when their national defence forces will have to focus their attention on the nuclear forces of potential enemies. The lack of warning time means that accidents can occur. Finally, nuclear weapons would not allow a state to keep a low-profile defence posture or to avoid hostile attention from their neighbours and the international community.

States seem to have learned the negative consequences of arming since the nuclear era began.[49] Learning involves using new knowledge to avoid unwanted consequences of a particular action and using more effective means to attain one's goals.[50] A more nuanced definition of learning characterizes it as "a change of beliefs (or the degree of confidence in one's beliefs) or the development of new beliefs, skills, or procedures as a result of the observation and interpretation of experience."[51] In the early stages of the nuclear era, there was a perception that nuclear weapons are like any others, though highly destructive, and that every security-conscious state needs them. As the nuclear age advanced, perceptions changed. More knowledge about nuclear weapons and nuclear war became available, and a new aware-ness developed of the need to control vertical and horizontal prolifer-ation. The Cuban missile crisis of 1962 made clear the dangers of nuclear "brinksmanship" and of the unrestrained arms race between the superpowers.[52] The overspill from the superpowers' discourse and conflict also affected lesser actors. Although strategists took the lead in formulating doctrines for managing the superpowers' relations, they also warned against using nuclear weapons for anything other than deterrence – for example, for offensive or defensive purposes.[53] Added to this was the scientific knowledge about radiation effects and the worldwide dissemination of these ideas. Peace movements helped to popularize these concerns.[54] Moreover, non-nuclear states have seldom bowed to the dictates of nuclear states because of a nuclear threat.[55]

CONCLUSIONS

This chapter proposes that the nuclear choices of technologically capable non–great power states are the result of their situations and regional contexts, their security interdependence, and their prudential calculations regarding the utility of unilateral acquisition of nuclear arms. The prudential calculations derive from anticipated losses to national security resulting from nuclear proliferation. States, especially in zones of low and moderate conflict, choose to forgo nuclear weapons to avoid generating negative security externalities and costly arms races, which may trap them in a condition of security dilemma. They also seek not to incite proliferation by other states. States' behaviour in this realm is thus consistent with the expectations of prudential realism.

Nuclear forbearance by a large number of states represents a fundamental change in international politics, transforming how states respond to the insecurity caused by introduction of a revolutionary weapon. Arming has been the historical route to security for states, both large and small. During the nuclear age, this approach has changed. Many states, especially in low- and moderate-conflict regions, seem to have realized that they can ameliorate the security dilemma if they refrain from actions that might cause their neighbours to arm. Nuclear forbearance thus constitutes a conscious effort by states to control or mitigate the effects and consequences of anarchy. Their choices are shaped largely by the nature and degree of conflict in their own regions. Thus in a high-conflict region, the propensity for nuclear acquisition is high, whereas in moderate- and low-conflict zones, it is low or non-existent.

States recognize that the pursuit of military autarky could harm their economic welfare. Economic well-being is a cardinal goal of most states, especially in regions of interdependence. A key underlying argument of this chapter is that even though the anarchic nature of the international system makes the security dilemma possible, the strategies that a state adopts to ameliorate or mitigate it can help determine whether it arms or disarms. States do have strategic choices to select from, and these choices need not always lead to arms races, and thereby the worsening of the security dilemma. Circumstances do matter, as nuclear choices are largely a function of a state's security environment.

I have also discussed the role of the nuclear non-proliferation regime. I question the claim of the universal significance of the regime and theories that establish it as a causal variable. My argument provides more of a semi-functionalist, yet nuanced explanation of the role of regimes. Regimes do not operate in a vacuum, and their effect varies with the state. Thus for states in low/medium–conflict zones and for small states, regimes matter most, while for those in high-conflict zones, they minimally constrain or facilitate nuclear forbearance. Regimes are most successful in dealing with states that experience security interdependence, and this often occurs in low- and medium-conflict regions.

PART TWO

Case Studies

CHAPTER THREE

Aligned Major Economic Powers: Germany and Japan

Germany and Japan, the defeated major powers of the Second World War, are two of the most advanced nuclear-capable states that have chosen not to acquire independent national nuclear-weapon capabilities. On a number of criteria these two states are comparable. In terms of civilian nuclear technology, they are two of the most advanced states in the world, with atomic power providing major portions of their national energy requirements. This civilian activity has created huge stocks of fissile materials that could be converted to weapon purposes if these countries chose to do so and were willing to break their commitments to the International Atomic Energy Agency (IAEA) and under the Nuclear Non-Proliferation Treaty (NPT). In 1998, Germany operated twenty nuclear power reactors, which generated over 31 per cent of the country's power production.[1] In the early 1990s, Germany was estimated to hold 8 tonnes of plutonium, while Japan's stockpile at the end of 1993 was estimated at 4.684 tonnes stored at domestic plants and an additional 6.197 tons in Britain and France destined for reprocessing.[2] Moreover, Japan has an ambitious fast-breeder reactor program, which by the turn of the century was expected to produce large quantities of refined plutonium.[3] Japan also produces fissile materials through fifty-three commercial reactors that generate about 35 per cent of the country's electricity output (1998 estimates), although all these facilities are under IAEA safeguards.[4] In February 1994, Japan launched the H-2 rocket, built with its own technology, thereby giving it an ICBM capability if the country's leadership decided to use it for military purposes.[5] Moreover, Japan's space agencies have successfully tested solid-fuel rocket systems, J-1 and M-5, with a payload and thrust comparable to American ICBMs, and they could use this capability to develop a strong missile program.[6]

Both (West) Germany and Japan had engaged in a bitter rivalry with the Soviet Union during the Cold War and were active participants in the American-led alliance against the Eastern bloc. Since the 1960s, they have made impressive economic progress and have developed the potential to become major military powers concomitant with their economic clout, if they chose to do so. Moreover, they both pursued low-profile security policies even during the height of Cold War tensions, despite being active partners in the Western alliance.

The end of the Cold War has, however, increased the differences in the security environments of these two states. While Germany is reunified, with all Russian troops removed from its eastern neighbours, Japan has witnessed only moderate change in its security environment. The Russo–Japanese territorial dispute continues, although the intensity of the conflict has decreased dramatically. In the early 1990s, Japan's smaller neighbour, North Korea, initiated a nuclear weapons program that caused considerable alarm in Tokyo, leading to suggestions that Japan would rethink its nuclear abstinence.[7]

Despite variations in their strategic environments, Japan and Germany have so far made quite similar nuclear choices. A strictly power-based explanation would have predicted these countries' increasing their political and military prowess in line with their economic power. There were pressures on them in the late 1950s (in West Germany's case) and late 1960s (in the Japanese case) to acquire independent nuclear capabilities. This chapter considers why these technologically capable nations chose not to acquire autonomous nuclear forces by examining the key factors that account for their forbearance. It also discusses probable changes in the international and regional systems that could force these states to initiate programs of nuclear weapons in the next century.

GERMANY

West Germany was one of the first states that forswore independent national nuclear weapons, yet paradoxically it also relied heavily on nuclear arms for its security. In terms of the amount of weapons stationed on a national territory during the Cold War, West Germany was third in the world, behind the United States and the USSR.[8] It was also likely to be in the forefront of a nuclear exchange in Europe in the event of a war between the Eastern and Western blocs, with large segments of its population and industrial strength threatened with destruction. Yet successive governments resisted pressure to acquire a national nuclear deterrent, even though they had built up strong nuclear energy programs. A discussion of the history of West Germany's nuclear policy can shed light on the evolution of a security approach that included forswearing an independent nuclear capability. For analytical purposes, I look at its nuclear policy in three periods: 1954–68, 1969–90, and after 1990. These periods correspond with major changes in international politics that had a bearing on (West) Germany's nuclear policy.

1954–68

During this period, several developments occurred with respect to West Germany and nuclear weapons. The most important was West Germany's signing of the Paris Accords of 1954 and the unilateral declaration of nuclear non-acquisition by Chancellor Konard Adenauer. According to the accords, West Germany pledged not to manufacture nuclear, chemical, or biological weapons on its territory.[9] The treaty, which returned West Germany sovereignty and allowed it to join the European Economic Community and the NATO alliance while stationing allied troops on its territory, was conditional on its accepting non-nuclear status. Though denied a totally independent foreign policy, West German leaders, especially Chancellor Adenauer, saw membership in NATO as a route to equal partnership in the Western alliance.[10]

Prior to West Germany's joining NATO, opposition by France had killed proposals for creating a European Defence Community with West Germany as a member, allowing it to pursue untrammelled rearmament. France's reluctance was one of the reasons for the West German pledge not to acquire nuclear weapons independently. This does not mean that West Germany was interested in obtaining nuclear capability. In the early 1950s, it showed little or no interest in developing atomic weapons partly because, under the Allied occupation, its scientists were restricted to elementary nuclear research. Even after the formation of the Federal Republic in 1949, scientists conducted their research as though Allied controls were continuing.[11] During the second half of the 1950s, however, West Germany attempted to play its nuclear card vis-à-vis its allies.

Despite pledges not to launch an independent nuclear weapons program, Defence Minister Franz-Joseph Strauss in 1957 undertook some diplomatic initiatives to acquire nuclear arms through a joint French–West German–Italian program. The plan was to produce nuclear weapons on French territory with West German technical and financial support. This was conceived as a way to circumvent West Germany's pledge to forgo nuclear production on its territory. West Germany would gain access to these weapons during an inter-state crisis. These plans, however, failed to materialize, despite initial talks and agreements on joint production of military equipment. In June 1958 the new French president, Charles de Gaulle, called a halt to the negotiations. De Gaulle adamantly believed in the creation of an independent French national nuclear force, devoid of any external participation.[12] After the failed attempts at co-operation with France, Strauss continued to pressure the United States to station nuclear weapons on West German soil. Washington was amenable to such pressures, as is evident in the proposal made at the North Atlantic Council meeting in December 1960 for the creation of a Multilateral Force (MLF) consisting of a submarine- or ship-based intermediate-range nuclear force under the joint control of the United States and NATO members, including West Germany. This proposal was discussed at a time when the NPT was in the negotiation stage. The Soviet Union vehemently opposed the MLF, arguing that it would make West Germany a de facto nuclear state. In 1965, the U.S. Johnson administration shelved the MLF proposal in favour of the NPT.[13]

West Germany's nuclear dilemma came into sharp focus during the NPT negotiations in the late 1960s. Chancellor Kurt Georg Kiesinger's coalition government had viewed the NPT as a West German commitment to its chief adversary, the USSR, and throughout 1965 and 1966 Bonn raised objections to the treaty. Strauss, now finance minister, led the opposition, arguing that West Germany, by signing the treaty, would allow the USSR to gain rights to interfere with West Germany's nuclear industry and technical development, military security, and foreign policy. The opposition's concern was that the growing U.S.–Soviet détente, as evident in the NPT, could weaken the American commitment to Europe and West Germany's security itself.[14] It also feared that the treaty would block Germany's nuclear-sharing arrangements with NATO and believed that the treaty should not be accepted without Soviet concessions on reunification. Opponents feared too that the U.S.–Soviet détente and U.S. arms-control negotiations with the USSR, including those that led to the NPT, would help formalize the territorial status quo in Central Europe and increase the legitimacy of the German Democratic Republic, thereby complicating efforts at reunification.[15]

Suspicion over the treaty also resulted from some West German decision-makers' perception that the treaty had been partly responsible for the demise of the MLF, as the USSR had linked the NPT to the scrapping of the MLF proposal. Opponents argued that the treaty would single out West Germany as the main proliferation problem and would question the validity of its 1954 non-proliferation pledge.[16] The Christian Democrats feared that the United States would curtail its supply of fuel for West Germany's power programs, especially for the fast-breeder reactors, and that the treaty would place production of plutonium under the control of nuclear states. They also worried that the states with nuclear weapons could restrict the growing West German reactor industry by refusing to share their technology with it. However, security concerns clearly were more significant. The West Germans worried that the u.s.–Soviet arms control process would relegate European and West German security concerns to a secondary level.[17]

1969–90

During this period, West Germany signed and ratified the NPT and reinforced its pledge not to acquire its own nuclear weapons. Its decision to do so was followed by the coming to power in October 1969 of Chancellor Willy Brandt of the Social Democratic Party (SPD). Adherence to the NPT was part of Brandt's new foreign policy posture, *Ostpolitik*, intended to encourage détente with the Soviet bloc. *Ostpolitik* was also partly a response to u.s. proposals for reduction of forces in Europe. The SPD believed that a co-operative relationship with the USSR would compensate for any possible lessening of u.s. commitment to Western Europe.[18]

Brandt rejected the previous government's arguments against the discriminatory aspects of the treaty by contending that it applied to all West German partners and that NATO would continue to provide for West Germany security. He also argued that peaceful nuclear pursuit would not be affected, that the treaty would not hinder European integration, and that the states with nuclear arms would undertake disarmament negotiations.[19] According to Brandt, West Germany's adherence to the treaty was a pre-condition for its normalizing its relations with Eastern European states, and its acceptance of the treaty would also undermine Soviet propaganda about West Germany as a state intent on acquiring nuclear weapons.[20] Although the Christian Democratic Party (CDU) and the Christian Social Union (CSU) opposed the treaty, in the end all but radical fringe groups were conscious of the disproportionate costs involved in not signing. However, it was only when *Ostpolitik* became West Germany's foreign policy framework in 1975 that formal ratification occurred. Continued CDU/CSU opposition had slowed the process.[21]

During this period, the stationing of NATO nuclear weapons in West Germany caused major debates within the country. The persisting ambivalence towards deployment of nuclear weapons on domestic soil manifested itself especially in the 1970s and the 1980s. Of particular significance was the West German position on the INF agreement of 1987 and the eventual removal of medium-range Pershing and Cruise missiles from its territory. Although West Germany was an active participant in NATO nuclear defence and Chancellor Helmut Schmidt was among those calling for INF deployments as early as 1977, Bonn was reluctant to implement the Montebello decision of 1983 to modernize NATO's nuclear forces. It also opposed U.S. proposals to modernize short-range Lance missiles.[22] Its strategy was to engage in the new NATO deployment as a way to get the USSR to agree to reduce and eliminate its ss-18 intermediate range nuclear missiles from Europe. Both the Schmidt and successor Kohl governments sought to downplay Bonn's visibility in this regard, by demanding multilateral deployment and sole U.S. control over the weapons in West Germany. Schmidt also played the role of a mediator to negotiate the INF accords.[23]

The controversy over the modernization of Lance missiles reflected West Germany's opposition to NATO's over-reliance on short- and medium-range weapons and on nuclear artillery pieces that could be used only on West German territory. All major parties, including the SPD and the CSU, supported major reductions in nuclear weapons in Europe.[24] Opposition groups, especially the Green Party, had argued that the deployment would increase East–West tensions and would make limited war more likely, while further fuelling the arms race. The SPD opposed deployment of the Pershing II, arguing that it would endanger détente and increase Western first-strike capabilities, deriving from quick time and high accuracy.[25]

After the Cold War

The post–Cold War era was heralded by the dismantling of the Berlin Wall in November 1989, followed by the reunification of Germany in 1990 and the collapse of the Soviet Union. The removal of Soviet/ Russian troops from Eastern Europe followed, radically improving Germany's security environment. The German non-nuclear policy was further reinforced by the agreements and assurances that Germany gave to the Soviet Union on this matter as a pre-condition for reunification. The Kohl–Gorbachev Agreements at Stavropol in July 1990 assured gradual withdrawal of Soviet forces from East German territory and implementation of German undertakings that recognized specific Soviet security interests and funded the social and economic costs of relocating Soviet forces. By this agreement, Germany unilaterally recommitted itself to its earlier pledges not to produce weapons of mass destruction, including nuclear weapons; obligated itself to sign non-aggression treaties with the Soviet Union and Poland; and reiterated its respect for existing state borders. Kohl also promised to keep East German territory as a denuclearized zone within NATO and off limits to non-German NATO troops.[26]

The subsequent commitments made by German leaders also suggest that they were acutely aware of Soviet sensitivities in the nuclear realm. On 12 September 1990, Germany signed the Two-plus-Four Treaty, and in article III of the treaty it agreed to abide by the commitments made by both West and East Germany regarding renunciation of nuclear, biological, and chemical weapons and application of the rights and obligations under the NPT. It also pledged to limit the size of its army and respect existing borders with neighbours.[27]

At the turn of the twenty-first century, Germany continues its non-nuclear policy. It shows no signs of altering the policy any time soon, despite the pessimism expressed by some scholars of hard realist persuasion.[28] In fact, Kohl's successor government, led by Gerhard Schröder, which came to power in October 1998, has been more anti-nuclear than any of its predecessors, because a key partner in its coalition has been the Green Party. The governing coalition put forth proposals such as NATO's adopting a no-first-use policy and Germany's closing down its nuclear power plants. But it had to shelve both proposals, the first because of opposition from other NATO countries, especially the United States, and the second because of domestic economic pressures.[29]

Why Did Germany Choose to Forswear Nuclear Weapons?

From a theoretical and empirical point of view, the important question is why West Germany, which had an active confrontation with a nuclear-armed superpower, chose not to acquire an indigenous nuclear force as did Britain and France. The most commonly accepted explanation is that it was forced to do so by the victors of the Second World War.[30] Subsequently, the American nuclear umbrella and the presence of massive U.S. forces forestalled any need for it to seek a national nuclear capability.[31] The United States acted as a pacifier and a "balancer of last resort" of Western European states such as West Germany and contained the challenger, the Soviet Union. By extending security guarantees to West Germany, the United States removed the major structural and systemic reasons for the pursuit of an autonomous defence policy. West Germany accepted a number of constraints, such as forswearing nuclear weapons and completely integrating its armed forces with NATO, because of the U.S. presence on the continent; without that presence, it has been argued, West Germany and other Western European countries would have pursued their own nuclear-weapons programs.[32]

It has been further argued that most of the American weapons in West Germany were under a dual-key control mechanism, in which the delivery systems were under the jurisdiction of the host country, while the United States controlled the warheads. This gave allied states such as West Germany "negative control" over the launching of nuclear weapons in case of a war.[33]

While these factors are extremely important in the West German calculations regarding nuclear weapons, especially up to the mid-1960s, a more nuanced explanation would look at other powerful variables that acted as constraints on the country's nuclear acquisition. I argue that in order to understand the non-nuclear policy, we must complement the alliance factor with other variables identified in this study. Such a viewpoint would give the agent, West Germany, a greater role in its nuclear choices, rather than seeing it as a passive actor unable to make decisions on its own in the face of formidable structural constraints. Thus we can attribute West Germany's non-nuclear policy largely to the asymmetrical security interdependence that Bonn entered into with its allies and adversaries in the post-1945 period. I argue that we should view its nuclear policy within the broader foreign policy that it had to devise, given its strategic and political position after the war. West Germany, during the Cold War period, was located in a mixed, high-conflict/low-conflict region, which was engaged in intense conflict with the Soviet bloc but in itself constituted an economically interdependent and low-conflict region. This mix of regional security environments shaped West German foreign affairs. West German policy stemmed from a conscious effort not to generate intense negative security externalities for its neighbours, with which it had fought two gruesome wars in the twentieth century.

Being in the forefront of a divided Europe, with its former territory partitioned by the ideological rift, West Germany's policy-makers had to be part and parcel of the Western alliance to deter potential attacks from the Eastern bloc. Yet Bonn had to be careful not to provoke the Soviet Union to a point at which war could become a possibility, which would spell disaster for West Germany, possibly more than for any other state in Western Europe. Administering a policy that did not give the impression of appeasement while not being overly confrontational was thus a constant dilemma faced by West German policy-makers during the Cold War era.[34]

This dualism became more pronounced during the 1970s and 1980s, when West Germany supported NATO decisions to deploy nuclear weapons on its territory while at the same time pursuing détente with the Soviet Union. The rationale of this "two pillar doctrine" was that armaments and détente were compatible and that "there could be no détente without military strength; military strength without détente would be precarious to be sure, but not impossible."[35] The simultaneous foreign policy goals – reunification, European integration, and fostering of the Atlantic community – forestalled an independent nuclear program that would have adversely affected all three objectives.[36]

West Germany thus was constrained by the asymmetrical interdependence in which it found itself during the post–Second World War era. This relationship tied its security to the other states in the European system and meant that unilateral nuclearization would have made it more vulnerable than secure as its allies and adversaries would have taken political and military counter-measures.[37] The West German dilemma over nuclear weapons resulted from its hostile historical interactions with its neighbours and from their lingering fears about a resurgence of German militarism.

Allied states were wary of an independent German nuclear capability. From their perspective, West Germany, uncontained through superior power capability, could again become a threat to their security.[38] France was the leading early opponent of West Germany's rearmament, especially through an independent nuclear-weapons capability. France was a key force behind West Germany's nuclear-renunciation pact in 1954 and under de Gaulle thwarted later proposals for Franco–German joint nuclear development. Bonn was equally cognizant of its need to be friendly to France. Its participation in NATO provided the best way to secure its security without excessively provoking its allies and adversaries and other smaller neighbours who were victims of German aggression in the preceding decades.[39]

A critical factor was the adverse implications that West German nuclear weapons would have created for the U.S.–West German relationship. That country's leaders had constantly emphasized the guaranteed American presence and involvement in Europe as the main pillar of West German defence and NATO as the formal framework for the West German–American security arrangement. They realized that they could gain more by being a responsible member of the Western alliance than by pursuing an independent nuclear venture. For West Germany, a multilateral defence structure under U.S. leadership provided a better security guarantee than a unilateral defence capability.[40] A nuclear capability would not have advanced any of its major goals in foreign policy and would have hurt prospects for peaceful German reunification, European integration, and removal of Soviet forces from Eastern Europe. The political and economic costs of a nuclear capability greatly outweighed potential benefits.[41] Additionally, West Germany's own ambitions regarding power and influence changed over time. Traditional military power seemed to have limited relevance to the creation of a stable, unified Europe. As well, West Germany could not create a unilateral security strategy without upsetting the European order. Unilateral nuclear acquisition could have reanimated "deep-seated fears of revived nationalist militarism in Germany" and therefore divided and debilitated Europe.[42]

The Soviet factor was extremely important in this respect. Soviet policy on nuclear non-proliferation was driven largely by fear of West Germany's acquisition of nuclear armaments, which would have multiplied Soviet hostility towards it, thereby intensifying Bonn's security dilemma. This hostility would have resulted in increased levels of Soviet military activity directed against West Germany, especially from East Germany. Moscow would also have delayed German reunification. This awareness was key to West Germany's policies towards the Soviet Union through the Cold War period, felt more intensely from the mid-1960s on.

West German decision-makers were conscious of Soviet opposition, and their decision to forgo a national nuclear capability was influenced by the need to allay Russian fears. In fact, many West German political leaders opposed even deployment of U.S. intermediate-range ballistic missiles (IRBMs) that could hit Soviet cities such as Leningrad and Moscow, on the grounds that it could provoke rather than deter the Soviet Union. In December 1957, NATO decided to deploy American-built Thor and Jupiter IRBMs in Europe following Soviet achievement of an ICBM capability. The West German government showed extreme reluctance to approve this deployment, arguing that the missiles were vulnerable to Soviet attack and that they would lead to withdrawal of U.S. forces from West Germany. Although it accepted the NATO decision, in the end no missiles were deployed.[43] The SPD's leading defence spokesman, Helmut Schmidt, rejected the proposal on the grounds that it would adversely affect NATO's strategy, destabilize East–West relations, and possibly provoke the USSR. In his words, supplying West Germany with "nuclear missiles capable of devastating Moscow or Leningrad would inevitably provoke the Soviet Union in just the same way as the supply of nuclear missiles to Cuba would provoke the United States."[44] During the INF debate in the 1980s, this concern again became prominent. The underlying opposition was based on the fear that the missile system would decouple the United States from European defence and that the United States would regionalize a potential military conflict.[45] Fear of an adverse Soviet response must have informed this opposition as well.

West Germany's economic interdependence with Western Europe and other leading global actors further enhanced its economic security and decreased its need for autarkic economic and security policies. The Western European states have created an interdependent economic order, interlinked by a political structure and by a confederal, pan-

European economy where national industries could prosper.[46] Germany has been the dominant advocate of further integration of Europe. Chancellor Helmut Kohl, especially, saw tighter integration as the only way to achieve his nation's vital economic, security, and political interests. The European Union provides Germany the best avenue for multilateral co-operation, enhances its economic interests through increased trade and investment, and improves its bargaining power vis-à-vis other major economic centres of the world.[47] With the collapse of Communism in Eastern Europe, Germany's economic and political interests in the ex-Communist states have increased dramatically. Germany has a vital interest in not turning this region into a zone of high conflict. Unilateral nuclear armament would run counter to German interests in integrating these economies and playing a larger role in these countries. With the end of the Cold War, Germany's security interdependence with other European states has increased, making it more difficult for it to acquire an independent nuclear capability.

JAPAN

Japan is a second major power that has declared a non–nuclear weapons policy, by acceding to the NPT of 1968 and by repeatedly proclaiming its intentions to remain non-nuclear. Japan in the post–war period confronted a nuclear Soviet Union and a nuclear China and engaged with the former in an active territorial conflict over the Kurile Islands, off northern Japan. Like (West) Germany, Japan has been under the U.S. "nuclear umbrella" since the 1950s, reinforced by the presence of thousands of U.S. troops on its soil and in and around its waters. Despite the American extended deterrence, Japan, by traditional power-political considerations, should have been a prime candidate for nuclear acquisition. It has possessed the necessary technology and materials for building nuclear weapons and could have quickly acquired a medium-level nuclear force. Periodic intense debates within Japan suggest the dilemma that Tokyo faced in this realm.[48] The political elite has often maintained that Japan has the technical capability but was not pursuing nuclear weapons. Some U.S. scholars had anticipated that Japan would become a nuclear power. For instance, Herman Kahn in 1970 and Zbigniew Brzezinski in 1972 predicted that it would acquire nuclear weapons.[49] But so far Japan has belied these predictions. For purpose of analysis, I divide Japanese nuclear policy into three phases: 1945–70, 1970–90, and 1991 and after. During these periods, major external changes occurred that had a bearing on Japan's nuclear policy.

1945–70

Being the first and the only country to experience an atomic attack, Japan was in the forefront of nuclear disarmament in the initial years of the post-war period. Domestic opinion against nuclear weapons had been strong, and images of Hiroshima and Nagasaki lingered in popular and elite perceptions. Yet systemic and sub-systemic changes, especially the advent of the Cold War and the outbreak of the Korean War in 1950, affected Japanese views on security and nuclear weapons.

Japan adopted a non-nuclear policy in the early post-war reconstruction period as part and parcel of the grand economic and political strategy that its leadership formulated in the aftermath of the country's defeat. It was clearly manifested in the Yoshida Doctrine, which declared Japan's intentions to pursue a low-posture international policy that would allow it to become prosperous. In security, the doctrine advocated a purely defensive posture via a modest self-defence force, which would be supported and strengthened by American security guarantees. This doctrine was part of a clearly defined foreign policy framework, tailored to overcoming the constraints that the post-war order placed on the Japanese leadership.[50] The u.s.–Japan Peace Treaty and the Mutual Security Pact of September 1951 were premised on Washington's desire to keep Japan as a bulwark against the spread of Communism in Asia and to block the Soviet fleet at Vladivostok and Soviet forces in the Far East if a war broke out.

The Yoshida Doctrine became institutionalized under the premierships of Ikeda Hayato (1960–64) and Sato Eisaku (1964–72). These leaders created a foreign policy framework that emphasized economic prosperity while avoiding ideological discussions, so as to create maximum domestic consensus.[51] It would avoid international and national security obligations in the implementation of this economics-first state policy. The objective was also creation of a "moratorium state," which reduced the role of military power and valued technological and economic strength. Sato expanded the Yoshida Doctrine when in 1967 he proposed three *non*-nuclear principles – not producing, not possessing, and not permitting introduction of nuclear weapons on Japanese soil. The u.s. nuclear guarantee helped make possible introduction of these principles.[52]

During the 1960s, two major incidents – China's testing of a nuclear device in October 1964 and escalation of the Vietnam War – heated up debate on nuclear weapons. Yet Japanese leaders in 1966, especially Foreign Minister Shhiina Etsusaburo, asserted Japan's place within the u.s. nuclear umbrella. Prime Minister Sato also declared during a November 1967 summit with President Lyndon Johnson that the U.S.–Japanese security treaty and the American nuclear umbrella defended Japan.[53]

None the less, popular pressure to maintain a non-nuclear policy continued even under increased security threats. Opposition to U.S. nuclear-armed ships visiting Japanese ports intensified, especially when the Japanese government decided in November 1967 to accept port calls by the aircraft carrier USS *Enterprise*. Domestic opposition to the visit contributed to adoption later of the three non-nuclear principles.[54] The crucial dilemmas for Japanese decision-makers during this period appeared to be how to remain non-nuclear while receiving American nuclear protection and how not to get entrenched in the U.S. nuclear buildup in the Pacific and thereby become a direct target of both China and the Soviet Union. The non-nuclear policy became more institutionalized despite threats arising out of the nuclear activities of China and the intensified conflict in Indochina, both of which profoundly affected Japan's security environment.

1970–90

These two decades witnessed significant changes in Japan's nuclear posture, especially the legalization of the non-weapons policy. Japan initially opposed the NPT, and although it *signed* the treaty in February 1970 (more than eighteen months after it was concluded), Tokyo took six years to *ratify* it. Its opposition should not be construed as a clever ploy by Japan to maintain its nuclear options, although some minor factions within the Liberal Democratic Party (LDP) feared that the treaty would foreclose Japan's future possibility of developing a weapons capability. More left-leaning groups feared that the treaty would perpetuate the nuclear monopoly of the five declared nuclear states. The bigger concern was that the NPT and the IAEA safeguards would adversely affect Japan's peaceful uses of nuclear energy. Japan also sought development of a fair and equal system of international safeguards. The delay in inserting article III of the treaty, which dealt with safeguards and peaceful nuclear co-operation, into the Soviet–American draft and the prior debate on Euratom versus IAEA procedures also caused Japan to hesitate. Japanese nuclear corporations were anxious about the frequency and intensity of IAEA safeguards inspections and the possibility of their facilitating commercial espionage.[55] Fear that the NPT safeguards might hinder Japan's civil nuclear energy program eased when the IAEA agreed to provide less intrusive safeguards and Japan received equal treatment with Euratom. Japan finally became concerned that if it did not ratify the NPT it might have difficulty in importing and exporting nuclear materials.[56] It ratified the treaty in June 1976.

Even while opposition to the NPT was increasing, a white paper on defence published in October 1970 made it clear that Japan would maintain its non-nuclear policy and respect article 9 of its constitution, which obligates the country to follow a non-aggressive policy. In practical terms, this policy involved imposing restraints on the quality and quantity of weapons, especially ones that would threaten other countries, such as ICBMs and strategic bombers. Although defensive nuclear weapons could receive exemption from this list, Japan would even then follow a policy of not acquiring nuclear weapons.[57] What the military planners meant by "defensive nuclear weapons" were small tactical nuclear weapons, such as nuclear mines and anti-air missiles, that could be useful in defence against hostile forces landing in Japan and that presumably would not pose a threat of aggression to other countries.[58] Notably, Japanese defence planners were aware of the need to reassure and not to provoke their Asian neighbours.

During this period, the U.S. nuclear presence in Japan caused more debates and helped to reinforce the public's nuclear allergy. In testimony before a U.S. Congressional Joint Committee, a former commander of the USS *Providence*, Rear Admiral Gene R. Laroque, stated that U.S. warships did not unload their nuclear arms when they made calls on Japanese ports.[59] A 1960 secret transit agreement, reportedly reconfirmed during talks between President Richard Nixon and Prime Minister Sato in 1972, permitted unrestrained transit of American nuclear weapons by air and sea on Japanese territory. Since no official text was available, Japan could deny the existence of such an agreement.[60]

The late 1970s and early 1980s were a period of increased Soviet military activity in the Pacific. Several factors – the Nixon Doctrine, the U.S. failure in Vietnam, the Soviet buildup of Backfire bombers and SS-20 missiles in Asia, the growth of the Soviet Pacific fleet, the stationing of Soviet troops in the disputed Northern territories, and Moscow's occupation of Afghanistan – increased pressures on Japan to refashion its defence policy. As well, there were U.S. demands that Japan end its security "free ride."[61] Under Prime Minister Yasuhiro Nakasone, military spending increased, along with fears of rising prospects of Japanese militarism. During this period, the security debate often involved four elite groups: Gaullists, political realists, military realists, and unarmed neutralists. The Gaullists, the smallest group, contemplated Japan's acquiring a strike force involving tactical nuclear weapons, but they were outshadowed by political realists, who believed in strengthening the U.S.–Japanese alliance in order to enhance security.

Even military realists, who clamoured for Japan to assume a greater military role in order to be prepared for a possible war with the Soviet Union, opposed acquisition of an independent nuclear capability.[62]

1991 and After

The end of the Cold War marked a watershed in Japan's security environment. The collapse of the Soviet Union altered Japan's perception of threats from its main opponent. At the same time, some Japanese strategic analysts raised concerns that Japan might lose its U.S. nuclear umbrella. Hence Japan's initial opposition to an indefinite extension of the NPT, which it would later recant.[63] In addition, massive importation of plutonium for the fast-breeder reactor program also raised questions about Japan's nuclear intentions.

The Gulf War, the first test of Japan's international activity in the post–Cold War era, challenged some of the traditional assumptions of security policy–makers. In June 1992, the Diet passed a law allowing Japanese Self-defence Forces to take part in international peacekeeping operations; their participation in Cambodia marked a sea change in Japan's foreign policy – the first time since the Second World War that Japanese troops were deployed overseas, though for peaceful missions.[64]

North Korean efforts to obtain nuclear weapons and the threat to withdraw from the NPT refocused international attention on Japan's nuclear potential. The North Korean crisis put tremendous pressure on Japan to rethink its nuclear policy. Pyongyang's program also involved development of medium range ballistic missiles capable of hitting the major cities of Japan. The test firing in May 1993 of Rodong I, a 1,000-kilometre-range missile that landed off the Noto Peninsula in the Sea of Japan, further aggravated the Japanese sense of insecurity.[65] During this time, a British government report revealed that "Japan has key bomb-making components, including plutonium and electronic triggers and has expertise to go nuclear very quickly."[66] Statements by various Japanese officials indicated a certain amount of rethinking. Foreign Minister Kabun Muto stated that if North Korean nuclear capability became a threat to Japan, "possessing the will that we can do it is important."[67] The easing of the North Korean crisis in 1994 reduced this impending threat and, along with it, speculations about Japan's nuclear acquisition.

The Indian and Pakistani nuclear tests in May 1998 raised considerable hue and cry in Japan, resulting in the government's imposing economic sanctions on the two countries. The North Korean test-firing of the Taepo-Dong I, with a range of 3,200 kilometres, over Japanese territory in August 1998 also increased Japan's security concerns. However, neither event seems to have fundamentally altered Japan's non-nuclear policy.[68]

Determinants of Japan's Nuclear Forbearance

The American nuclear umbrella has been a necessary condition for Tokyo's non-nuclear policy, as it has allowed Japan to concentrate on economic policies. Yet a comprehensive understanding of Japan's non-nuclear policy would complement the alliance variable with other compelling factors identified in this study. A culturalist explanation based on nuclear allergy and embedded anti-militarism holds some strength, but it has difficulty in providing a dynamic explanation, because a worsening external security environment could weaken the allergy, as the political elite would be forced to choose radical options and mould public opinion to support its actions.[69]

During the Cold War era, Japan was situated in a mixed high–moderate conflict zone and had nuclear states as enemies. Although tensions with the Soviet Union placed it in a high-conflict zone, the conflict level in East Asia affecting Japan was usually of a moderate nature, with Japan not engaged in any serious enduring rivalry/conflict. Relations with China and North Korea were hostile, but still not involving militarized disputes or armed clashes. However, based on its security context, and left alone, Japan would have been a strong candidate for nuclear acquisition. I argue that its asymmetrical security interdependence vis-à-vis allies and adversaries powerfully constrained its acquiring an independent nuclear capability. This factor was relevant during the Cold War and has increased in salience since then.[70]

The Japanese forbearance of nuclear weapons has been the result of cost–benefit calculations by successive governments and the adoption of a low-posture defence policy purported to project the image of a benign trading state, not interested in aggressive military policy. Acquisition of major military systems such as nuclear capability would have generated intense negative security externalities for neighbours (both allies and adversaries) with which Japan had fought aggressive wars in the past, especially those that Japan had occupied. A turbulent international order in which Japan acquired weapons of mass destruction was perceived from the early days of the post-war era as antithetical to projection of such a benign image. Because of the historical baggage of aggressive Japanese nationalism, neighbouring states, especially the USSR and China, as well as the smaller Asian states, would have viewed a Japanese independent nuclear capability with intense suspicion, if not hostility. Moreover, unlike in the 1930s, in the post-war era Japan became a major player in the liberal international economic order. Japan's prosperity and economic security became enmeshed in the global web of financial, production, and trading interdependencies.[71] Japanese dependence on foreign sources for key raw materials, food, and energy has forced it to adopt a policy posture of "being friendly with everybody," or at least not making serious enemies anywhere – as in the posture of *happo-yabure* (defenceless on all sides) used in Japanese fencing (*kendo*). A Japanese military buildup would have seemed a dangerous sign to some such countries and persuaded them to increase their military readiness vis-à-vis Japan.[72]

As with West Germany, anticipated negative responses by neighbours, allies, and adversaries constitute a significant disincentive that helps explain Japan's non-nuclear policy. The perceived hostility from neighbouring Asian states and the Soviet Union are critical in this respect. The Yoshida Doctrine of a low-posture defence policy, with small amounts of armaments, was indeed premised on the fear of adverse effects on neighbouring countries. U.S. Secretary of State John Foster Dulles had desired rearmament of Japan, but its leaders made choices contrary to requests to that effect.[73] In 1967, Prime Minister Sato called together a small group of officials and scholars to examine whether Japan should possess nuclear weapons independently. They reported that it was technically feasible but politically unacceptable – a nuclear weapons program would be costly, it would alarm neighbours, and it would not receive a majority of public support.[74] Although the group placed the cost factor on top of the list of constraints, by the 1970s increased prosperity would have allowed Japan to foot the bill for such a program. Alarming the neighbours remained a critical dissuasive factor even as economic constraints faded in importance.

Asian states that had experienced Japanese aggression would have been extremely hostile to Tokyo's acquiring a nuclear capability. Japan's increased dependence on Asian states for markets, raw materials, and economic investment made it imperative that Japan heed the sensitivities of its Asian neighbours.[75] Additionally, the smaller Asian neighbours that Japan conquered in the 1940s are no longer passive colonial states, but major economic and political actors in the Asia–Pacific region. In 1995 the ASEAN countries concluded a nuclear-free-zone treaty for South East Asia, with the aim of preventing states in the region from acquiring nuclear weapons. These states are likely to react vigorously to a Japanese nuclear program and might form counter-alliances and thereby neutralize any advantages that Japan might obtain in security through possession of nuclear weapons.

South Korea especially would have been most reluctant to see Japan rearm. Some analysts there already call Japan an "associate member of the nuclear club," and they perceive Japan as a future security threat to Korea, especially after reunification of the Korean peninsula. The historical legacy of Japanese imperialism still reverberates powerfully in South Korean minds. Evidence of this can be seen not only in academic discourse, but in popular writings as well. The novel *The Rose of Sharon Has Blossomed*, "in which North and South Korea cooperate in developing nuclear weapons that save the South in a war with Japan," was a national bestseller in 1991.[76]

It is not likely that the response of Japan's major ally, the United States, would be positive to a Japanese nuclear weapons program. The U.S. security relationship has been pivotal to Japan's security and economic well-being, and it has allowed Japan to pursue incremental changes in its defence policy.[77] The United States, despite the end of the Cold War, has shown no inclination to withdraw from the Pacific, as evident in its active pursuit of the Asia Pacific Economic Forum (APEC) to expand economic co-operation among Asian countries. As long as Japan remains non-nuclear and possesses a weak conventional military capability, the United States could maintain hegemony in a region that it perceives as likely to be economically the most dynamic in the world in the next century.

Since the end of the Cold War, the United States has shown keen interest in continuing its security relationship with Japan. The U.S.–Japanese security treaty was revitalized in September 1997 with new guidelines, which upgraded defence co-operation. The guidelines clearly stipulate Japan's role in future conflicts in the region. They include supply of air and naval facilities, materials, and fuel, but not of weapons or ammunition. The security arrangement thus continues to limit Japan's offensive capabilities and military operations in the region. One of the key elements of the renewed co-operation has been the extra efforts made by Japanese and American officials to brief and reassure Asian countries, especially China, about the defensive nature of the revitalized pact. A mechanism for the periodic briefing of neighbouring countries on joint activities will be formalized in the future.[78]

During the Cold War era, Japan's nuclear acquisition would have pushed the Soviet Union more into a politics of confrontation. Moscow could have built up its air and naval forces in the Pacific, hardened its position on the disputed northern islands, used the Japanese nuclear issue to obstruct arms-control negotiations with the United States, and, in a worst-case scenario, engaged in a pre-emptive blockade or strike against Japan.[79] These concerns were evident in Japan's foreign policy towards the Soviet Union during the 1970s, when it made every effort to reassure Moscow that it was not forming an anti-Soviet alliance with

China. Tokyo would "attempt to keep the door open for expanded Soviet ties should Soviet diplomatic strategy toward Japan change."[80]

A related major constraint on Japan's nuclear option has been its assumed difficulty in building an invulnerable second-strike capability without provoking its potential targets, Russia and China. A nuclear opponent bent on destroying Japan could do so by placing a few bombs on key cities and industrial sites.[81] The damage that Japan could inflict on Russia, in contrast, would be limited. According to a study in 1980, as the Soviet Union had only a handful of cities in the Far East, a Japanese tactical nuclear attack could probably have resulted in a million casualties, while a similar assault on Japanese cities could have resulted in 40 million casualties. A Japanese theatre nuclear force would not constitute a deterrent to Russian attack because of the radioactive fallout on Japan itself. Japan's chief hope then would be a strategic force based on SLBMs, but the lead time for acquisition of such a force would be at least a decade. However, such a force could have increased the Russian military threat to Japan.[82]

Because Japan is a densely populated island nation, fixed silos or bomber bases would remain vulnerable to enemy attack. Japan might have to develop mobile launchers and keep dozens of nuclear-armed aircraft permanently airborne, with the attendant problems of safety. A Polaris-type submarine force could, however, provide a limited second-strike capability.[83] Such a system would be capable of hitting targets in China and eastern Russia but would attract the wrath of these two countries. Japan would not be able to develop such an invulnerable second-strike capability without provoking hostile responses from the United States, Russia, China, and neighbouring countries in East and South East Asia. Some analysts think that the end of the Cold War has reinforced Japanese vulnerability in this respect. Even if Japan acquired nuclear weapons, its highly valued urban centres and dense population would mean that a non-industrialized nuclear state such as North Korea (if it ever acquired such weapons) or a nuclear state with great territorial depth such as Russia could threaten it with a nuclear first strike.[84]

Some observers cite the anti-nuclear feelings or the nuclear allergy of the Japanese public as a critical factor in the non-nuclear policy. Living in the only nation that has ever experienced a nuclear attack, the Japanese public has been extremely hostile to these weapons. In addition, succeeding generations of political leaders have been sensitive to this factor. Strong anti-nuclear movements arise from the public's fear that nuclear possession would excite its neighbours and cause war rather than deter it.[85] Although this factor seems important, major alterations in Japan's security environment, caused by drastic external changes, could alter public perceptions of the utility of nuclear weapons. Public opinion could also be remoulded by a determined political leadership if it were able to portray an impending security disaster in the face of deteriorating circumstances if a nuclear deterrent were not available. However, modest changes in the security environment are unlikely to diminish the nuclear allergy. In that sense, the allergy exerts a modest, but conditional influence.

The same argument applies to self-built institutional and legal factors.[86] The Basic Atomic Energy Law of 1956 and the U.S.–Japan Security Treaty of 1958 permit Japan to use nuclear energy only for peaceful purposes. Article 9 of the constitution also indirectly prohibits it from acquiring nuclear weapons, although some constitutional experts and policy-makers disagree. Following the first Chinese nuclear test, the government announced that "under the present circumstances nuclear weapons are subject to the prohibitions of the constitution, but that if nuclear weapons are developed which could properly be construed as defensive, then the constitution could not be said to prohibit them," implying that the constitutional provision is not absolute.[87] However, developing a weapon purely for defensive purposes seems highly questionable. The established utility of nuclear weapons has been their deterrent value, rather than defence. Most of the elements of a second-strike capability – heavy bombers, ICBMs, and SLBMs – are also offensive weapons, even if intentions are defensive. Japan is unlikely to succeed in convincing its neighbours that such a second-strike capability is defensive only.

Other legal arrangements, such as the ban on dispatch of military forces overseas and on export of arms, the three non-nuclear principles, the ceiling of 1 per cent of GNP spent on defence, the five principles for SDF participation in peacekeeping operations, and prior approval by the Diet of such dispatches, should prevent potential militarization.[88] But these legal arrangements reflect Japan's security interdependence. Strategic notions such as "non-offensive defence," which exclude acquisition of the capacity to invade or threaten other countries, and the notion of "minimum necessary defense capability" clearly reflect a desire not to be seen as provocative to neighbouring states.[89] Legal and institutional instruments, however, reflect the existing policy preference against nuclear acquisition and are therefore not determinants. Like nuclear allergy, legal arrangements can be manipulated if and when the security environment changes radically. These instruments, however, exert a modest influence on Japan, preventing it from altering policies suddenly in the face of limited external challenges.

What role does the NPT play in Japanese nuclear forbearance? I argue that the treaty is not a determinant, but largely a manifestation of Japan's non-nuclear commitment. Japanese nuclear facilities have been comprehensively safeguarded by the IAEA. For instance, in 1990, 25 per cent of all IAEA inspections took place in Japan.[90] Neither domestic nor international institutional constraints are causes or determinants of Japan's non-nuclear policy. They contribute to its maintenance to the extent that they give other states some confidence with respect to Japan's intentions and prevent possible hostile countervailing measures. Security interdependence is a more crucial causal factor in determining the sustenance of Japan's non-nuclear policy.

Japan's rethinking of the value of nuclear weapons has resulted from its changed view of power and influence since its defeat in 1945. To some Japanese scholars, nuclear weapons have not elevated the power and prestige of second-tier states. Japanese views about power and prestige differ in some sense from those of the traditional realpolitik school. Opposition in the 1970s to its becoming a superpower was based on concern that Japan would have to devote much more energy to the military aspect of national capability. To many Japanese a second-class international status was preferable to the "risks, costs, and tensions of first class status."[91] Anticipated hostile responses from allies and adversaries have powerfully affected Japanese perceptions of power and influence.

OPTIONS FOR GERMANY AND JAPAN

Some analysts have argued that Germany should and would acquire nuclear weapons and that selective proliferation in states such as Germany would enhance international security. According to an analysis in 1985, a (West) German mini-nuclear force would have been more credible and safer than the American extended deterrent.[92] To neo-realists such as Waltz and Mearsheimer, structural changes would force Germany and Japan to pursue national nuclear-weapons programs.[93] Despite these predictions, in the German case, the end of the Cold War greatly reduced the short- and medium-term possibilities of nuclear acquisition. Germany is no longer engaged in a protracted conflict with Russia, and its borders are secure with the end of Communism in Eastern Europe and the re-establishment of a buffer between it and Russia. Germany has integrated further in the European Union. Unilateral acquisition of nuclear arms could jeopardize Germany's security more than such a course of action would benefit it. If Germany (as well as Japan) goes nuclear, the non-proliferation regime would suffer its biggest setback, as major powers' going nuclear would have larger implications than smaller actors' doing so. The end result could be a resurgence of nationalism and renewed hostility towards Germany by its neighbours, especially France. It would also undermine the progress made so far in European integration. German statements and behaviour since the end of the Cold War give ample evidence that Germany is keenly interested in strengthening the European Union (EU) and further integrating the continent by enlarging the EU to include Eastern European states.

In attempting to strengthen the EU, the German leadership has been making sure that Germany does not revert to the politico-military strategy followed up to 1939, which resulted in what German historian Friedrich Meinecke called "the German catastrophe," which "caused the country's ideological and political isolation and its encirclement by unfriendly neighbors."[94] A number of changes in the European land-scape suggest the continuation of a non-nuclear policy by Germany. Deepening economic interdependence and the transformation of Europe into a low-conflict zone are significant in this respect. The economic interdependence of today is different from any in previous eras in terms of institutions, scale, and depth.[95]

In addition, political and institutional structures exist to allow the orderly management of this interdependence and thereby reduce the prospects of future conflict. Even if incentives for conflict exist, there are mechanisms available, such as the European Commission, the Council of Ministers, the Parliament, and the European Court, to contain it. These institutions also provide "warning lights" if any of the member states attempt to go above them and pursue autarkic policies.[96] Moreover, for Germany, reunification has resolved a central issue over which conflict could have erupted. Germany clearly has no interest in forcefully changing the territorial boundaries of Europe now that the relative value of territory has depreciated for an advanced, industrialized state.[97] The biggest constraint on Germany's assuming a larger role is the perceived and actual responses of neighbouring states. In this sense, a united Germany continues to share some of the constraints felt by the old West Germany. In the eyes of its neighbours, Germany still lacks the legitimacy needed to become a normal military power. Although it participated in the conflict in Bosnia and Kosovo in 1999, its peacekeepers were under NATO command and did not represent unilateral, assertive military behaviour.[98]

A drastic change in the international system, resulting in the resur-gence of enduring rivalries among great powers, is the most likely condition under which Germany would pursue an independent nuclear capability. Such a transformation would be the result perhaps of the failure of the international economic order that has so far benefited Germany, of the rise of one or more great powers in Europe or elsewhere as enduring rivals with threatening military and economic policies, or the total withdrawal of the U.S. security guarantees.[99] While such possibilities cannot be ruled out entirely, the historical progression in Europe suggests the reverse. High levels of institution-alized co-operation did not exist during previous eras when major states pursued mercantilist policies with a vengeance.

In the Pacific, a significant factor restraining Japan from going nuclear would be the persistence of Japan's security interdependence with its neighbours and U.S. security guarantees. The rise of regional nuclear powers hostile to Japan, the emergence of an enduring rivalry between Japan and China, and a simultaneous withdrawal of U.S. secu-rity guarantees would be the necessary conditions for Japan's nuclear-ization. However, a total American withdrawal from the Pacific or the emergence of a hostile relationship between Washington and Tokyo is unlikely in the short and medium terms. The United States has well-entrenched interests in the Pacific. The rise of Asia–Pacific as an eco-nomically vibrant region in the next century would make it imperative that the United States maintain its involvement in the Pacific.[100]

Both Japan and Germany have the latent capability to become nuclear states if they choose to do so. This potential itself could act as a virtual deterrent on a prospective aggressor. Japan's industrial and technolog-ical capabilities have seemed to some analysts equivalent to a latent deterrent.[101] This implicit military capability has allowed Japan to pursue a "virtual deterrence strategy." Although this capability may not prevent a surprise attack, the potential aggressor is unlikely to use nuclear weapons in the initial stages of a conflict. The defensive capability that Japan and Germany possess could make an attacker's task of conquest of either more difficult. This, combined with the alliance relationship, could restrain an adversary from launching an attack on these states.

A significant reason for Japan to convert its latent nuclear capability to an active weapons program would be a worsening of its security environment following a loosening of the U.S. security commitment. Since 1976, Japanese defence policy has assumed that a full-scale military clash between East and West was unlikely. However, in the past, the fear of China's targeting its nuclear weapons on Japan did not materialize.[102] In addition, the nuclear acquisitions of India and Pakistan have also provoked less security concern than anticipated. North Korea's nuclear program is likely to increase calls for Japan to acquire an independent nuclear capability; reunification of the two

Koreas could also increase Japanese security if the new country follows a pro-nuclear policy. However, overt nuclearization is unlikely in the short and medium terms.

A second rationale for Japan's acquiring nuclear weapons – power and prestige – proved less significant as the nuclear age continued. Many political leaders believed that "enhanced military strength does not necessarily correlate with enhanced security." The post-war Japanese conception of power has been based on the notion of "global civilian power," assuming that "a major military buildup in Japan, already one of the world's biggest economic powers, is neither in the national interests nor would it serve the cause of international order." Japan has become a major economic power without possessing nuclear weapons or even a massive conventional capability. Changing conceptions of national power and the elevation of economic power have strengthened Japan's position without its possessing weapons of mass destruction, which would inevitably antagonize neighbours and other key actors in the international system.

The development of defensive technologies could help Japan deploy a fairly reliable defensive system against nuclear attacks, avoid building costly nuclear systems, and decrease the chances of a potential nuclear attack. A theatre missile defence (TMD) based on anti-ballistic defence systems would not increase first-strike capability, as it probably would for a nuclear state.[103] In the wake of the North Korean nuclear crisis, Washington was reportedly working with Japan on deploying a region-wide anti-missile system.[104] Japan's most probable types of danger – interdiction of its merchant shipping, conventional air bombardment, and invasion – could be deterred by adequate defensive and deterrent capabilities. However, even an SLBM-based force might not provide an invulnerable deterrent for a densely populated Japan.

Japan's nuclear future will also depend on China's rise as a military power in the Pacific and any threatening postures towards Japan. China's continued rapid economic growth and its military modernization could give Beijing a major capability in the region.[105] China has hitherto not been viewed as a major threat to Japan, partly because it lacks a blue-water navy in the Pacific powerful enough to threaten Japan's coastlines. The growing economic interdependence of the two countries could also forestall Chinese aggression. If China pursues aggressive military policies in the Pacific, Tokyo might be forced to acquire deterrent capabilities, including nuclear weapons, or to strengthen the security relationship with the United States.

Before concluding this chapter, I would like to consider why the constraints identified in this book are not applicable also to France and

Britain, two other key states situated in the low-conflict region of Western Europe. The main difference is that both Britain and France were winners of the Second World War and became accepted great powers following the war, a position reinforced by their status as permanent members of the UN Security Council. As I showed in chapter 2, great powers' security calculations are generally global in nature, as they tend to perceive nuclear acquisition as essential to keeping their dominant power position in the international system. Although both Germany and Japan were great powers until their defeat in 1945, they are no longer accorded that status. After the war they reoriented their military and economic polices and eventually became great economic powers. In the military/security area, they act almost like middle powers, with much of their security focus confined to their immediate region. Although their relative power positions have declined since the war, both Britain and France still maintain higher military profiles and global interests than do Germany and Japan. Consequently, their nuclear policies are driven by global rather than by regional considerations. If Germany and Japan ever decided to reorient their strategies and become great military powers and thereby break their security interdependencies, factors relevant to the great powers identified above might influence them. Such a transition could occur largely because of deteriorating international security relations, especially involving these states and other great powers. By the model in this study, the main impetus for nuclear acquisition for Germany and Japan could thus come from the rise of enduring rivalries involving other nuclear powers.

CONCLUSIONS

The nuclear choices of Germany and Japan provide valuable clues about state policies regarding weapons of mass destruction. Their past and present non-nuclear policies have not been simple accidents or the function of a single variable but rather the result of conscious foreign policy postures aimed at maximizing economic and security goals within the constraints imposed by asymmetrical security interdependence with allies and adversaries. The effect of this interdependence is manifested in the two countries' desire to follow low-posture security policies that could preclude hostile interactions with their adversaries and allies. Legal and institutional constraints and distinctive anti-militaristic cultures (of late) may have played a secondary and facilitating role in their policies, but, as I argued, they are not key determinants. Finally, American security guarantees provided these states necessary protection against a Soviet nuclear attack, obviating their need for independent nuclear capabilities.

CHAPTER FOUR

Aligned Middle Powers:
Canada and Australia

Among the states that have forgone independent nuclear arms, Canada
and Australia are notable because they could create a nuclear force in
a short period if they chose to do so. These states have been two of
the biggest producers of uranium in the world, they possess a large
pool of scientists, and they both have been active in providing support
services for the U.S. nuclear deterrent. Canada especially had acquired
the technological potential to develop nuclear weapons of its own long
before other nuclear states, except the United States, built their weapon
systems. It had gained this expertise through its participation in the
Manhattan Project and its development of civilian nuclear-reactor
technology and infrastructure in the early stage of the atomic era.
These technological achievements included the globally marketed
CANDU reactors, which produce plutonium as a by-product. Canada
also had developed an internationally competitive aircraft industry
during the early post-war period, which would have allowed it to
construct an appropriate nuclear delivery system. Although Australia
initially lagged behind in nuclear technology, by the 1970s it had
attained sufficient technical potential to develop its own bomb in a
matter of years, if it chose to do so.

These cases provide two somewhat similar states for comparison in
terms of size, culture, substantial Anglo-Saxon origins, political systems, place in the international system, and reliance on alliance partners
– first Britain and then the United States – as their main security guar-
antors. They also have been trading states that depend on exports of
natural products for a major portion of their gross national product.
As middle powers with modest influence in international politics, both
pursued strategies that placed them within the Western alliance, and at
the same time they established roles in the collective security efforts of
the United Nations and in its peacekeeping operations and disarmament

efforts. During the Cold War era, they both confronted the problem of "alliance dilemma," or the issue of how firmly to commit themselves to the dominant alliance partner's conflict interactions with its chief adversary, the Soviet Union.[1]

However, in some measures their situations vary. In a geographical and strategic sense, Canada is closer to the United States, and this factor makes it imperative that Canadian security be linked heavily to U.S. security. While Australia's geographical distance from the major conflict centres of the world, especially during the Cold War era, provided it with a somewhat benign security environment, Canada's location between the United States and the Soviet Union gave it a higher profile in a possible nuclear exchange between the two superpowers. Yet the presence of key communication installations in Australia for the U.S. nuclear strike force meant that the Soviet Union might have targeted that country as well for a nuclear attack in the early stages of a third world war. This chapter first centres on Canada, then looks at Australia, and then offers an analysis of their nuclear forbearance and its theoretical implications.

CANADA

The Canadian non-nuclear policy reflected deliberate choices that the country's leadership had made and a continuation of a low-key defence policy that relied heavily on American and NATO military strategies. Yet Canadian non-nuclear policy was not always driven solely by the wishes of the dominant partner. For instance, after acquiring jointly controlled nuclear weapons from the United States for its forces stationed in Europe, Canada, under Prime Minister Pierre Trudeau, decided to remove those weapons from Canadian control. Unilateralism was evident in that choice, made by the most independent of all prime ministers in Canadian history. I argue that we can understand Canadian non-acquisition of nuclear weapons only within the larger context of a low-profile security policy pursued by successive governments. This policy also entailed serious efforts to maintain a middle-power, internationalist position, in which Canada could exert influence in global affairs, including in nuclear non-proliferation, by emphasizing legal norms, international organizations, and collective security measures.

The Canadian policy towards nuclear weapons changed significantly during the first three decades of the Cold War era. During the 1940s, Canada took part in the initial development of the atomic bomb through its involvement in the (U.S.) Manhattan Project. Participants included the Canadian government, industry, and academe, along with their American and British partners. Canada also supplied the project with uranium from the Eldorado mine on Great Bear Lake and with plutonium produced at nuclear facilities in Montreal.[2] However, U.S. passage of the McMahon Act in 1946 ended trilateral co-operation, as the United States wanted to prevent third countries from acquiring material for nuclear weapons. While Britain resented this unilateral action, W.L. Mackenzie King's government said almost nothing. It was as if Ottawa had already decided to pursue only peaceful applications of atomic technology.[3]

When the Second World War ended, Canada's position on nuclear weapons was already focusing on international control of the atom. This stance was articulated by Canada's ambassador to the United States, Lester Pearson. In a memorandum to the Department of External Affairs prior to the Washington conference in November 1945 of the "ABC" powers – "America," Britain, and Canada – Pearson argued that the advent of nuclear weapons represented a revolutionary development in world politics and that it could not be kept secret for more than five years. Any industrial state with knowledge of atomic technology could manufacture it, resulting in "the most bitter and disastrous armament race ever run." He proposed that the ABC powers use their temporary advantage to bring the atom under international control. They should keep nuclear knowledge in trusteeship with the UN until an international commission could be established to investigate national nuclear facilities and control atomic energy development worldwide.[4]

On 5 December 1945 C.D. Howe, minister of reconstruction, while answering a question in the House of Commons, stated: "We have not manufactured atomic bombs, we have no intention of manufacturing atomic bombs."[5] On 9 November 1949, Prime Minister Louis St Laurent told the Combined Policy Committee (CPC) of the ABC powers: "We did not want to make bombs, neither to have title to them nor to use them."[6] Despite these statements, historians have not yet found any meetings of the cabinet or government committees that dealt with nuclear weapons. However, it seems that after helping develop the atomic bomb, Canada sought containment of the revolutionary weapon in the interests of the world community. There is no indication that Canada received any external pressure in this matter.[7]

Although Canada did not pursue an independent nuclear capability, it provided materials and support to Britain and the United States. The Chalk River facility near Ottawa continued to produce plutonium even after 1945, and Canada sold nuclear materials to its two partners' nuclear weapons programs for over twenty years. By 1959, Canada's annual uranium exports reached over 12,000 tonnes, worth $300 million, ranking it fourth-highest in value among the country's exports.[8]

Canada's contribution to the American nuclear deterrent, providing ancillary services to the U.S. nuclear forces, increased steadily. Canadian territory became significant to U.S. strategic planning in intelligence gathering, forward-basing of aircraft to strike Soviet targets, and early warning and early defence against a Soviet attack.[9] The period saw establishment of the North Atlantic Treaty Organisation (NATO) in 1949 and of the North American Air Defence Command (NORAD) in 1958 (renamed North American Aerospace Defence Command in 1981).[10] NORAD institutionalized U.S.–Canadian co-operation by setting up early warning of Soviet strategic bombers approaching the United States over the North Pole during a war.

Nuclear issues dominated the Canadian debate on defence policy during this period, especially the 1958 decision to acquire nuclear weapons from the United States, which caused considerable turmoil within the country and in relations between the two countries. The dispute was a result of Canadian vacillation in implementing the 1958 decision. The systems to be transferred included the short-range ground-to-air Bomarc B missile, the Honest John artillery rocket, the F-104 Starfighter aircraft, and the CF-101 Voodoo interceptor aircraft, all expected to carry nuclear weapons.[11] Prior to the agreement to transfer nuclear weapons, Canada had initiated development of the nuclear-capable Avro Arrow aircraft system, which was cancelled in February 1959 apparently because of high manufacturing costs.

The decision to acquire American nuclear weapons for Canadian forces followed NATO's 1957 decision to adopt tactical nuclear weapons as part of a European deterrent. In 1958, Canada, under the Progressive Conservative government of John Diefenbaker, agreed to buy the Bomarc and Lacrosse missiles without specifying whether they would have nuclear or conventional warheads. It did so after considering two choices – letting Canadian forces exclusively control nuclear weapons, developed through domestic efforts or acquired internationally, or allowing American weapons to be transferred to the Canadian forces in Europe. It had ruled out creating an independent nuclear force for lack of compelling strategic reasons to do so. It would pursue the NATO strategy: Canadian forces stationed in Europe would receive American nuclear weapons under dual U.S.–Canadian control.[12]

However, the Diefenbaker government showed extreme reluctance to accept the weapon systems, even though it had concluded the agreements in the first place. It deployed the BOMARC and the CF-101 Voodoos in Canada and the Lacrosse and later Honest John missiles with the Canadian NATO contingent in Europe and assigned to it conventional weapons, although they were effective only with nuclear warheads.[13] Diefenbaker and Secretary of State for External Affairs

Howard Green viewed Canada's close nuclear co-operation with the United States as a risky strategy. They feared that Canada's acquisition of nuclear weapons would mean abandonment of its long-standing efforts at the United Nations for arms control and disarmament.[14] Green also believed that Canada had only a limited ability to promote disarmament internationally and that it was therefore all the more important that it do what it could: "set a good (non-proliferating) example by refraining from acquiring or storing nuclear weapons on its soil."[15] He believed that acquisition of American weapons would result in Canada's losing its sovereignty and reduce the government's ability to make defence policy independently.[16]

The government's indecision resulted partly from the intense debate that the issue provoked. Although a majority of the public supported nuclear acquisition to honour the commitment, significant sections of the political elite opposed the decision.[17] While the Department of National Defence favoured the action, External Affairs showed opposition. The defence minister, Douglas Harkness, strongly supported the nuclear deal, as did the Royal Canadian Air Force.[18]

Diefenbaker was particularly concerned about the U.S. nuclear strategy, as evident in his hesitation to alert Canadian forces during the Cuban missile crisis. The prime minister believed that President Kennedy took the alert decision hastily and without consulting him. Although he officially ordered an alert two days later, during the crisis Canada rejected U.S. requests to disperse nuclear-armed fighters in bases across Canada. However, Ottawa approved shipping of nuclear warheads to U.S. bases in Canada, at Goose Bay in Labrador and Stephenville in Newfoundland, but only eight of 640 requests to fly nuclear-armed B-52 bombers over Canadian airspace. However, the bombers of the Strategic Air Command (SAC) went on alert and were dispersed over Canadian territory.[19]

Diefenbaker's indecision on nuclear warheads was partially responsible for the Conservatives' narrow defeat in the 1963 general election. His reluctance to acquire nuclear weapons was criticized by the Kennedy administration, which expressed its displeasure before the election. The U.S. administration was determined to convince Canadians that allied states needed nuclear weapons and found support for its position in Canada's Liberal Party.[20] Lester Pearson's new Liberal government agreed to enter into negotiations with the United States. This led to a decision on 16 August 1963, under which Canada agreed to acquire the four weapons systems carrying nuclear warheads. The United States would retain custody of the nuclear warheads but would share with Canada control over release of the weapons, similar to the joint-control arrangements that it had with other NATO countries. By the end of the year, the first nuclear warheads arrived on Canadian bases.[21] With this step, Canada became a partial nuclear state, controlling nuclear weaponry, with its superpower patron, in violation of its stated non-proliferation policies.

While changing his own policy, the Liberal leader argued that Canada had to honour past commitments, although some leading Liberals such as Pierre Trudeau opposed the decision, contending that it was made under American pressure and that it constituted a step towards nuclear proliferation.[22] The new Liberal policy was a reversal of the party's formal resolution on nuclear weapons, approved in January 1961, which had posited that acquisition of nuclear weapons by additional countries would increase the chances of accidental nuclear war and jeopardize efforts to eliminate the weapons. It further pledged to withdraw Canada's interceptor role in NORAD and stop deploying Bomarc missiles in Europe.[23] Sensing the mood of the Canadian majority in favour of acquiring nuclear weapons, the Liberals had changed their policy in January 1963. Pearson had argued that since Canada supplied uranium to Britain and the United States and was protected by the U.S. strategic deterrent, it must honour its previous commitments and accept nuclear warheads.[24] Moreover, the Liberal leadership saw the weapons as simply on "restricted loan."[25] It is unclear whether Pearson was driven by the desire to win the next election or by the principle of honouring a commitment made by Canada.

Canadian policy underwent a sea change under Liberal prime minister Pierre Trudeau, who vehemently opposed Canada's possession of nuclear weapons. In 1961, Trudeau had opposed resumption of nuclear testing by the superpowers, and in 1963 he had staunchly criticized Pearson's decision to accept American nuclear arms. In 1968, he argued that the danger of nuclear war increased in proportion to the number of nuclear states and contended that NATO's nuclear policy and capability were "dangerously provocative and something in which Canada should have no part."[26]

In 1970, the Trudeau government announced its decision to remove by 1972 nuclear weapons deployed with Canadian troops in Europe, dismantle Bomarc missile sites in Canada, and replace the locally deployed CF-101 interceptor aircraft by the mid-1980s.[27] A foreign policy review in 1971 called for complete transfer of nuclear weapons to the United States and reduction of troop commitment to NATO, although Canada would remain in the alliance and in NORAD.[28] The government contended that American strategic weapons and the presence of North American troops in Europe were sufficient to deter a Soviet military offensive in Europe and that theatre nuclear weapons were not credible as deterrent forces and were destabilizing.[29] This abandonment of foreign-acquired nuclear capability was an act of forbearance that Canadian decision-makers made independently, without any U.S. pressure.

Trudeau also made some unilateral moves on arms control and nuclear non-proliferation. In his speech at the UN Special Session on Disarmament in 1978, he called for constraining the technological impulse that drove the superpowers' arms race. He proposed a "strategy of suffocation" to halt development of new weapons systems, including flight testing of all new strategic delivery vehicles. Ironically, in 1983 his government agreed to allow the testing of U.S. air-launched cruise missiles on Canadian territory. He justified the decision by contending that Canada was obliged to allow such tests by its commitments to NATO and NORAD and that Canadian defence manufacturers would benefit by way of supplying parts.[30]

The election of Brian Mulroney's Conservatives in 1984 strengthened Canada's alliance with the United States. Canada actively participated in the Reagan administration's aggressive nuclear strategy, although Canadian public opinion had shifted against nuclear weapons, fearing the dangers of East–West nuclear exchange. Canada's participation was somewhat reluctant, as evident in its initial opposition to joining research on the Strategic Defense Initiative (SDI, or "Star Wars"). Several negative opinion polls prompted the government in September 1985 to adopt a policy that ruled out direct government participation in SDI but allowed private involvement.[31] The most significant area of defence co-operation was in continued testing of U.S. Air Launched Cruise Missiles (ALCMs) on Canadian territory, despite strong public opposition.[32] With the end of the Cold War, Canada continued its alliance with the United States and its participation in NATO, though at a reduced level. Canada took an active role in extending the NPT in perpetuity in 1995 and the conclusion of the Comprehensive Test Ban Treaty (CTBT) in 1996. Despite its non-proliferation activism, Canada has not unequivocally declared a non-nuclear policy or support for global nuclear disarmament. It continues to be a participant in American nuclear preparedness, weapons testing, and forward defence.

In 1999, Jean Chrétien's Liberal government did make some efforts at reducing the role of nuclear weapons globally and at changing NATO's nuclear policy, especially on first use of nuclear weapons. In December 1998, the parliamentary Standing Committee on Foreign Affairs and International Trade recommended wide-ranging policy changes to promote nuclear disarmament. Its report urged Canada to strive consistently to reduce the political legitimacy of nuclear weapons and work with its NATO allies to promote nuclear disarmament and "de-alerting" of these weapons. The Canadian government accepted most of the recommendations, except the call for a convention on nuclear disarmament, which it described as "premature."[33] Canadian disarmament efforts at NATO's fiftieth-anniversary conference in Washington, DC, in April 1999 did not succeed. Canada's proposal that NATO recognize that the NPT called for eventual elimination of nuclear weapons and Canada's "belief that nuclear deterrent was valid only against a potential nuclear attack and not aggression in some other form" did not muster any support. The conference decided to maintain nuclear weapons in order to "preserve the peace and prevent coercion in any kind of war."[34]

Explaining the Canadian Nuclear Policy

Since the late 1940s Canada has had the capability to build an independent nuclear force. From 1963 until 1969, Canada jointly owned U.S. nuclear weapons, and there was a certain amount of U.S. pressure to maintain those jointly held nuclear forces on Canadian territory. Thus Canada had at least two windows of opportunity if it wanted to pursue an autonomous nuclear capability. In both instances, Canada chose of its own volition to forgo nuclear weapons. Why did it become a non-nuclear state? There are two common explanations. First, U.S. hegemony and security guarantees meant that Canada did not need to develop its own nuclear weaponry. Second, Canadian policy was norm-driven, which precluded actions that would encourage nuclear proliferation. I argue that both these factors carry some weight and, combined, help explain Canada's policy.

Two critical factors account for the Canadian policy: the benign security environment in North America and the credibility of the U.S. extended deterrent, largely as a result of geographical proximity and long-standing close politico-economic relations. These factors allowed successive Canadian governments to pursue a low-profile security strategy. The U.S. guarantee thus has been a necessary condition for the non-nuclear policy, but overemphasis on that variable takes away any independent role for Canada on the nuclear question. Moreover, Canada maintained an active conventional force. What made the difference in the nuclear realm? Why did its wartime allies Britain and France, which were also under the nuclear umbrella, develop nuclear weapons, but not Canada? In fact, Canada seemed to have made the choice to remain non-nuclear even before NATO came into being in 1949. An independent capability would probably have enhanced Canada's power and influence within the alliance. Moreover, for a period of time, the United States was eager that Canada possess nuclear weapons as part of the NATO nuclear deterrent.

I argue that situational variables significantly determine Canada's low-profile security policy and its non-nuclear policy. To a great extent, Canada's security threat (in modern times in terms of cultural penetration) came from the United States. The last war between these two states ended in 1814, and early in the twentieth century Canada dropped all war plans against the United states. Since then, the Canadian–u.s. border has emerged as the longest undefended frontier in the world. Conventional capability, let alone nuclear weaponry, seemed unnecessary in this context.

The Soviet Union was a threat to Canada in large part because of Canada's alliance with the United States and other NATO countries. The geographical proximity of major Canadian cities to Soviet-targeted American cities also meant that the radiation effects of a nuclear war would spread to Canada. In addition, the presence of American facilities and jointly operated facilities such as NORAD in Canada meant that the USSR would have targeted Canadian territories early in a nuclear war. Canadian possession of independent nuclear weapons would have aggravated this Soviet threat rather than reducing it. By the model in this study, Canada was situated in a low-conflict/high-conflict region during the Cold War, but the high conflict was not the result of its individual pursuits. It perceived an independent nuclear force unnecessary and even harmful to its own security interests. It rejected even a jointly held nuclear force because of these considerations and its own image as a middle power pursuing non-proliferation.

Canada's behaviour constitutes a conscious effort not to generate negative security externalities for other countries and not to incite others to acquire nuclear weapons. A domestic nuclear force, it thought, could give incentives to other technologically capable states to go nuclear. Non-proliferation was in Canada's self-interest. This consideration was evident in statements by Mackenzie King, C.D. Howe, Louis St Laurent, and Lester Pearson, clearly suggesting that non-proliferation strongly influenced official thinking in the 1940s and 1950s.

Support for international institutions and the norms and principles inherent in them has been a key element of Canadian security policy. During the post-war period, Canada pursued a functionalist approach towards international organizations, whereby states would exercise influence in accordance with their expertise in particular fields. Canada's advanced status among non-great powers in international trade, aviation technology, and nuclear technology contributed to this policy posture. "The underlying purpose was political – the assertion of the interests of lesser states against those of the greater,"[35] even while they benefit from association with the major powers. Peacekeeping was a key area reflecting Canadian functionalist internationalism in subsequent years.

Despite these positions, Canadian nuclear policy contained a certain amount of ambiguity and contradiction. On the one hand, it was actively supporting the nuclear activities of its American and British allies, while on the other it refused to build its own forces and opposed the spread of nuclear weapons. This contradiction may be the result of a dual role and the foreign perception arising from Canada's being a member of the NATO alliance with close links to the Western Cold War players. It was also based on the perception that it was in Canada's interests not to contribute to nuclear proliferation, an area in which Canada could achieve autonomous foreign policy goals. Moreover, it often fitted well with the policy preferences of Canada's great-power patrons, Britain and the United States. The contradiction has continued beyond the Cold War as Canada has become a staunch advocate of non-proliferation but has failed to articulate a clear policy on a world free of nuclear weapons.

Some scholars have argued that the rise of the Cold War created a climate that allowed Canadian leaders to accept blindly the u.s. view of international relations and thereby u.s. hegemony on matters of defence and security.[36] It is true that the geographical proximity of the United States and Canada's participation in the u.s.-led alliance system somewhat nullified the rationale for an independent Canadian nuclear force. In this sense, Canada enjoyed the most credible extended deterrent protection from the United States among all its allies. Thus during the Cold War it believed that the Soviet Union could not attack Canada without provoking a u.s. nuclear response.[37] Canadian decision-makers assumed the central role that the u.s. capability played in continental defence even before establishment of NATO and NORAD, more precisely from the signing of the Ogdensburg Agreement of 1940. Accordingly, Canadian governments paid little attention to developing an independent defence capability but were interested more in maintaining "national integrity of its forces within integrated command structures."[38] However, the Soviet Union never directly threatened Canada, nor was there a historical antagonism between the two countries. The Soviet threat came largely as a result of Canada's proximity to, and close alignment with, the United States.

Despite the u.s. protective shield provided, Canada's participation in the alliance also brought attendant costs. It deeply embedded Canada in the American nuclear strategy and thereby increased the chances of

Canada's getting entrapped automatically in any nuclear exchange between the superpowers. The Canadian refusal to station U.S. nuclear weapons on its territory further complicated the process. Thus it has been a delicate balancing act to be a member of the alliance without nuclear weapons stationed on its territory.[39] Decision-makers sometimes opposed the American nuclear strategy, as evident in 1950 when Harry Truman hinted at using nuclear weapons in Korea, and during the Cuban missile crisis of 1962. Most prominently, the Canadian rejection of American requests to station aircraft of the Strategic Air Command (SAC) and of the U.S. air force (as early as 1951) in Canada's north is another example. The United States again pressed Canada in the 1960s to store air-to-air nuclear missiles at Harmon Air Force base in Newfoundland and at Goose Bay, Labrador; anti-submarine nuclear munitions at Argentia in Newfoundland; and nuclear bombs for the SAC at Goose Bay.[40] Canada opposed storing these weapons for long periods for fear of becoming a target of nuclear attack in the first phase of a nuclear war. Its reluctance to participate fully in the SDI research, its opposition to the sharing of weapons, and its sometimes-critical positions on arms control attest to its fear of nuclear entrapment. During the early stages of the Cuban missile crisis and the Middle East crisis of 1973, Canada refused to go along with the U.S. nuclear alert.

Even when Canada was active in the Western alliance, its opposition to nuclear arms was evident, although it was under the U.S. nuclear umbrella. It was in the interests of Canada that the role of nuclear weapons and nuclear deterrence be minimized in world politics, so as to diminish Canada's dependence on the United States for security and its vulnerability to American defence policy pressures. Canada believed that the superpowers' arms race centralized power within the international system and "deepened the subordinate status of the lesser members of each bloc."[41] Anti-nuclearism became embedded in Canada's security policies, as evident in its strong support for nuclear arms control and non-proliferation. This support manifested itself more concretely in Canadian interest in the CTBT in the 1970s and 1980s and in doing research on a verification regime for CTBT if and when it came into force.[42] Canada assisted, along with Australia and South Africa, in getting an agreement on extending the NPT in perpetuity in 1995 and in the signing of the CTBT in 1996.

Canada's calculations of power and prestige differed from the assessments of military power by great powers. Many Canadians have been historically distrustful of military institutions and hence never equated military power with national sovereignty. Throughout the Cold War and later, the Canadian military faced difficulties in getting budgetary allocations for new and sophisticated weapons systems. For Canada, it looked as if power and influence could be accrued through non-acquisition of nuclear weapons. Additionally, a Canadian nuclear force would have encouraged the spread of nuclear weapons to additional countries.[43] Canada was an early sponsor of the international efforts aimed at curtailing the spread of nuclear weapons, despite its support for the U.S. nuclear deterrent in Europe and its inadvertent contribution to proliferation through its supplying potential nuclear countries with reactors and fissile materials, especially the Canadian Deuterium Uranium (CANDU) reactor, run on natural uranium/heavy water, which can produce weapons-grade plutonium. However, by 1976, Canada had enacted stringent safeguards requiring all countries importing Canadian uranium, nuclear fuels, and reactors to accept full-scale safeguard agreements with the IAEA.[44]

Hegemonic persuasion cannot explain the Canadian policy towards nuclear weapons. Such persuasion in fact worked in the other direction, forcing Canada to accept American nuclear weapons on its soil. This policy was eventually reversed, largely on Canadian initiative. Canada's benign security environment in North America and its desire not to provoke further proliferation produced its policy of a low security posture and in turn the non-acquisition of an independent nuclear force. Norms and interests coincide in this case. The norm of non-proliferation fits well into Canada's security and power calculations. Canada views as advantageous a world where military power receives low priority, as diplomacy and economic capability would provide it with a major role in the international arena. If international politics is dominated by considerations of military power, this could limit Canada's role as an honest broker largely because of its lack of hard power resources.

AUSTRALIA

Australia has possessed some key ingredients for a nuclear program, and it could have acquired operational weapons within a decade of beginning active pursuit. Australian scientists worked in the wartime British nuclear project, and Canberra provided sites for British atomic tests in the Monte Bello Islands in 1952 and at Woomera and Emu Fields in 1953. British rockets were also tested at the Woomera facility throughout the 1950s.[45] In addition, Australia possessed large deposits of natural uranium. Between 1955 and 1963, it produced about 6,000 tonnes of uranium oxide, which Britain and the United States used for nuclear weapons.[46] From 1945 till the early 1960s, Australia showed great interest in acquiring nuclear weapons through a joint project with Britain.[47]

In 1958, the chairman of the Australian Atomic Energy Commission (AAEC), J. Philip Baxter, recommended construction of an atomic reactor at Mount Isa (where large uranium deposits were found) that could produce weapons-grade plutonium at an expected cost of £10 million and an annual maintenance cost of £8–10 million.[48] Baxter stated in 1972 that Australia could build a facility capable of producing enough enriched uranium for assembling fifty atom bombs a year, at an initial cost of $50 million and an annual cost of about $20 million.[49] In 1975, Australia launched a 500-megawatt reactor at Jervis Bay, which was expected to produce plutonium for a small nuclear force.[50] According to one estimate, with over $200 million, or 20 per cent of its defence budget, in the late 1970s, Australia could have produced 150 twenty-kiloton plutonium-based warheads and 100 cruise missiles and developed an adequate command and control system for such a force.[51]

Like Canada, Australia chose not to acquire an independent national nuclear deterrent. But unlike Canada, policy-makers in Australia pondered the issue for well over a decade. During the 1950s and 1960s there were calls for Australia to develop its own nuclear weapons or acquire them from Britain or the United States, but the mainstream political parties opposed such a course. The main proponents were the right-wing Democratic Labor Party (DLP); some officials of the AAEC, especially its chairman, Baxter; and defence officials, especially in the air force and the Ministry of Supply. The Australian Labor Party (ALP) vehemently opposed nuclear weapons.[52] Supporters anticipated that nuclear weapons would spread like conventional weapons and thought that Australian armed forces should have the most lethal weapons of the era, like any other modern defence forces. This would also serve well Australia's collective security arrangements with Britain and the United States. Newly released classified documents suggest that from 1956 to 1963 defence officials attempted to procure tactical nuclear weapons from those two allies. From 1964 to 1972, they sought to develop indigenous capabilities.[53]

The debate in Australia in the 1950s took place among high level defence officials, who made serious efforts to acquire tactical weapons from Britain and the United States. The minister for air, Athol Townley, wrote to Defence Minister Philip McBride on 12 September 1956 asking him to raise with the U.S. government the possibility of its equipping the Australian air force's Sabre and Canberra aircraft with tactical nuclear weapons.[54] McBride brought up the issue at a meeting of the Defence Committee in November 1956. The committee suggested that "the effectiveness of all Australian services would be considerably increased if they were equipped with low-kiloton nuclear weapons" and recommended approaching the British and the Americans for such arms.[55] Such internal debates compelled Prime Minister Robert Menzies to rule out nuclear possession. In September 1957, Menzies declared that nuclear acquisition would be costly and an irresponsible contribution to proliferation and that additional nuclear states would increase the chances for nuclear war. However, he added that he did not mean to "exclude the possibility of future procurement."[56] Despite his public pronouncements, there is evidence that he twice raised the issue with his British counterpart, Harold Macmillan, during their meetings. The subject was also on the agenda during the visit of the British Air Chief Dermont Boyle to Canberra in March 1957 and meetings between Menzies and Macmillan in January and February 1958. That the British did not totally oppose the idea was clear when, in August 1958, Macmillan agreed to provide Australia with information about nuclear weapons but not actual possession of such devices. Both leaders agreed on the undesirability of such an action at that time, given delicate British–U.S. negotiations. A later decision could depend on the U.S. Congress's amendments to the McMahon Act.[57] Despite their concern about the impact of Australian nuclearization on Britain's nuclear co-operation agreements with the United States and their fear of nuclear weapons spreading to additional states, various British officials favoured helping Australia because of its Commonwealth ties and their desire to sell British-made nuclear delivery aircraft. Australian defence officials were interested in buying nuclear-capable delivery systems, such as the V Bomber, TSR-2, and Bloodhound Mark III missiles. In addition, they wanted U.S. F-111 aircraft.[58]

The Australian nuclear debate (mostly within the government) heated up when UN committees were tabling or discussing nuclear arms control and non-proliferation proposals. The U.S.–Soviet negotiations on the nuclear test ban in 1961 and the proposals for establishing listening posts in Australia as part of test-ban monitoring, prompted Menzies to state that "Australia should insist on a nuclear weapons on demand" agreement for joining any treaty. This would allow Canberra to acquire nuclear weapons in the event that major countries in the Asia–Pacific region did the same.[59]

Following the Chinese nuclear test in 1964, the Australian government again thought of acquiring nuclear weapons. The Chinese test unleashed latent nuclear ambitions among Australian defence planners, for they viewed China's nuclear capability as a threat to Australia's security. During the 1960s, the decision by Britain to withdraw military forces from the Pacific also accentuated Australian insecurity. The arrival of John Gorton's government in December 1967 was critical, as Gorton was a supporter of Australia's acquiring nuclear weapons.

During this time, AAEC Chairman Baxter also stepped up his advocacy of nuclear weapons: "Plans for the purchase of a reactor with considerable potential for the easy manufacture of plutonium were nearly signed in the context where Australia's accession to the recently concluded NPT was uncertain."[60]

Although Australia signed the NPT in 1970, defence planners in Canberra did not completely abandon the idea of an independent nuclear force until 1973, when Australia ratified the treaty.[61] The three-year delay in ratification, largely over fears of the treaty's impact on construction of nuclear reactors based on domestically produced fuel and of possible restrictions on Australia's uranium exports, appeared to some analysts a sign that Canberra was keeping its nuclear options open. This (alleged) tacit interest, ambitious plans for an indigenous nuclear energy program, and interest in peaceful nuclear explosions probably all contributed to the delay in ratification.[62]

The NPT negotiations touched off intense debate in government circles. The superpower-led NPT deliberations forced Australia in 1968 to consider whether it needed an independent nuclear capability. A senior defence committee studied the issue and rejected the idea. First, nuclear weapons would not be an effective deterrent against low-level attacks by regional adversaries, which would believe that Australia would not respond with nuclear weapons in such situations. Second, developing an effective deterrent to match major powers' arsenals would be "prohibitively expensive." And third, Australia could rely on the U.S. extended deterrent in any eventuality, whereas its development of nuclear weapons might upset relations with Washington.[63]

Discussions at various levels and official reports hinged on the point that Australia had a rational interest in nuclear weapons' not spreading. It was argued that the NPT would constrain nuclear development in Asia, the most likely source of a potential security threat. Development of nuclear weapons would attract hostile responses from allies and adversaries, with the United States opposing such an action vehemently, creating strains in the U.S.–Australian relationship. Non-acquisition also seemed a way to confirm Australia's position as a responsible state and signal its peaceful intentions towards its Asian neighbours.[64]

The signing of the NPT by several important countries, especially Japan, West Germany, and other Asian states, strengthened the position of proponents of Australia's following suit, lest Australia be one of the few industrialized countries not to adhere to the treaty.[65] The Gorton government decided to sign the treaty, with the understanding that Australia would not be constrained in its nuclear options until it ratified the document. However, the pro-NPT Labor Party won the

1972 election, paving the way for Australian ratification in 1973 and cancellation of the Jervis Bay reactor program.[66]

With ratification, Australia emerged as an avid champion of nuclear non-proliferation. Its policy towards nuclear weapons in general changed under Bob Hawke's Labor government, which came to power in 1983. It accepted the Palme Commission's report on common security as the basis for Australian policy on arms control while opposing nuclear superiority and the war fighting doctrines of the u.s. Reagan administration.[67] A 1981 government review of Australian defence policy identified low-level contingencies such as smuggling and attacks on isolated military facilities as the most likely threats and ruled out the likelihood of a full-scale invasion. A follow-up report in 1984 by a Joint Committee on Foreign Affairs and Defence proposed that the defence forces prepare themselves for rapid response to low-level threats in an essentially benign strategic environment. American support in such a crisis would be a bonus rather than a "central element of Australia's response capacity."[68] The government argued that Australia's participation in the Western alliance did not mean subservience to the United States. Australian positions on the comprehensive test ban, as well as on the South Pacific nuclear-free zone, reflected this independence.[69]

The Hawke government also undertook a number of unilateral initiatives in arms control. It increased the budgetary allocation for research on arms control and disarmament, appointed Australia's first ambassador for disarmament, stepped up the campaign for the CTBT, and, most significant of all, sponsored the South Pacific nuclear-free zone.[70] In 1985, the government refused u.s. aircraft use of Australian bases to monitor MX missile tests; rejected invitations to participate in SDI research, especially in rail-gun research technology, an area of Australian expertise; and, finally, decided to stop research in this field completely.[71] Despite these steps, there are some indications that Australia sought to maintain a nuclear-weapons option by accumulating plutonium. Its initial concerns revolved around the possibility of Indonesia's acquiring nuclear weapons, but Jakarta's accession to the NPT and lack of progress in acquiring nuclear facilities reduced that concern.

Japan's accumulation of plutonium spurred Foreign Minister Hayden's proposal for Australia's maintaining limited activities designed to reduce the lead time in acquiring nuclear weapons if a contingency arose. Hayden aired his interest in the government's increasing its support for nuclear research at a meeting of a small group of ministers, including Prime Minister Hawke, in November 1984. According to the proposal, the AAEC would be given new equipment and a new reactor.

Australia could also extract weapons-grade fissile materials from its current reactors. Hayden intended that Australia should possess the technical know-how to be able to assemble a bomb in the shortest possible time, if developments in the region warranted.[72] Despite his personal interest, there is no evidence that the government showed any enthusiasm for developing a virtual nuclear capability.

Many Australian decision-makers had misgivings about the alliance with the United States; they showed their discomfort in the "alliance dilemma," especially the complete enmeshing of their country in u.s. nuclear strategy during the Cold War, which made it a strategic target of the Soviet Union. The nuclear dilemma in the South Pacific expanded with France's continued testing of nuclear weapons until the early 1990s on the Muroa Atoll, in French Polynesia, missile testing by all the nuclear states, use of transit routes and port facilities for craft carrying nuclear weapons, and dumping of nuclear waste. Opposition to nuclear activity in the region led Australia to take the lead in concluding the Raratonga Treaty of August 1985, which declared it a nuclear weapon–free zone. The treaty forbids its adherents from developing, manufacturing, acquiring, or receiving from others nuclear explosive devices, stipulates that export of nuclear materials must be conducted under strict international safeguards, and bans permanent stationing of nuclear weapons on land, inland waters, or seabeds within the territories of signatories.[73]

However, anti-nuclear activism was much more evident in neighbouring New Zealand than in Australia. By passing the Nuclear Free Zone, Disarmament and Arms Control Bill in June 1987, New Zealand became the "only country in the world which has attempted to legislate disengagement from nuclear deterrence" by prohibiting visits by nuclear-propelled or -armed warships and aircraft.[74] The Australian position on this dispute was not to isolate New Zealand completely as the United States did. Despite sending a disapproving letter in January 1985 to New Zealand, the Hawke government expressed its sympathies with its neighbour. Yet the alliance with the United States seemed useful, as it provided a link with Western states and a channel of communications to the highest levels of the u.s. government.[75]

Why Australia Chose Not
to Acquire Nuclear Weapons

I argue that the benign security environment in the South Pacific is probably the primary reason for Australian's non-acquisition of independent nuclear weapon capability. The anzus alliance with New Zealand and the United States provided a bulwark against the least-likely, worst-case contingencies of large-scale aggression by other nuclear states, such as the USSR and China. Successive Australian governments have recognized the utility of the ANZUS alliance. However, since the 1970s, Australia has been compelled to engage with Asian neighbours while maintaining ties with Britain and the United States. Australia has also created a number of strategic partnerships and defence co-operation programs with neighbouring states.[76] The Australian debate on nuclear weapons has been a mellow affair, involving members of the political, scientific, and bureaucratic elite. U.S. security guarantees to Australia contributed to this lack of interest in nuclear weapons. However, the ANZUS Treaty does not involve an explicit nuclear guarantee like NATO's.[77] None of Australia's immediate neighbours possesses nuclear weapons, and the region's benign security environment itself would have probably prevented Australian nuclearization. The low-conflict environment and the lack of credible security threats from Asia led to Australia's low-posture defence policy.

Some scholars have argued that bureaucratic politics, changes in executive leadership, and the popular perception of nuclear weapons account for Australian nuclear choices. According to one study, the security factor is not a strong one: Australian officials made their most ardent efforts to acquire nuclear weapons between 1956 and 1961, when their nation enjoyed its highest level of security. "Moreover, all of Australia's moves towards a nuclear weapons options came in spite of the ANZUS Treaty."[78] Although there is some merit in the bureaucratic-politics argument, it is still unclear, however, whether the bureaucrats would have been able to launch a nuclear weapons program without dramatic changes occuring in the external security environment. Australia's relationship with other regional powers, including China, was not enduring rivalry, and there has been no indication that China's nuclear weapons were directed against Australia. Without active neighbouring nuclear rivals hostile to Australia, it was unlikely that pro-nuclear bureaucratic and political elements could have pursued a weapons program vigorously. However, changing perceptions of the need for nuclear weapons seem to have encouraged Australian forbearance.

Two influential studies by the Australian United Services Institution published in 1975 found that the country's acquisition of tactical or strategic nuclear weapons to deter conventional attacks would be counter-productive, as it would encourage potential adversaries to build their own nuclear forces. Because half of its population was concentrated in a few cities in the southeast and key industries were in the LaTrobe Valley and Wollongong, a potential invader could engage in nuclear blackmail. One of the studies contended that "Australia's broad security interests lay in supporting to the fullest extent

the control of nuclear weapons." According to the other, "the acquisition of nuclear weapons by one or more regional powers, particularly
Indonesia or Japan," should be the chief rationale for an Australian
decision to acquire nuclear weapons.[79] It feared that Australia would
have difficulty in building an effective nuclear force capable of deterring nuclear powers such as China. It was also not clear whether
nuclear acquisition would increase Australia's power and influence in
South East Asia, the region of immediate strategic interest, or whether
it would have diminished "Australian security by arousing unnecessary
and hostile reactions by it neighbours." Additionally, nuclear acquisition would have antagonized Australia's chief allies and trading partners – Britain, Japan, and the United States. Washington especially was
expected to oppose any efforts by Australia to undermine global non-
proliferation efforts.[80] Australian external affairs and defence ministers
reported to the cabinet that the NPT, if successful, would confine the
nuclear risk in Asia to China. If India developed nuclear weapons, this
would not have threatened Australia, as it would be in the context of
India's conflict with China. Besides China, threats to Australian strategic interests in the foreseeable future would come from subversion,
infiltration, and insurgency-type activities, which nuclear weapons
could not deter. Australian opposition to the NPT could have reduced
U.S. support for Australia to confront a non-nuclear-threat scenario.
Moreover, it was argued that Indonesia would feel threatened and
might seek protection by nuclear powers.[81]

Australian decision-makers had realized that a domestic nuclear
force could put tremendous pressure on other regional states, especially
Indonesia, to acquire their own nuclear forces or to seek nuclear
guarantees from other nuclear powers. The result would be a local
nuclear arms race, as well as the "possibility of a disarming attack on
an embryonic Australian nuclear force."[82] Some Australian bureaucrats had recognized this constraint early. A memorandum by E.H.
Bunding, Secretary in the Prime Minister's Department, warned in
1958 that the Australian position in Asia would be adversely affected
by its nuclear acquisition. "At the moment, I do not think Australia
rates very high as a target priority, but if we possessed the weapon we
would also enhance our strategic position in the eyes of our enemies,
which may increase our target rating," forcing Australia to launch a
costly civil defence program.[83] Thus potential hostile attention from
other states, especially nuclear ones, discouraged the country's pursuit
of independent nuclear weapons. Australia would need a second-strike
capability to deter possible use of nuclear arms by the major powers,
while a tactical capability could be used against invading troops only

after they arrived in Australia. Such a tactical attack would harm Australian civilians as well.[84]

Australian opposition to nuclear weapons became clear in the threat assessments of successive governments. Security threats emerging from maritime interdiction were viewed as the most probable ones, with the nuclear war–fighting doctrines of the superpowers likely to cause major damage to Australian security if a war broke out. Australia would be inadvertently entrapped in the conflict, given the presence of American communications facilities on Australian territory. During the Cold War era, the deterioration of superpower relations was viewed as most threatening to Australia's security. The Hawke government regarded the nuclear arms race and nuclear war–fighting strategies as policies from which Australia should disengage.[85]

A number of objections were raised on the viability of the u.s. alliance. First, it was perceived to be not reliable for confronting all kinds of military situations, leaving Australia vulnerable to small-scale military threats. Second, the alliance would curtail the manœuvrability of the junior partner, Australia, in defence and in other spheres as well. Third, the alliance would make Australia "suspect in the eyes of the opponents of the u.s. and non-aligned countries and consequently [restrict] the role Australia could otherwise play in regional and global politics."[86] None of these objections, however, led to dissolution of the alliance. Breaking this highly interdependent economic and security relationship would have been very costly for Australia, especially in political and economic terms.

The cost of an independent nuclear force was another consideration during the 1950s. In the early years of the nuclear age, Australian leaders had argued that development of nuclear weapons was costly. Prime Minister Menzies told Parliament in 1957 that the country could not develop an independent nuclear capability "because of the prodigious expenditures involved."[87] By the 1970s, these arguments began to fade as the cost was calculated to be not too burdensome. Moreover, Britain had withdrawn from Australasia, and China had acquired nuclear capability. After the Vietnam War, the u.s. commitment to Australian security seemed insufficient to meet the most probable regional threats. Small-scale conflicts involving South East Asian states, especially Indonesia, were unlikely to have obtained American military support, whereas threats by the Soviet Union or China during the Cold War would probably have provoked Washington's assistance.[88]

The chances of Australia's acquiring nuclear weapons on its own decreased further when it signed the NPT in February 1970 and ratified it in 1973. A majority of public opinion favoured the NPT, as Australia had a major stake in preventing proliferation, which would have caused more instability globally and regionally.[89] Australia's nuclearization could have complicated its position on arms control and disarmament. Although not a leading player internationally, unlike Canada, in nuclear non-proliferation, Australia has been the dominant force in the region for arms control. It took the initiative in 1984 for the conclusion of the South Pacific Nuclear Weapon Free Zone Treaty. It, along with New Zealand, had approached the International Court of Justice at The Hague for a stop to French nuclear testing in the region. Australian credibility in this respect would have evaporated, especially with New Zealand and other South Pacific countries, if it had acquired nuclear capability.

In the 1990s, Australia took additional steps on nuclear disarmament. In 1995, the government appointed a panel of distinguished scholars and statesmen (the Canberra Commission) to study ways to create a nuclear-free world. The commission produced its report in August 1996, which has since received much international attention. It proposed several immediate and long-term steps by the nuclear states to eliminate nuclear arms once and for all.[90] Australia was also a key player in extending the NPT in perpetuity, despite questions about the treaty's unequal nature and its legitimization of monopoly rights of the states with nuclear weapons. In 1996, Australia also took the initiative in bringing the CTBT to the UN General Assembly after India objected to its passing by the Geneva-based Disarmament Committee.

CONCLUSIONS

Canadian and Australian policies towards nuclear weapons serve as cases of states in alliances with the United States and in somewhat benign security environments pursuing low-profile defence policies intended to maintain their middle-power status. Independent national nuclear capabilities would have upset security strategies based on minimalist defence postures and foreign policies founded on middle-power internationalism. Such capability not only would have attracted hostile responses from allies and adversaries, but it would have hurt these nations' status as trading states as well. These countries thus perceived from the beginning the utility of remaining non-nuclear, despite occasional pressures to acquire independent capabilities, most notably in the Australian case.

Although the behaviour of these states appears interest-driven, norms do play a modest part in their policies. The norm of non-proliferation fits well into their security and power calculations. These middle powers regard a world where military power is given low priority as one to their advantage, as diplomacy and economic capability would give them major international roles. If international politics is dominated by military considerations, their lack of hard power resources would limit their role as honest brokers. Norm-driven behaviour is often congruent with a middle power's internationalist position, especially vis-à-vis control of nuclear proliferation. These states also have often made efforts not to entrap themselves in a possible nuclear war, as evident in their independent initiatives to distance themselves from a number of u.s. positions on nuclear war–fighting and their unwillingness to store u.s. weapons on their territories.

CHAPTER FIVE

Neutral States:
Sweden and Switzerland

The non-nuclear policies of two European neutral states – Sweden and Switzerland – offer insights into the security strategies of countries that are not formally covered by nuclear umbrellas or security assurances through superpower alliances. Arguably, the possession of an independent nuclear capability by these states would have strengthened their defence postures, which are based on armed neutrality, making them less dependent on outside states for protection in the event of a European war. Some early proliferation theorists had predicted that neutral states were the most probable candidates for nuclear acquisition after the major powers. Strict neutrality prohibited their getting aid from any external sources during wartime, and if there were any implication of support, the neutral states could lose their legal status.[1] The nuclear age posed particular problems for the defence of small neutral states. In the pre-nuclear era, only a hostile state's entering the territory of the neutral state violated its neutrality, whereas in the atomic age a nuclear state could engage in a nuclear attack without ever entering the territory of the neutral state.[2]

Since the late 1950s, both Sweden and Switzerland have had the technological and material capabilities necessary to launch independent nuclear weapon programs. Sweden possessed uranium deposits and technological capability; Switzerland, though less capable, also possessed the basic ingredients required for acquiring nuclear weapons. Until the mid-1960s, both countries contemplated nuclearization; debates in both centred on obtaining a tactical nuclear capability. Such a capability, it was argued, would compel an invading army to disperse rather than concentrate its forces, fearing a tactical nuclear attack on large troop formations. It would also reduce defence expenditures by lowering the amount spent on conventional military capability. Both countries considered a strategic nuclear capability unfeasible because of concern that it lacked credibility and that a countervalue strategy was contrary to the classic deterrence-by-denial strategy of neutral states.[3]

The argument in this chapter is that the two neutral states decided not to acquire nuclear weapons to forestall possible hostile attention from major powers during peacetime and a preventive attack during wartime. Nuclear possession would have increased their insecurity, while making their neutrality policies less effective. They have based their security strategies on most-probable-threat scenarios and designed their defence strategies to rely on conventional deterrence. They have seen nuclear weapons as not enhancing but rather constraining their capacity to deter and defend.

SWEDEN

Among the technologically capable states that forswore the nuclear option, Sweden is a unique case, because its military and political elite seriously contemplated acquiring an independent nuclear capability in the late 1950s and decided in the end to forgo it. From 1947 till 1972, Sweden kept the nuclear weapons option open. A report in 1994 suggested that Sweden, even after foreswearing that option, still maintained an interest in a virtual deterrent capability by continuing laboratory-based nuclear weapons experiments. The report alleged that in the 1960s Sweden had employed 350 scientists at the National Defence Research Establishment (FOA) for nuclear weapons research and that about twenty-five people continued the endeavour well into the 1980s. Moreover, plutonium derived from the decommissioned reactor in the Stockholm suburb of Agesta was used for this research. Although the 65-megawatt reactor officially closed in 1974, it was kept ready to be restarted on a relatively short notice of a few months under this virtual weaponization program. The Swedish scientists also reportedly possessed an "archive of preliminary design and technical data on nuclear weapons, the legacy of Sweden's Cold War era bomb project."[4]

Despite this report, there is little evidence to show that Sweden has seriously pursued the nuclear option since the early 1970s. By most measures, Sweden is a non-nuclear state that could have acquired nuclear weapons if it chose to do so. Laboratory-style research experiments seem to occur in almost all industrialized countries that have powerful civilian programs. Sweden had both the technical capability and the window of opportunity prior to signing the NPT if it wanted to acquire nuclear weapons, for it had built up a strong nuclear industry, including indigenous light-water reactors. In addition, it has been home to Western Europe's largest concentration of uranium reserves, estimated at about 15 per cent of the world's total supply.[5]

The plutonium produced in Swedish power reactors would have been sufficient for developing medium-type nuclear weapons.

The Swedish case is all the more important for this study, as during the Cold War era it faced threats from the Soviet Union, especially in the form of submarine incursions in Swedish waters. Sweden has a coastline of over 2,000 kilometres and contains several archipelagoes, whose security was of major concern. Despite protests in the early 1980s, intrusion by Soviet submarines increased, creating a major security challenge. During the same period, the Soviet naval buildup in the Kola Peninsula grew dramatically. These naval facilities would have permitted rapid deployment of forces capable of offensive operations.[6] In normal circumstances, a state confronted with such a threat would either seek to balance the power of the threatening state by joining an alliance or acquire effective, independent countervailing capabilities, possibly including nuclear weapons, to deter the potential adversary.

Moreover, Sweden has been spending lavishly on acquisition and maintenance of conventional weapons. This investment generated a substantial defence infrastructure, industries, and sophisticated weapons systems. Its air force was as powerful as that of the other medium powers of Europe – Britain, France, and (West) Germany. Therefore Sweden probably would not have had to spend much more for aircraft-based delivery systems. Sweden also had to take into account the nuclear capability of its opponents, as evident in its production of interceptors and dispersal of aircraft.[7] Swedish strategic doctrine has assumed that "self-protection required at least rough parity with any force likely to be fielded against them."[8] From a worst-case perspective, it is not clear, however, whether such a posture alone could have deterred a determined nuclear adversary.

For maintaining strict neutrality, a nuclear capability would have been useful.[9] Tactical nuclear weapons would have had a strong deterrent effect, given their potential to thwart a Soviet attack prior to the landing of invasion forces on Swedish territory. Sweden's policy of armed neutrality depended heavily on its capacity to deter attacks and to defend itself if deterrence failed. This capacity, according to former defence minister Anders Thunborg, depended on Sweden's ability to mobilize quickly a trained force of 600,000 to 700,000 and its possession of a qualitatively and quantitatively superior air force and a strong civil defence program.[10] Moreover, Sweden had learned from the Second World War that its neutrality and armament policies had worked and that its security would depend largely on its own resources, national mobilization within the concept of total defence, and well-equipped armed forces.[11] Successive governments have viewed a self-sufficient military-industrial policy as essential for the peacetime credibility of its non-aligned position and for its neutrality during a possible war. Security planners agreed that any military threat would arise primarily from the East–West conflict in Europe.

Sweden has been a pioneer in nuclear research. Its program is almost as old as that of the United States and France, as it began with the appointment in 1945 of a royal commission and the establishment in 1949 of AB Atomenergi, a conglomerate of private business and government.[12] Sweden had shown interest in nuclear weapons immediately after the U.S. atomic attacks on Hiroshima and Nagasaki. The supreme commander of the Swedish armed forces asked the FOA to conduct research on an atom bomb, with special funds allocated to the program. During the 1950s the FOA directed several studies, and in the early 1960s it conducted critical research.[13]

At the same time, Sweden embarked on a massive development of nuclear technology, including nuclear reactors and fuel-cycle facilities. It linked civilian and military nuclear research from early on. In 1950, AB Atomenergi and the FOA reached a secret agreement that stipulated free flow of personnel, know-how, and raw materials between the two and, in the event of a military crisis, FOA's absorption of AB Atomenergi.[14] In December 1952, the commander of the Swedish air force, Lt-Gen. Bengt Nordenskiold, called for development of nuclear weaponry. An official report in 1954, by a committee headed by Chief of General Staff Gen. Nils Swedlund, recommended a tactical nuclear program.[15] The superpowers' development of tactical weapons transformed Swedish calculations. By the end of 1954, the superpower arsenals were inducting tactical weapons, especially the low-yield variety mounted on artillery pieces. Nuclear weapons were thus no longer confined to air-delivered systems.[16]

The debate on nuclear weapons, however, divided the political parties. In 1955, Prime Minister Tage Erlander of the Social Democratic Party declared that Sweden had no intention of becoming a nuclear power. The Conservative Party called for nuclear acquisition, while the Liberal and Centre parties supported continued research without immediate acquisition. The divisions were also apparent in the armed forces, with the supreme commander and the air force in favour of nuclear acquisition and the army divided on the issue.[17]

In January 1957, the director general of the Swedish Institute of National Defence, Hugo Larson, declared that Sweden had the capability to acquire nuclear weapons within seven years. The commander-in-chief of the armed forces supported this statement.[18] For many defence planners, tactical nuclear weapons were essential to deterring a potential adversary from engaging in an isolated attack against Sweden similar to the Finnish–Soviet Winter War. A tactical nuclear capability would substantially improve the Swedish capacity to "impede an invader" crossing the borders or coming from the sea.[19]

The Swedish government attempted to divert public opinion on the issue even as a majority supported nuclearization. In 1958, leaders of the major political parties met privately and decided not to launch an explicit weapons program but to keep the options open. It supported the large civilian nuclear program as a way to acquire enough weapons-grade plutonium in case Sweden wanted a weapon developed in the future. The government acquiesced to the Conservative Party's demand for greater defence appropriations in return for the Conservatives' agreeing to postpone a final decision on acquisition.[20] In 1959, the political debate reached a turning point when the government approved a compromise plan to postpone a final decision until the civilian program was further advanced. It decided not to launch any rapid production of weapons-grade nuclear materials or to design and test deliverable warheads.[21] This plan brought the debate to a temporary close. In 1960 Parliament defeated a Conservative motion to commence research on nuclear weapons.[22] Despite this political inaction, Swedish scientists continued their nuclear research and by 1968 made major strides, especially in the design, dynamics, and neutronics of a nuclear explosion and its initiation. They also conducted research on the design of weapon triggers and the safe storage of nuclear arms.[23] This scientific progress, however, did not translate into operational weapons.

By the mid-1960s, a change in the views of the Swedish military was already apparent. From having strongly supported acquisition of tactical nuclear weapons, the Swedish General Staff, in its five-year plan presented in 1965, simply recommended laying the foundations of a scientific program to shorten the time required for building a nuclear force.[24] In February 1968, a special government defence committee recommended that "it is not in our nation's security interests to acquire nuclear weapons. If developments over the long run lead to a situation in which nuclear weapons become common place in the arsenals of small nations, then the question of Swedish atomic weapons may be raised."[25] One analyst attributes the Swedish rethinking to the internal debate within the military, which produced a strong faction in support of conventional defence. The Swedes realized that it would be difficult to possess both strong conventional and nuclear capabilities simultaneously.[26] Sweden signed the NPT in August 1968 and ratified it in January 1970, thereby legalizing its non-nuclear status.[27]

Sweden continued this status all through the Cold War, despite increased Soviet naval activities in Swedish waters. The end of the Cold War has dramatically improved Sweden's security environment. The independence of the Baltic states has created a buffer between Russia and the Nordic states. Sweden's joining the European Union in March 1994 also helped to improve its long-term security environment and to facilitate its insertion into a future European security arrangement.[28]

Why Sweden Chose Not to Acquire Nuclear Weapons

The evolution of Swedish attitudes towards nuclear weapons reflected the trends of the times. During the 1950s and 1960s, many observers saw tactical nuclear weapons as potentially part of a strong armed force, and many armies expected that they were militarily useful. By the 1970s, with fear of an impending war in Europe having decreased, Swedish thinking also changed. Sweden abandoned efforts at nuclear acquisition because of a strategic assessment in which the anticipated responses of friendly neighbours and adversaries played a major role. Political leaders calculated that the "costs and risks of nuclear weapons outweighed any potential benefits."[29] The Swedes believed that possession of nuclear capability would only invite a potential adversary, such as a major nuclear state, to use such weapons against Sweden in a possible conflict and increase the probability of Sweden's becoming involved in a future war. The strategic analysis pointed out that even though Sweden might be reserving nuclear arms for tactical purposes, the opponent need not view such a capability in that way and would attempt to wipe it out early in a war. Because Sweden is a small state, its use of tactical weapons inside its own territory would be suicidal and therefore the threat of such a war not credible to a potential attacker.[30]

A 1955 analysis for the government argued that the Soviet Union would view Sweden as a dangerous neighbour and would drag it into any war in the early stages, anticipating that Stockholm would switch to the West sooner or later.[31] In the event of a conventional war, the attacker was unlikely to escalate into the nuclear level on the Swedish front unless Sweden possessed such weapons. Sweden's chances of deterring a war were higher if it possessed only powerful conventional forces, which might dissuade an adversary from attacking. Tactical weapons were unlikely to deter a conventional attack, because Sweden, if attacked, would either surrender or introduce tactical nuclear weapons early on and thereby invite a massive retaliatory strike. Such an attack would wipe out the country – a situation that the presence of a nuclear force was supposed to prevent.[32]

The analysis discounted possibility of a major attack on Sweden by a nuclear state. It assumed Sweden's "marginality" – Sweden carried minimal value to both superpowers, which would devote only marginal forces to confronting Sweden in the case of a war.[33] Swedish military planners also assumed that a superpower military confrontation around the North Cape and the Baltic need not inevitably involve Sweden.[34] With the superpower allocating only marginal conventional forces to Sweden, the chances of occupation decreased as the costs of conquest increased.[35]

Swedish defence policy sought to impose marginal costs on the opponent rather than defeating it completely. It would deter a potential attacker by imposing a series of growing costs rather than risking total destruction of Swedish cities.[36] Sweden's geographical and strategic location was the main impetus for adoption of a less obtrusive defence posture. Sweden belongs to a zone of moderate conflict, partly because the Scandinavian peninsula is difficult to pass through and provides only limited strategic gains for an invader.[37] Sweden could become involved in a war only through a general conflict in Europe between the superpowers. As a result, minimizing superpower confrontation became a major strategic objective for Sweden during the Cold War era.

The Swedes were convinced that a low-profile defence policy would maintain a somewhat benign strategic environment in the Nordic region. They assumed that the major powers had a common interest in keeping the region less tense. They believed that the "Soviet Union [had] more to lose than to gain from promoting a military buildup in the North, for that would threaten its major naval bases."[38] From this point of view, Swedish acquisition of nuclear weapons would have increased major powers' attention to the region. Within the region, democracy, high levels of economic prosperity, and social democratic policies had led to internal stability as well. Further military preparedness might undermine the twin pillars of Nordic stability and security, both internally and externally.

The Swedes also feared that a domestic nuclear force might compel neighbouring states, particularly West Germany, to acquire nuclear weapons. Any further diffusion of nuclear arms would be detrimental to Swedish and international security. Sweden championed nuclear disarmament and non-proliferation at the UN and in other forums and helped to build international opinion against nuclear weapons. It also believed that the only way it could "defend against nuclear weapons is by trying to reduce the risk that such weapons will ever be used."[39] Prime Minister Erlander argued in his memoirs that Sweden should make every effort to outlaw nuclear weapons. The credibility of its efforts in this respect would be undermined if it were to nuclearize.[40] Dominant sections of the Social Democratic Party, which ruled Sweden for most of the post-war era, also believed that nuclear forbearance could set an example for other countries. Moreover, Sweden was a supporter and initiator of major disarmament proposals; it created a cabinet post for disarmament and proposed reducing NATO and

Warsaw Pact nuclear and conventional arsenals.[41] Sweden was one of the first nations to propose the NPT and a comprehensive test ban, and it was an active member of the Geneva-based Eighteen-Nation Disarmament Committee (ENDC). Sweden's inclusion as one of the eight non-aligned members of the ENDC in 1962 had a major impact on domestic politics. Swedish delegates in Geneva played a major role in the test ban negotiations and spoke for the developing countries. Any full pursuit of a nuclear bomb would have jeopardized this carefully cultivated image and hurt the country's prestige and influence in international politics.[42]

SWITZERLAND

A second neutral state that has forsworn nuclear weapons is Switzerland. Like Sweden, it considered tactical nuclear weapons to strengthen its armed neutrality, and it kept the option open until 1969, although it never took concrete steps to develop such weapons. From a purely military perspective, tactical nuclear weapons would have augmented Switzerland's capacity to deter direct invasion during a war in Europe. Some Swiss legal experts had argued that the Hague Convention on neutrality of 1907 allowed a neutral power to resist attempts to violate neutrality by all means, including force. From this viewpoint, based on the principle of self-help and the international law concerning neutrality, no legal barrier prior to its signing the NPT prohibited it from acquiring nuclear weapons or using them to thwart a conventional attack.[43]

Nuclear research in Switzerland began in November 1945 when the government established the Atomic Energy Committee (SKA). In April 1957, it launched the SAPHIR swimming-pool-style reactor, which it had bought from the United States in 1955. The reactor was capable of producing 10,000 kilowatts of power and was the backbone of nuclear fission research in Switzerland for many years. In 1962, Switzerland began construction of an experimental power plant in Lucens. Major construction ensued, and by the 1980s about 40 per cent of Swiss electricity came from nuclear sources.[44] Switzerland had acquired uranium and plutonium as part of its nuclear development, and until 1977 its nuclear facilities were not fully safeguarded by the IAEA because Switzerland ratified the NPT only that year. Some Swiss scientists were also trained in the Manhattan Project. With its high levels of technical development, Switzerland could have become a nuclear state by the late 1970s.

Independent national defence always constituted a key element of Swiss armed neutrality, which was adopted in 1815. Since then, Switzerland has been able to avoid military invasion. It maintained

independence during the world wars, although how it did so is an
unresolved issue. Revelations in 1997 suggested that the Swiss helped
the Nazis by trading looted gold from occupied countries and concentration camp victims and maintaining bank accounts for Germany to
ward off an invasion of Switzerland. A U.S. government–sanctioned
study also found that Switzerland supplied Germany with many vital
commodities and war materials, such as "arms, ammunition, alumi-
num, machinery and locomotives."[45] However, likely destruction of
Swiss industrial sites and the threat of guerrilla warfare seem to have
dissuaded Hitler from invading Swiss territory. The East–West conflict,
however, magnified the perception at home that Switzerland could not
afford to take its independence and neutrality for granted. The Swiss
attempted to steer clear of the Cold War and protect their neutrality
by maintaining a well-trained and well-equipped armed force, which
in a war would have given it the highest density of military forces
proportionate to terrain in Europe.[46]

Swiss military strategy relied on a high level of deterrence or dissuasion of an opponent. The strategy posited intense armed resistance
aimed at making the "price of entrance" too high – an offensive would
be costly, time-consuming, and unprofitable.[47] In order to buttress this
strategy, Switzerland had fortified the entrance to and the centre of the
Alps and had placed hundreds of permanent demolition devices on all
strategic points, such as bridges, so that enemy tanks could not cross
into the country. In addition, it had built a massive civil and military
shelter program, which was expected to provide a safe haven to major
portions of the army and civilian population in the event of a war.
The Swiss population was also trained in civil defence and could
mobilize about 700,000 troops in two to four days.[48] This high level
of military preparedness and the strategy of dissuasion would have
been strengthened by tactical nuclear weapons and the capacity to
deter an invasion by any nuclear-armed nation.

Switzerland's relations with the Soviet Union were not at all cordial
during the Cold War years, despite its neutrality. From 1918 to 1946,
Switzerland had had no diplomatic relations with the USSR. Moscow
had gone so far as to institute an economic boycott of the country in
1923 in retaliation for Switzerland's successful efforts to prevent Soviet
membership of the League of Nations. After 1946, Swiss territory was
also the scene of extensive espionage activity by the KGB.[49]

Like Sweden, Switzerland began its interest in nuclear weapons early
in the atomic age. The 1945 mandate of the SKA included investigation
of all aspects of nuclear weapons, preparation of every way to protect the
army and the population against the impact of a nuclear attack, and
study of the requirements for developing nuclear weapons. According

to Bruno Pellaud, a top atomic energy official from Switzerland serving with the Vienna-based IAEA, "until the signing of the NPT in 1969, and its ratification by Parliament in 1977, Switzerland indeed kept politically open the option of national nuclear weaponry."[50]

The Zurich daily *Tagesanzeiger* published previously classified materials on the nuclear program in 1995.[51] The sequence of events relating to development of nuclear weapons suggests that the Swiss army was very keen on acquisition. In 1946, the Federal Council gave secret guidelines to the SKA to create a bomb. The move assumed greater momentum during the late 1950s, when the army strongly pushed for tactical nuclear weapons.

Military strategists did not openly debate the nuclear issue until 1954, when a number of them urged Switzerland to acquire tactical nuclear weapons as a way to strengthen its defence capabilities "in an age of rapidly changing war technology."[52] NATO was considering tactical weapons for its principal members on a dual-key basis, controlled jointly by the United States and its allies. The Swiss leadership estimated that nuclear proliferation was a fait accompli and that Switzerland should also possess nuclear weapons.[53] The Swiss army viewed tactical nuclear arms as battlefield weapons, almost like another powerful form of artillery. Since Switzerland had a high proportion of infantry troops, an attacker with such weapons could concentrate and force a breakthrough into Swiss territory. But if Switzerland possessed such armaments, it could make such an attack costly: the army could go to the rear of the invading forces and destroy their logistics and communication lines. One Swiss strategist saw this as the conventional approach of dissuasion – i.e., making the price of attack too high, the key basis of modern Swiss defence strategy.[54]

The Defence Committee of the Federal Council debated a proposal by the army's chief of staff in November 1957. A study that year by a committee of army officers had suggested that Switzerland acquire tactical nuclear weapons and delivery aircraft to destroy as many units of the invading forces as possible before they arrived on Swiss territory. The committee also recommended abandonment of static defence in order to achieve greater mobility for the armed forces – a requirement for atomic warfare.[55] Tactical nuclear weapons would force the enemy to disperse its troops, disable a strong attack, increase Swiss political clout after a possible war, and prevent Switzerland from becoming an East–West nuclear battlefield. There was, however, a consensus that conventional military capability should not be reduced, as the committee believed that too weak a conventional force could lead to a desperate use of nuclear weapons.[56] A report by the Federal Military Department (EMD) to the Federal Council in May 1958 contended:

"We are completely defenseless against bombers flying at a high alti-tude. The acquisition of atomic surface to air weapons is our highest priority." The report concluded that the army urgently needed its own nuclear weapons and that neither international law nor Switzerland's neutrality policy prohibited their acquisition.[57]

In July 1958, following the shock of the Hungarian Revolution of 1956, the Swiss government announced that the army must be equipped with tactical nuclear weapons to preserve the country's inde-pendence and neutrality.[58] However, plans for nuclear acquisition caused considerable opposition from the superpowers. The Soviets especially condemned the move as counter to Switzerland's tradition of neutrality.[59] The Swiss announcement led to a domestic debate involv-ing the public, political parties, and the media. In December 1958, the Federal Council voted to order the EMD to find out about manufactur-ing these weapons in Switzerland, if necessary with the co-operation of other countries. In early 1960, the chief of staff applied to the head of the EMD for permission to conduct inquiries about acquiring nuclear weapons from abroad.[60] However, in 1960 the government recognized that, because of the great powers' nuclear monopoly, the weapons were not obtainable from abroad and that Switzerland was not yet capable of producing them. Switzerland must follow developments in the atomic field carefully so that if one day the atomic monopoly ended, Switzerland would review acquisition.[61] However, the debate continued through the early 1960s, involving the Federal Council, the military, political leaders, leftist groups, pacifists, and theologians. Left-leaning political groups wanted Switzerland to forgo its nuclear weapons option. Proponents of acquisition argued that tactical nuclear weapons could be employed in a discriminatory way and that a potential enemy would use such devices if Switzerland did not possess them. Opponents contended that atomic weapons would destroy what Switzerland wanted to defend, including its own population or that of a friendly country, in the name of preventing an attack.[62]

Two constitutional initiatives were launched, the first by the Social Democrats on 1 April 1962, "forbidding Switzerland to produce, import or permit the transit, storage or utilisation of nuclear weapons or any parts of such weapons." This referendum was overwhelmingly rejected. In May 1963, the majority faction of the party introduced another initiative, which stated simply that the government must con-sult the electorate before it acquired nuclear weapons. This initiative also went down to overwhelming defeat.[63] The Swiss public thus gave its government *carte blanche*. These referenda also showed its clear opposition to a constitutional ban on nuclear acquisition.

Despite its popular mandate, the government did not pursue the nuclear option vigorously. In October 1963, Chief of Staff Jakob Annasohn ordered a team of prominent physicists to determine whether Switzerland had the ability to build a nuclear weapon. The scientists concluded that it could develop uranium bombs. They estimated that acquisition of enriched uranium bombs of 60 to 100 kilotonnes to be delivered by aircraft would take thirteen years.[64] By the end of 1963, with tensions in Europe receding and the PTBT signed, the government began to lose its enthusiasm, although the army remained interested. Switzerland signed the Partial Test Ban Treaty (PTBT) in August 1963. In a 1966 policy statement, the government expressed its hope for an effective treaty on nuclear non-proliferation, which would remove the threat of a nuclear war.[65]

Switzerland initially opposed signing the NPT, saying that the document did not clearly define the safeguards. It also wanted to maintain its right to reject any IAEA inspectors it deemed inappropriate. Bern wished to retain the ability of Swiss industry to use atomic energy for peaceful purposes, sharing of data on nuclear weapons (if they could be used for peaceful purposes), a "no-use" pledge by nuclear states against non-nuclear states, and the right to engage in peaceful nuclear explosions. It was equally unhappy with the treaty's lack of security guarantees.[66] Aversion to the treaty was particularly strong in Parliament. The domestic nuclear industry also opposed it, fearing adverse effects. Bern was especially concerned about the economic impact of the treaty on the import and export of nuclear technology and materials and the comparative advantages of states not subject to NPT controls.[67] However, in 1969 Switzerland signed the document, although it delayed ratification until 1977. Only in response to growing domestic and international pressure did it finally ratify the treaty.[68]

Why Did Switzerland Reject Nuclear Weapons?

The Swiss decided to forgo tactical nuclear weapons so as to preclude hostile responses from potential adversaries. As with Sweden, Swiss leaders believed that nuclear weapons would make their country an early target of nuclear attack, while a non-nuclear posture, based on a very strong conventional capability and guerrilla strategy, would possibly maintain neutrality in the event of a war in Europe. Despite high levels of military preparedness, successive governments perceived that their territory did not constitute a key target for military operations by either Warsaw Pact or NATO forces. The prime theatre was expected to be northern Germany, while Switzerland could get involved as a secondary target as a result of an operation in southern Germany. Thus the strategic reality was that during wartime, "neither NATO nor the Warsaw Pact would send first echelon mechanised divisions and air power to a secondary theatre of operations." The equipment of these troops, especially tanks, was comparable to Switzerland's, whose strong anti-tank capacity could destroy invading tanks.[69] Switzerland viewed its immediate region as friendly, with neighbouring states having no territorial ambitions against it, and it perceived no need for a nuclear deterrent to withstand threats from them.

The blurring of the line between defensive and offensive capabilities as a consequence of nuclear possession was another major consideration. As the early optimism faded that a tactical nuclear weapon could be used for battlefield objectives without collateral damage resulting, the Swiss realized that nuclearization would make them a prime target of hostile states' nuclear attacks. Pre-emption would become a possible motive for starting a war against Switzerland. The Swiss defensive and dissuasive strategy entailed war avoidance by all means. Nuclear possession could attract a military response from an adversary such as the USSR early in a war, as that adversary would have little assurance that Swiss capability was not meant for offensive purposes. As in the Swedish case, tension between the security needs of a neutral state and the particular character of nuclear weapons was noticeable in the Swiss dilemma.

Switzerland, however, took a possible nuclear war in Europe very seriously, as is evident in its elaborate preparations for civil defence, including extensive shelters against nuclear or chemical attack. It undertook strong precautions to protect as much civilian life as possible in the event of a nuclear war. By the early 1960s, the Swiss had built an extensive civil defence program under the aegis of 3,000 communities to train and organize well-equipped shelters in the event of a conventional, chemical, or atomic attack. By 1988, about 85 per cent of the population had access to shelters within ten to fifteen minutes if an emergency required evacuation.[70] Its confidence in its civil defence also meant that Switzerland could reduce the potential incentive for a nuclear power to use nuclear weapons against the country.

While deciding to sign the NPT, the Swiss leadership believed that accession would strengthen Swiss security while decreasing the chances of further nuclear proliferation.[71] It increasingly recognized that proliferation posed the most serious danger, since nuclear weapons in the hands of small, aggressive states could start a bush-fire, dragging the superpowers into their minor conflicts. Having additional countries target Switzerland with their nuclear weapons was not in the Swiss interest.[72]

CONCLUSIONS

In the early stages of the nuclear era, there was a belief in Sweden and Switzerland that tactical nuclear weapons were another powerful conventional device that could be used for dissuading a potential aggressor. As the nuclear age continued, it became clearer that such weapons carry an offensive quality to them, although they were meant for deterrence, and thereby generate negative security externalities for other states. Others, especially potential adversaries, would take nuclear possession as an aggressive step, as it would blur the line between the neutral state's traditional insistence on defensive capabilities and the exigencies of nuclear warfare. Even a highly defensive-oriented neutral state would be reluctant to use nuclear weapons against an invading army already on its territory. Thus the neutral state would have to cross the border and attack, or use the weapon in a neighbouring state's territory, before the attacker crossed into its territory, thereby violating the principles of neutrality. Nuclear adversaries, not knowing whether these weapons were for deterrent or offensive purposes, would be tempted to pre-empt them, seeing the capability of Sweden and Switzerland as part of the Western force. Neither Sweden nor Switzerland ever considered acquiring strategic nuclear weapons, which would have increased their offensive capabilities – a substantial violation of neutrality. Such a high-profile nuclear strategy would have automatically turned their countries into Soviet nuclear targets, eliminating their chances for non-involvement in a potential war in Europe. Not getting militarily involved in the wars of their neighbours had been a crowning achievement of the Swedes and the Swiss for over a century and a half.

Both nations provide valuable cases of neutral states that initiated nuclear weapons programs but later chose to rescind them. Having been spared the Second World War and war in general since the Napoleonic era, they chose not to acquire an independent deterrent. Their decisions were the result of a conscious cost–benefit analysis and the belief that nuclearization might upset their neutrality. The two neutral states under study here chose to forgo their nuclear options in order to maintain a benign strategic environment and avoid the excessive attention of nuclear powers during peacetime and in the event of war. The concept of marginality carried with it a strategic choice of not becoming an early target of nuclear attack in the event of a major European war, and the guarantee for that was nuclear abstinence.

Swedish and Swiss flirtation with nuclear weapons in the 1950s and 1960s was largely the result of the mindset of the times, when there was a general expectation of nuclear proliferation – all technologically capable states would acquire them sooner or later. It was not based on considerations of power or influence. Both states saw a strong army as essential to maintaining neutrality, but not as an instrument of international influence. The nuclear forbearance of these countries occurred before the NPT entered into force, although their signatures on the treaty confirmed and formalized their non-nuclear status.

CHAPTER SIX

Non-Allied States:
Argentina and Brazil

The decisions by Argentina and Brazil to sign the Nuclear Non-Proliferation Treaty (NPT) in 1995 and 1996, respectively, present significant theoretical and policy puzzles. These two states opposed the non-proliferation regime because of its discriminatory nature and its alleged negative impact on their independent nuclear energy programs. For well over three decades they had kept their options open by conducting research and development on technology and acquisition of materials useful for a nuclear weapons program. At the time of their nuclear forbearance, both, especially Argentina, were advanced enough to fabricate a small nuclear force quickly.[1] Moreover, both had pronounced their interest in peaceful nuclear explosions. Although both states faced only limited security threats in comparison with countries in South Asia or the Middle East, the Argentines confronted a nuclear Britain during the Falklands/Malvinas War; their possession of a mini-nuclear deterrent would probably have prevented a British military counter-assault in 1982. The war also proved to Argentina that it could not rely much on outside help in a military crisis.

Why in the early 1990s did these two formerly rival states choose to forgo their nuclear options after several decades of opposition? Moreover, the way they became non-nuclear – through a bilateral process, with hardly any help from the IAEA or major-power actors – also points to divergent routes to non-nuclear status that compromise domestic political imperatives and normative judgments about the international nuclear order.

A hegemonic-dissuasion explanation would give credit to constant pressures from powerful actors such as the United States and other nuclear suppliers. A regime-based explanation would cite the influence of the non-proliferation regime, especially the NPT and the norms and principles enshrined in the regime. These explanations, however, are insufficient. U.S. pressure indeed pushed these states to maintain their opposition to the non-proliferation regime. Dissatisfaction with nuclear hegemony encouraged nationalistic tendencies in these two countries and reinforced their desire for autarkic nuclear policies.[2] Moreover, the United States played no direct role in the regional nuclear rapprochement.

An international regime–based explanation is also not accurate because these states saw the regime as impeding their nuclear energy programs and constraining their independence. The non-proliferation regime came into the picture only after these states themselves decided to become non-nuclear and to create a regional mechanism to monitor their civilian nuclear activities. Their preference for a bilateral regime is clearly evident in their creation of the Brazilian–Argentine Agency for Accounting and Control of Nuclear Materials (ABACC) prior to signing up for the full-scope IAEA safeguards.[3] Such a bilateral mechanism is unique since all other non-nuclear states rely exclusively on the IAEA or supplier countries for inspecting their nuclear facilities.

A more promising explanation looks at domestic factors such as the advent of democracy and economic liberalization that brought about changes in the nuclear policies of Argentina and Brazil.[4] Even this explanation has problems, however, as the move towards nuclear rapprochement had already begun under military rulers. Moreover, these countries never actually fabricated a weapon. As I argue below, the resolution of territorial disputes and the desire of civilian rulers to reduce conflict in the region were critical factors. The absence of an intense, enduring rivalry of the India–Pakistani or Arab–Israeli variety was pivotal in achievement of the desired changes.

The non-nuclear policy, I argue, arose from cost–benefit calculations made by civilian leaders of the two countries who came to view nuclear acquisition, even maintenance of a weapons option, as hampering their economic and security co-operation and as leading to a technological race with military implications. The transition of the "Southern Cone" from a moderate- to a low-conflict zone since the late 1980s helps explain the nuclear choices of these states. However, a larger set of variables – domestic, bilateral, and regional – needs to be explored if we are to understand fully the transformation of the two states.

The relations between Argentina and Brazil have vacillated from conflict and competition to minimal cooperation throughout the twentieth century, although mutual distrust was a characteristic feature up until the early 1990s. Several factors made the relationship competitive. Asymmetry in size and economic and military capacity affected mutual relations. Both states vied for regional leadership and export markets in Latin America, while lingering territorial disputes prevented mutual accommodation. The launching of high-profile national nuclear energy programs increased the conflict. Although the prime motivation behind the nuclear programs was energy development, each country viewed the other's successes in this area in a "zero–sum" perspective, or as a loss for itself, with potential security implications.[5] The Brazilians perceived Argentina as an impediment to their achieving regional hegemony. They believed that Argentina was attempting to isolate Brazil in Latin America, especially among the Southern Cone nations. This conflict of interest was indeed a hangover from the days of the Chaco War (1932–35) and the world wars.

In the post-1945 era, the Brazilian perception of threat reached its height during Argentina's Peronist era (1946–55). Juan Peron's nationalist regime signed a number of commercial and cultural agreements with Bolivia, Chile, Paraguay, Peru, and Uruguay. Peron's launching of a nuclear energy program in the 1950s and Argentina's relative advantage in nuclear development in later years aroused Brazil's continuing suspicion.[6] During the 1970s, General Alejandro Lanusse pursued an active diplomatic campaign in Latin America against Brazil, which "brought to the surface all the latent antagonisms."[7]

The perceptions of mutual threat increased each time either country acquired new civilian nuclear technology or reactors. When Argentina signed a contract with Siemens of Germany for the construction of the Atucha I reactor in 1968, Brazil's worries increased. The Argentine military rulers were probably exploring the nuclear option more seriously as a counterweight to Brazil's increasing strength in conventional weapons.[8] The Brazilian–West German nuclear deal of 1975 and the Argentine efforts to acquire a third nuclear reactor in 1979 increased mutual suspicions and competition. The 1979 decision by Jorge Videla's government in Argentina to acquire the reactor from Switzerland seemed to have encouraged Brazilian President João Baptista Figueiredo to send the president of NUCLEBRAS to Argentina to explore co-operation in nuclear energy. The settlement of the dispute over electric development in the River Plate Basin helped to ease political tensions; by early 1980 the two countries had exchanged visits by high-ranking nuclear energy officials. In May 1980, Figueiredo visited Argentina and signed a two-way co-operation agreement that called for bilateral technical collaboration and joint ventures for the production of reactor components and fuel elements, with the aim of minimizing dependence on Western supplier countries.[9] With the end of military rule in both states, civilian leaders perceived that covert nuclear programs were impeding their efforts at bilateral, regional, and international economic co-operation.[10] Developing a non-threatening security policy became the key to co-operation. Continued non-transparent development of national nuclear programs would result in mutual mistrust and hostility, a condition antithetical to regional economic and security co-operation.

A Bilateral Approach

Both Argentina and Brazil pursued a bilateral approach to nuclear nonproliferation. The involvement of the IAEA and other multilateral nonproliferation agencies was not noticeable in this process. The two states followed a step-by-step approach for well over a decade and along the way signed several bilateral accords, preceded by general improvements in political and economic relations – a process that had begun under military rule. The major step in this direction was the signing of the 1979 agreement that created a framework for resolution of the disputes in the River Plate area. Having settled their territorial disputes, these states began to focus on the nuclear issue. The first important measure was the Argentina–Brazil agreement of April 1980 for peaceful use of nuclear energy, which established co-operation in the nuclear fuel cycle and co-ordination of nuclear policies. The Foz do Iguazu Declaration of 1985 was the next milestone, followed by the president's declarations at their meetings in Brasilia (1986), Viedma (1987), Ipero (1988), and Buenos Aires (1990). During this period, a significant "ad hoc process of reciprocal head of state and technicians visits to indigenous and non-safeguarded nuclear installations was established."[11] The visit to each other's nuclear facilities by President Raul Alfonsin of Argentina and Jose Sarney of Brazil was a critical confidence-building measure.

The culmination of this bilateral approach occurred on 28 November 1990, when the new presidents of Argentina and Brazil, Carlos Menem and Fernando Collor, respectively, signed the Declaration on the Common Nuclear Policy of Brazil and Argentina at Foz do Iguazu. The document established a common system of Accounting and Control of Nuclear Materials (SCCC), and it envisaged negotiations with the IAEA for a full-scope safeguards agreement based on a bilateral system. The declaration also called for "initiatives conducive to the full entry into force" of the Treaty of Tlateloco.[12] In July 1991, Argentina and Brazil concluded a bilateral agreement to use nuclear materials and facilities "exclusively for peaceful purposes" and to prohibit "testing, use, manufacture, production or acquisition by any means of any nuclear weapon," including peaceful nuclear explosions (PNEs), and the "receipt, storage, installation, deployment or any other form of possession of any nuclear weapon."[13]

The bilateral efforts were institutionalized with creation in July 1992 of a joint accounting and inspection agency, ABACC, headquartered in Rio de Janeiro. The agency has been conducting mutual inspections by sixty specialists (thirty from each country) at nuclear facilities on a cross-national basis. These inspections include verification of inventories of nuclear materials, unannounced and short-notice inspections, and inspections carried out along with the IAEA.[14] The agency coordinates activities with the IAEA, whose officials also conduct separate inspections. National safeguards authorities periodically send ABACC reports on the accounting of nuclear materials.[15] These bilateral safeguards measures are more thorough than the IAEA's system, and verification of inventories has proved to be a major confidence-building measure.

Milestones in the nuclear rapprochement between the two countries include a quadripartite agreement signed in Vienna in December 1991, involving Brazil, Argentina, the IAEA, and ABACC. Both countries agreed to disavow peaceful nuclear explosions – a major change in policy. The agreement and its protocol, which came into force in March 1994, set up comprehensive safeguards for the export and import of nuclear materials and implemented article 13 of the Treaty of Tlateloco regarding application of IAEA safeguards.[16] Argentina in January 1994 and Brazil in May 1994 also ratified the Treaty of Tlateloco, which establishes a nuclear-free zone in Latin America – another step towards transparency in their nuclear programs. These countries had earlier signed the treaty but refused ratification. The accession of Argentina to the NPT in 1995 and of Brazil in 1996 completed all the key formalities for non-nuclear status.

ARGENTINA

Argentina has been a pioneer among developing states in the development of nuclear technology. Endowed with an abundant supply of uranium, it launched an ambitious nuclear energy program in the 1950s, hoping for full mastery of the nuclear fuel cycle.[17] The starting point of atomic energy development was establishment in 1950 of the Comision Nacional de Energia Atomica (CNEA). The rationale for creation of atomic energy facilities and the importance given to this area by successive governments is multi-faceted. One primary motive was to reverse Argentina's relative decline from one of the world's richest countries in the 1940s to an isolated, poor nation, which had lost its trading position.[18] When Juan Peron launched the program, his intention was to bring back grandeur to Argentina by acquiring the "cutting edge" technology of the times – nuclear technology. Nuclear autonomy was part and parcel of a larger inward-looking, autarkic development strategy. This was one of the few areas where national consensus developed, as both Peronists and non-Peronists supported nuclear autonomy – i.e., lessening of foreign dependence – and the CNEA received unparalleled national support even during periods of political and economic turmoil.[19]

Successive military regimes viewed nuclear technology in terms of the Peronist vision and pursued a statist and "zero-sum"-oriented security policy, premised on creation of an economically and militarily self-sufficient and autonomous state able to confront an unequal international system.[20] Competition with Brazil and fear of a possible U.S.–Brazilian alliance also encouraged Argentine rulers to pursue a nuclear program. In order to counter Brazil, Argentina attempted to gain regional leadership by implementing a maritime strategy focusing on the South Atlantic and sub-Antarctic regions.[21] Competition with Brazil drove the military component of the program. The massive growth of Brazil's population and economy and international recognition of Brazil as the leading power of South America increased the Argentine sense of inferiority.[22] Although the Argentines did not fear an external attack by any of their neighbours, they wanted to obtain military equality with Brazil and preponderance over Chile in order to maintain a balance of power in the region and to prevent any politico-military alliances between these two countries. In addition, Argentina sought political and economic relationships with Bolivia, Paraguay, and Uruguay to keep these countries as a buffer against Brazil.[23]

The main component of the Argentine nuclear energy program has been the power plants – Atucha I, the Embalse Reactor, and Atucha II. Atucha I, built with the collaboration of the German company Siemens, is a natural uranium–fuelled, heavy water–moderated reactor. Canada built the 600-mW Embalse CANDU-style heavy-water reactor. The 745-mW Atucha II is also a heavy-water reactor.[24] In 1998, Argentina produced over 11 per cent of its national power through the nuclear source.[25] Until 1995, it had maintained nuclear facilities without IAEA safeguards. The most important facility from the proliferation point of view was the gas-diffusion enrichment plant located at Pilcaniyeu in Rio Negro province, the existence of which was revealed in 1983 after it had operated secretly for about five years. Although this facility was expected to produce only 20 per cent–enriched uranium (suitable for use in research and power reactors and not for weapons), manufacturing weapons-grade materials there was possible in the long run.[26] Other unsafeguarded facilities included a small reprocessing plant and a fuel-fabrication facility at the Ezeiza research complex near Buenos Aires and an experimental pilot-scale heavy-water facility near Atucha I and II in Buenos Aires province. The reprocessing facility has been expected to separate 15 kilograms of plutonium from spent fuel each year and then fabricate the plutonium into fuel.[27]

Although no specific weapons program was authorized, by the 1970s it was apparent that Argentina was developing technology suitable for such a program. In 1983, CNEA President Admiral Castro Madero announced that Argentina had acquired the technology to enrich uranium.[28] Argentina also would have been able to convert some of its military aircraft, such as Skyhawks, Super Etendards, and Mirage III, into nuclear-carrying delivery aircraft.[29] It had missile technology and was on its way to building the IRBM Condor Missile II, which the Menem government cancelled in August 1991. This missile was expected to carry a payload of 500 kilograms with a range of 1,000 kilometres and would have been a good nuclear-delivery system. A handful of crude, first-generation nuclear weapons were likely to be effective against amphibious forces, such as the British task force that was sent to the South Atlantic in 1982.[30] Although the risk of British retaliation would have made any Argentine threat of nuclear use less credible, the sheer uncertainty it would have generated might have provided a limited deterrent against a British assault.

Successive military regimes maintained an ambiguous position on nuclear weapons. Although Argentina never went far enough to build a bomb, it refused to sign the NPT and failed to ratify the Tlateloco Treaty. Its declared policy was always to reject any plans to build a bomb.[31] It finally ratified Tlateloco on a conditional basis and refused to waive the requirement that the treaty not come into full force until all Latin American states had ratified it and all nuclear states had ratified the appropriate protocols. This nullified Argentine adherence, because Cuba had not become a member of the treaty.

The Falklands/Malvinas conflict with Britain temporarily increased the Argentine military's desire to acquire nuclear weapons. The defeat, however, further delegitimized military rule, and the civilian regime of Raul Alfonsin took office in December 1983. Civilian governments asserted their opposition to the military's secret nuclear program. They knew that the military would use the defeat in the 1982 war as a pretext to speed up the nuclear program. In their endeavour to make Argentina less isolated, they focused on change in the nuclear domain.

Why Argentina Chose to Forgo Its Nuclear Option

The military defeat in the Malvinas War discredited the national security ideas held by the military. The process of bilateral nuclear co-operation started under the last military regime and accelerated under Alfonsin, but it received more concrete and active direction from Alfonsin's successor, Carlos Menem. The slow but steady change from conflict to cooperation can be traced back to 1976, when Argentina appointed as ambassador to Brazil Oscar Camilion, who worked diligently to improve relations between the two countries. The settlement of the Itaipu Dam dispute in 1979 and the Falklands War in 1982 transformed Argentine perceptions of Brazil. The Brazilian position (officially neutral, but slanted in favour of Argentina) during and after the war was viewed favourably by Argentina. Defeat in the war resulted in introspection by the Argentine elite, and the geopolitical and conflict-oriented views of the military strategists were now challenged by "cooperative, integrationist" ideas of civilian analysts.[32] Progress towards settlement of the Beagle Channel dispute with Chile reduced Argentina's sense of "encirclement." More and more Argentines began to view Brazil as a partner, albeit a senior partner, and not as a threat.[33]

The changes occurred out of realization by the Menem government that Argentina's nuclear policy blocked co-operation with Brazil and economic integration with the region and the rest of the world, especially in trade, finance, and investment. The Argentines realized that they, with a population of less than 30 million, could not take on Brazil, which had 120 million people and was the eighth-largest economy in the world. Although a superior nuclear capability might have worked to Argentina's strategic advantage, Brazil's acquisition of a similar capacity would have neutralized its effect. The consequence was a policy of co-operation resulting from recognition of Argentine inability to challenge Brazil in the long run.[34] Argentina also realized that Brazil was unlikely to sign the NPT in the short run and that a bilateral arrangement was feasible for domestic political reasons in both countries and would be consistent with opposition to the inequitable non-proliferation regime.

The larger changes in foreign policy initiated by the Menem government included befriending the United States, quitting the non-aligned movement, suspending the Condor II ballistic missile program, and sending frigates to the Persian Gulf during the 1991 war as part of the U.S.-led coalition. In addition, Argentina decided to join the Nuclear Suppliers Group (NSG), the Missile Technology Control Regime (MTCR), and other non-proliferation arrangements. In April 1992, a presidential order decreed that sale of missile, chemical, and nuclear materials must be consistent with the guidelines set by MTCR, NSG, and the Australia Group. Cutting off co-operation with Egypt and Iraq in the missile field was a significant step in this regard. The key change was, however, Argentina's joining the NPT in 1995, which has strengthened its non-nuclear credentials.

BRAZIL

Brazil's nuclear program, unlike Argentina's, has been affected by the vagaries of domestic politics. It has been heavily state-managed, while Argentina's involved more private initiatives. Brazil's also lacked the ideological and political consensus and continuity characteristic of Argentina's.[35] As a result, in 1998 the country operated only one nuclear reactor, which generated less than 1 per cent of the country's electricity.[36] Yet Brazil has been a pioneer in the developing world in nuclear research and development. It possesses an estimated uranium reserve of 300,000 tonnes, the world's fifth-largest, and a thorium reserve of 80,000 tonnes.[37] It also has a strong aircraft industry and was making headway in a missile program when the non-nuclear policies were adopted.[38]

Brazil initiated research in nuclear technology as early as 1945, when it signed a nuclear co-operation agreement with the United States. Early activities were exploration for thorium and uranium and development of facilities for nuclear energy. In 1954, Brazil launched the National Nuclear Energy Commission (CNEN); under the Atoms for Peace Plan, the United States provided three research reactors. With the establishment of military rule in 1964 the armed forces began to show interest in nuclear technology for security objectives. In 1967, the military-run National Security Council declared nuclear energy capability a permanent national objective, as one of the most important goals in the country's national security doctrine.[39]

Not surprisingly, therefore, Brazil opposed the NPT. It saw the non-proliferation regime as ensuring the developed nations' monopoly of nuclear technology; non-nuclear signatories would be giving up both their right to build nuclear weapons and access to the benefits derived from peaceful uses of nuclear energy. Brazil also feared that adherence would give it a "dependent nuclear status and so endanger or restrict future development schemes." It doubted the treaty's security guarantees and resented the manner in which the superpowers negotiated it, making it a fait accompli for the developing countries.[40]

Despite opposition to the NPT, in 1972 Brazil managed to sign a contract with the U.S. energy company Westinghouse for construction of its first nuclear reactor, Angra I. However, following the Indian nuclear test of 1974, the United States hardened its policies regarding the supply of nuclear technology and materials to all "threshold" states. The U.S. Atomic Energy Commission (AEC) in 1974 decided not to renew its guarantee to Brazil for the supply of enriched uranium. As nuclear co-operation with the United States stalled, Brazil turned to West Germany, which wanted to strike lucrative commercial deals with it. In June 1975, Brazil and West Germany signed an $8-billion agreement that provided Brazil with complete fuel-cycle technology and two power reactors, with an option to buy six more. Complete implementation of this agreement would have resulted in Brazil's generating 10,000 mW of electricity from nuclear sources by 1990. By 2010 over 40 per cent of the country's energy was to come from the nuclear sector.[41] Although the agreement provided for more stringent international inspections than standard IAEA arrangements, it was feared, especially by the United States, that the uranium-enrichment and spent-fuel reprocessing facilities could provide Brazil with weapons-grade materials that it could divert to a future weapons program.[42] This agreement has, however, not met original expectations.

International suspicions intensified as Brazil's nuclear intentions became clouded in secrecy when the military began a parallel program in 1975 under the presidency of General Ernesto Geisel. This program was beyond the jurisdiction of civilian authorities such as CNEN and under full military control. It included a gas-centrifuge unit at the navy-run Aramar facility near São Paulo and a laboratory-scale reprocessing facility, also at São Paulo. Plans were afoot for a graphite reactor at an army-controlled facility near Rio.[43] The Aramar plant was expected to produce less-than-20-per-cent enriched uranium for nuclear power and research reactors and, more important, for nuclear submarine reactors, which Brazil had been developing.[44] Financing of the nuclear program came in a clandestine way. According to the president of the CNEN, Jose dos Santos, in 1989 secret bank accounts under the pseudonyms Delta I, II, and III, became known. The National Security Council, which loosely coordinated nuclear activities, divided the money among diverse military organs, in charge of different nuclear activities, while keeping the CNEN out of the picture. The different activities of the armed forces – laser enrichment by the air force, centrifuge enrichment by the navy, and a graphite reactor by the army – reveal the extent to which the military was pursuing nuclear weapons. Only the navy succeeded in enriching uranium (at a cost of $1 billion), but not enough for weapons.[45]

Although the parallel program had been in full swing since 1979, in the 1980s some rethinking began among the Brazilian leadership. Under President General Figueiredo, a foreign debt crisis and opposition by leading nuclear scientists such as Jose Goldemberg, David Simin, and Luiz Pinguelli Rosa slowed the program. The end of military rule heralded major changes in nuclear policy. The civilian

President Jose Sarney appointed Goldemberg as president of the Sao Paulo State Company for Electricity, and the government adopted his recommendation for restructuring CNEN. However, the military still retained full control over the parallel program.[46]

In September 1990, the new president Fernando Collor de Mello, received a fifty-page classified report on the bomb project, code-named "Solimoes," after the Brazilian river. He met the chiefs of the army, navy, and air force and asked them to stop the project. On 18 September 1990, Collor took the military heads to Cachimbo in Central Amazon and "threw a symbolic shovelful of cement into a hole four feet in diameter and 1050 feet deep," designed for underground nuclear tests. The military was awaiting 20–30 pounds of enriched uranium with the hope of testing a Hiroshima-type bomb in a year or two.[47] Collor later elevated Goldemberg, a staunch opponent of the military program, as the head of the entire Brazilian nuclear energy program.

Twelve years of summit meetings with Argentina produced a host of agreements that made Brazil forswear nuclear weapons. Several developments – inclusion of a provision in the Brazilian constitution in 1988 that nuclear energy was to be used only for peaceful purposes, the agreements with ABACC and IAEA for full-scope safeguards, the signing and ratification of the Tlateloco Treaty, and Brazil's joining the MTCR in October 1995 – all reaffirmed the non-nuclear policy. The decision to sign the NPT signalled a dramatic change in attitude towards nuclear non-proliferation. President Fernando Henrique Cardoso, in June 1997, submitted the proposal to Congress, which approved it in July 1998. Congress also ratified Brazil's accession to the CTBT in July 1998. On 13 July 1998, Cardoso signed the instruments of ratification of both the NPT and the CTBT in the presence of the UN secretary general, Kofi Annan, thereby formalizing Brazil's non-nuclear status.[48]

Why did Brazil Choose to Give up Its Nuclear Program?

Brazil's nuclear ambitions derived from considerations of power and prestige and to a certain extent from its competition with Argentina. Brazil's perceptions of threat have been more elusive than that of any other threshold nuclear state. Unlike India, Israel, or Pakistan, Brazil did not face any serious military threats to its security.[49] It also held conventional superiority over all major Latin American countries. It was competition with Argentina that drove Brazil's actions and reactions in nuclear weapons. Argentina's lead in the race aggravated Brazil. Sections of the military became anxious when Argentina announced its completion of the fuel cycle and its achievements in missile technology. Army Minister Leonidas Pires Goncalves declared in September 1985 that Brazil could not stay behind if Argentina built a nuclear bomb.[50]

The Brazilian military also viewed nuclear acquisition, or at least the capacity to obtain nuclear weapons without actually producing them, as a way to bolster Brazil's power and prestige in the world and Latin America in particular. Brazil wanted to become a major world power and a participant in crucial international decisions. It saw the NPT as a binding commitment that would have frozen the global power structure and closed off Brazil's chances to become a major power. The military believed that Brazil would become the dominant power of Latin America during the twenty-first century and saw nuclear status as necessary for achieving that goal.[51]

Brazil was the first nation to propose a Latin American nuclear-free zone in September 1962, and Mexico took up the idea later. In 1964, Brazil's military rulers, along with Argentina, refused to ratify the Tlateloco Treaty, as the two countries wanted to remove its restrictive clauses, which they perceived as constraints on their independent nuclear policies.[52]

Why did Brazil decide to forswear nuclear weapons in the 1990s? What made the transformation possible? The key variables were bilateral and regional as well as domestic. The major determinant was fear of provoking a nuclear arms race with Argentina. Because of the latter's lead in nuclear technology, it was unlikely that Brazil could have achieved superiority in this realm. A nuclear arms race, Brazil feared, would only harm its security environment.[53] Brazil's conception of power and prestige also changed with the arrival of civilian regimes. Although sections of the civilian elite and the military still harboured the traditional goal of dominance in Latin America, the realization began to dawn that co-operation was the better route to regional leadership. This change was most evident in improved relations with Argentina, achieved after 1976 by a variety of co-operative mechanisms. The Argentine defeat in the Malvinas War ensured that Argentina would not undertake another military venture anytime soon. Brazilian leaders perceived that a stable Argentina as a neighbour was in Brazil's interests. Depoliticizing the relationship appeared essential for enhanced co-operation.[54] The simultaneous transition to democracy in the two countries increased the pace of co-operation. The elite realized that nuclear weapons do not provide much power or influence in relationships between neighbouring states that do not harbour military hostility or territorial claims against each other. The end of the Cold War further helped change Brazilian conceptions on security: Brazil has to become part of the global economy and thereby an economic power. The new civilian economic and security polices were driven by that goal.

Can Brazil revoke its non-nuclear policies? Such a decision would devastate its relations with Argentina and other states in the region, as well as with its major trading partners. Moreover, according to the CNEN's president, no major interest in the armed forces favours nuclear weapons – Brazil is "the only country that allows external inspectors (ABACC and IAEA) inside military facilities." Total civilian control means that secret funding is no longer feasible.[55]

CONCLUSIONS

The main conclusion of this chapter is that a major change occurred in the perceived utility of nuclear weapons when Argentina and Brazil resolved their territorial conflicts. Changes in domestic power structures accelerated and reinforced the process. The military regimes valued these weapons for maintaining their autarkic policies, and they expected that nuclear possession would bring grandeur to their countries. Once territorial disputes were settled and civilian regimes assumed power, security-conscious worst-case assumptions changed to assessments of most-probable threat. Ambiguity over nuclear intentions seemed to forestall economic policies of regional co-operation and opening up to the larger international market.

The civilian regimes realized that their mutual nuclear competition blocked regional rapprochement. The leadership in both countries understood that nuclear acquisition would transform the somewhat benign security environment in the Southern Cone and intensify the limited political, economic, and cultural rivalry. Nuclear acquisition by one state would compel the other to follow suit and thereby undermine co-operation, which they both desired. Thus the clear catalyst for nuclear rapprochement was mutual concern about a possible nuclear arms race. The two states initiated policies that played down geopolitical competition, and these small steps led to a larger thaw. The moderate level of conflict and the absence of intense, protracted conflicts allowed this process.[56] The resolution of territorial disputes was a key precursor of this change. Economically exhausted leaderships in both nations determined to abandon the Cold War–era national security doctrines based on high military spending and worst-case assumptions. Their building of a free-trade zone called "Mercosur" made them realize that economic integration would not be feasible if the military competition continued.[57] Regional stability was essential for economic

co-operation, and bilateral nuclear forbearance became a crucial building block for a stable regional order. The evolutionary nature of this
change supports the argument presented in chapter 2 – that nuclear
non-acquisition is largely a function of political processes occurring
regionally as political elites rethink a high-risk security policy based
on nuclear weapons. It also supports the main argument of the study
– that nuclear forbearance is possible in moderate- and low-conflict
zones that do not have intense enduring rivalries and protracted
conflicts, characterized by militarized disputes and crises.

CHAPTER SEVEN

Nuclear Choices of South Africa, Ukraine, and South Korea

In this chapter I look at three additional states – South Africa, Ukraine, and South Korea – that have decided to forgo nuclear weapons to see whether the theoretical framework outlined in chapter 1 can explain their choices. Although these cases, drawn from three regions of the world, are not identical, as they possess varying levels of nuclear development, they are comparable on the most crucial criterion: they gave up their nuclear options despite strong security reasons for maintaining or building the weapons. Ukraine confronted a nuclear neighbour, while for South Korea, the nuclear activities of North Korea constituted a major security threat. South Africa and Ukraine possessed nuclear weapons when they proclaimed a non-nuclear policy, although the latter inherited them from the former Soviet Union. Ukraine gave up its nuclear weapons even when a limited nuclear capability could have acted as a military deterrent against any Russian revanchism.

SOUTH AFRICA

South Africa had assembled six nuclear devices and was on the way to developing a seventh when it gave up its program in 1990 and chose the non-nuclear path. Its transformation from a covert nuclear nation to a non-nuclear state has important theoretical and policy implications. Indeed, it is the only state in the world that had developed nuclear weapons on its own and then chosen to abandon them. In a purely realpolitik sense, maintaining nuclear weapons would have given South Africa a deterrent capability and a potentially significant power resource in regional and global politics.

South Africa has been a pioneer in nuclear research and uranium production. As a result, it sat on the board of governors of the International Atomic Energy Agency (IAEA) until 1977, when it was expelled for covert nuclear activities. South Africa has also been one of the leading producers of uranium and a major supplier to Western countries.[1] It began construction of an unsafeguarded pilot uranium-enrichment plant in 1971 at Valindaba, outside Pretoria, where in 1977 it began producing enriched uranium at 80 per cent, which it later used for the nuclear weapons program.[2] According to IAEA estimates, by 1989 South Africa had produced between 200 and 400 kilograms of weapons-grade uranium, enough to make between twelve and twenty-four nuclear weapons.[3] Its decision to produce weapons-grade enriched uranium was driven partly by U.S. sanctions. In 1977, the Carter administration, as part of its global non-proliferation policy, decided to suspend the U.S. contract to provide low-enriched uranium to the Koeberg reactors unless South Africa acceded to the NPT. The United States formalized this ban in 1978 through the Nuclear Non-Proliferation Act (NNPA). Pretoria viewed the cutoff as a unilateral abrogation and initiated its own enrichment program, which helped it to accumulate substantial quantities of highly enriched uranium for making weapons.[4]

The weapons program began in 1974 when Prime Minister John Vorster authorized a small-scale program and construction of an underground test facility in the Kalahari Desert. The active militarization of the program began in April 1978, when Vorster approved a document outlining the country's nuclear course. In July 1979 a committee appointed by Prime Minister P.W. Botha recommended manufacture of seven nuclear weapons.[5] By 1991 South Africa had about six nuclear devices and was developing implosion and missile technology.[6] The delivery systems would have been Canberra and Buccaneer aircraft and possibly Jericho missiles supplied by Israel. According to Waldo Stumpf, South Africa in 1977 completed the first full device using enriched uranium, which it expected to test at the Kalahari site, but it later abandoned the testing idea.[7] It built a second, smaller device in 1978 and manufactured additional weapons at the facility of the Armaments Corporation of South Africa (ARMSCOR) at Pelindaba, near Pretoria, beginning in December 1982. According to Stumpf, the program was reviewed in September 1985, and the government decided to limit it to seven fission gun–type devices, of which only six were completed.[8]

The South African nuclear strategy was reportedly to use the bomb as a political tool to achieve its security objectives.[9] This strategy involved three phases. In the first, the South African government would adopt a policy of neither confirming nor denying its nuclear possession to maximize uncertainty. The second phase would occur if the country were militarily threatened. Pretoria would then secretly inform Western governments, especially the United States, of its nuclear status to try to persuade it to come to South Africa's rescue. If such appeals did not produce the expected results, South Africa would move on to the third phase – acknowledging openly, or testing publicly, a nuclear bomb that would compel the West to intervene on South Africa's behalf.[10] The strategy has been termed "catalytic deterrence," based on arousing concerns in the West about Pretoria's using nuclear weapons in a crisis and thereby encouraging the West to intervene to protect it. The leadership believed that "the calculated ambiguity of neither confirming nor denying nuclear weapon possession, and having an ability to test rudimentary devices," would be "sufficient to ensure nuclear coupling with the West."[11]

Although the decisions were made within a psychological framework of racial hostility and exaggerated perceptions of threat, we must assess the underpinnings of the threat scenario if we are to understand South Africa's nuclear choices. The conflicts in Southern Africa in the 1970s and 1980s played a large role in South Africa's perceptions. The rulers believed that the Soviet Union was bent on destroying South Africa's racially based political system of apartheid through its support for the liberation struggle within South Africa and in other "frontline" states. P.W. Botha, a former defence minister, and Admiral Bierman, commandant-general of the South African Defence Forces (SADF), believed that such an assault was inevitable[12] and that South Africa had no allies to withstand a Communist onslaught.

These anxieties increased with the liberation of Angola and Mozambique in 1974 from Portugal and intensified with South Africa's active involvement in the civil wars in these two countries. In Angola, South Africa sided with the National Front for the Liberation of Angola (FNLA) by sending 3,000 troops to fight along with it. These forces confronted 15,000 to 20,000 Cuban troops who were defending the Marxist People's Movement for the Liberation of Angola (MPLA), and South Africa had to withdraw in 1976. South Africa also perceived high stakes in the increased guerrilla warfare in Namibia and Rhodesia and got actively involved in the operations there as well. South Africa's abandonment by the West and the end of white rule in Rhodesia (later Zimbabwe) in 1979 increased the elite's sense of isolation.[13] The South African nuclear weapons program sprang from this security environment, characterized by protracted conflicts and enduring rivalries and its near-isolation by the international community.

Why Did the Transition Occur?

Despite the threat scenario confronted by South Africa, nuclear acquisition was indeed short-lived. Just over a decade after acquiring the first devices, South Africa gave up its nuclear weapons, closed the plant that was making enriched uranium, downgraded the enrichment level of uranium to make it unsuitable for nuclear arms, and shredded the blueprints for nuclear weapons. The transition occurred following the changes in Southern Africa's security environment and along with the transformation of the apartheid regime and its collapse in 1991.[14] It also coincided with the collapse of Communism in the Soviet Union and Eastern Europe.

The timing of the decision shows how regional changes can powerfully influence national choices in the nuclear realm. The tripartite agreement between South Africa, Angola, and Cuba in December 1988 for a phased withdrawal of Cuban troops from Angola, South Africa's granting of independence to Namibia in 1989, and the end of the Cold War contributed to the decision. The election of F.W. De Klerk as president in September 1989 was the beginning of major political reforms and changes in foreign and domestic policies.[15] The ending of conflicts in the region made irrelevant a military strategy based on the conception of "total onslaught." Thus the earlier transition of the region from high to moderate conflict assisted this change in approach. In the transformed environment, security threats were no longer crucial, and nuclear weapons seemed unnecessary symbols of a bygone era.[16]

De Klerk's inauguration in 1989 marked a watershed in the transition to non-nuclear status. The president ordered a halt to nuclear weapons making and the decommissioning of the pilot enrichment facility. He appointed an expert committee, consisting of senior officials from the Atomic Energy Commission, ARMSCOR, and the defence forces, to consider abandonment of the nuclear weapons program and dismantling of the assembled weapons. On its recommendations, he ordered the uranium-enrichment facility shut down in February 1990. Subsequently, he appointed Waldo Stumpf to oversee dismantling of the weapons. By July 1991, the process was completed; there followed destruction of blueprints and technical data on nuclear weapons.[17]

Although South Africa had acceded to the NPT in July 1991, De Klerk announced the fact only on 24 March 1993.[18] What motivated him to give up nuclear weapons? In his speech, he stated that with the withdrawal of Cuban troops from Southern Africa, the end of the Cold War, the cease-fire in Angola, and the tripartite agreement on the independence of Namibia, a nuclear capability had "become not only superfluous, but in fact an obstacle to the development of South Africa's international relations."[19] The program clearly lost its rationale with the end of the protracted conflicts in Southern Africa. With domestic political reforms, a secret nuclear program was untenable. In addition, nuclear forbearance became essential for ending South Africa's isolation and its joining the international mainstream as an advanced state in areas such as nuclear energy and space technology. Improving relations with the West and African countries was part of the new strategy.[20]

Will South Africa revert to its pro-nuclear policy under a future government? Although leaders of the African National Congress (ANC) had expressed reservations about De Klerk's failure to consult them, the party's policies have been strongly anti-nuclear. Even before gaining power, the ANC had called for making South Africa a responsible member of the international non-proliferation community by striving for an African nuclear-free zone, full participation in IAEA activities, and non-allocation of resources and scientists to produce nuclear weapons.[21] The ANC government of Nelson Mandela did follow through on the party's pledge, and South Africa has increased its non-proliferation credentials by accepting nuclear-supplier guidelines for export of nuclear materials, by taking the lead in arranging a nuclear-free zone in Africa, and by helping the process of extending the NPT.[22] It played a pivotal role in the extension of the NPT in perpetuity in 1995. When the UN conference deadlocked over a timetable for nuclear disarmament, South Africa introduced a proposal that emphasized the obligations of the nuclear powers to fulfil their disarmament pledges and measures to strengthen the treaty's periodic review process. The president of the conference, Ambassador Jayantha Dhanapala of Sri Lanka, used the proposals as a way to satisfy the principal requirements set forth by several major countries for the indefinite extension. Although the decision involved several other players and delicate negotiations and manoeuvring, the South African contribution was pivotal.[23]

The South African case confirms the main hypothesis of this study. A technologically capable state acquired nuclear weapons in response to security threats during a period of intense protracted conflicts and enduring rivalries, marked by several militarized interstate disputes. The end of these conflicts allowed it to initiate a process of nuclear dismantlement. It saw military capability that it had accrued as a result of nuclear possession as no longer necessary and as inhibiting its acceptance into the international community. The ANC government, in its desire to avoid conflict with other significant states with which it interacts, continues the non-nuclear policy. It views the maintenance of a nuclear capability as antithetical to its goal of creating a zone of peace and co-operation in Africa.

UKRAINE

On 1 June 1996, Ukraine became a non-nuclear nation when it completed the transfer of the last batch of 1,900 strategic nuclear warheads to Russia for destruction.[24] The denuclearization process took three years and followed a concerted effort by the United States and Russia to get Ukraine to commit itself to a non-nuclear path. Along with two other successor states, Belarus and Kazakhstan, Ukraine inherited its nuclear weapons from the Soviet Union when it broke up. At the time of dissolution, Ukraine possessed about 4,400 nuclear warheads, making it the third-largest nuclear power in the world. These weapons had constituted a key part of the Soviet deterrent against the West.[25] Not only did Ukraine have the weapons on its territory, it also held a large pool of nuclear scientists, had the capability to make nuclear and missile components, and possessed the industrial infrastructure to maintain a small nuclear force.

According to a hard-realist account, Ukraine should have retained its nuclear capability as a deterrent against Russia and as a hedge against possible expansionist forces taking power in Moscow. This would not only have protected its security but also promoted regional stability.[26] However, the Ukrainian decision to sign the NPT and transfer nuclear weapons, especially tactical warheads, to Russia for destruction challenges some of the hard realists' predictions of states' nuclear choices. The tactical nuclear weapons were the first to be transferred in 1992, although this capability could have constituted the most effective deterrent against any military assault by Russia.

Ukraine chose to give away its nuclear weapons in return for economic assistance and security assurances from the United States and Russia. The Ukrainian decision to accede to the NPT followed a trilateral agreement between Presidents Leonid Kravchuk, Bill Clinton, and Boris Yeltsin in January 1994. The security assurances that Ukraine received were extremely important for that country, especially Russian willingness to honour existing borders, the commitment by the three nuclear powers (Britain, Russia, and the United States) not to use or threaten to use force, particularly with nuclear weapons, or to employ economic coercion against Ukraine.[27] Ukraine ratified START I in February 1994 and the NPT in November 1994.

The Ukrainian decision to forbear nuclear weapons confirms my arguments in this study. Ukraine falls in a zone of moderate conflict, despite the possibility of conflict with Russia. Contrary to writings by some Western analysts, my interviews with Ukrainian policy-makers and scholars reveal that they perceive only a low possibility for a direct military threat from Russia, citing historical and cultural factors and ethnic closeness. A more probable threat would be an economic squeeze, as Russia still supplies 70 per cent of Ukraine's gas and 85 per cent of its oil and constitutes the biggest market for Ukrainian products.[28] Despite a history of Russian aggression and occupation, the current relationship is not an enduring rivalry, involving active, militarized inter-state disputes. Russia and Ukraine had initial disputes about the Black Sea Fleet in Sevastapol and other issues relating to the division of assets of the USSR. The intergovernmental agreements of May 1997 resolved much of the dispute with a leasing arrangement and Russia's acceptance of Crimea and Sevastapol as Ukrainian.[29] The Ukrainian leadership debated the costs and benefits of keeping the nuclear capability but decided that Ukraine could increase its security and international prestige and improve relations with Russia and the West by forfeiting nuclear arms. Although it could have kept the weapons for a while, the costs of their maintenance – in economic, political, military, security, and environmental terms – seemed to outweigh the benefits, which were unpredictable at best.

Within Ukraine there were elements that wanted to keep nuclear weapons. However, after the withdrawal to Russia of all tactical nuclear weapons by mid-1992, the Kravchuk government viewed strategic weapons as only bargaining chips. Later President Leonid Kuchma also followed his predecessor's nuclear policies.[30] Barring some small sections of the officer corps, the military was very much in favour of nuclear disarmament in return for getting more spending for conventional forces. The military hierarchy believed that the maintenance costs of nuclear weapons would swallow the scare resources needed to provide basic support to the armed forces. The military "understood the cost of command, communications and intelligence (C3I) and Ukraine's technical problems in maintaining a nuclear force over the long term."[31]

The leadership realized that continued nuclear possession would hurt Kiev's prospects for becoming accepted by the international community, especially by the West;[32] it would force Russia to increase pressure on Ukraine, preventing a Russo–Ukrainian accommodation. The Western European states would ostracize Ukraine, and American opposition would effectively isolate Ukraine from the global community. The country's immediate problems were economic development and consolidation of independence, and it required external assistance for fulfilling both these objectives. Nuclear possession would only exacerbate the new nation's basic economic, political, and social problems.[33] When making a case to the Rada (parliament) to ratify Ukraine's accession to START I, Foreign Minister Anatoly Zlenko argued that the economy could not sustain a nuclear program and that other countries would scale back relations with it and even impose sanctions.[34] Its strategic warheads were all targeted towards the United States, which clearly was not in the interests of Ukraine. Conversion of those missiles to tactical missiles would have been possible, but at a high cost.

Some nationalists in the Rada attempted to link nuclear possession with power, prestige, and international influence. In 1992, second thoughts began to develop among Ukrainian officials, as some believed that their country could follow the model of France as a nuclear state. In late 1992, opinions began to change as the president publicly demanded credible security guarantees as the major condition for nuclear disarmament. These Russian and u.s. guarantees were crucial for his gaining the Rada's support for disarmament. Officials valued these guarantees for their symbolism and their usefulness as recognition of Ukraine's independence and sovereignty.[35] Gaining maximum financial rewards for disarmament also became a motive of the leadership around this time. To beef up its non-nuclear credentials, Ukraine agreed to follow the guidelines of the Missile Technology Control Regime (MTCR).[36] American, British, and Russian willingness to concede to most of Ukraine's demands eventually enabled the government to follow through on its promise of nuclear disarmament.

Ukraine's decision to forgo nuclear weapons challenges some of the axioms of hard realism, especially vis-à-vis the security dilemma in an anarchic world. It suggests that Ukraine clearly adopted a policy to reshape its security environment and ameliorate the effects of anarchy by opting for a low-key security policy. The maintenance of an effective nuclear deterrent would have magnified the threats surrounding Ukraine. This also would have meant Ukraine's pursuing a high-profile security policy, thereby provoking adverse responses from Russia, the United States, and other Western countries with which it was attempting to build close economic and political relations. If Ukraine had had an enduring rivalry with nuclear-armed Russia, it probably would not have dismantled its nuclear weapons.

SOUTH KOREA

The decision by South Korea in the 1970s to give up its plans for nuclear weapons, and its reluctance in the 1990s to initiate a program in the face of North Korean nuclear threats, shows us how a dominant ally's security shield and close economic relationships discourage a state in a high-conflict region to acquire an independent nuclear capability. Ever since the Korean War of 1950–53, South Korea has been engaged in an intense protracted conflict/ enduring rivalry with North Korea, with troops of the two countries separated only by an eighteen-mile-wide demilitarized zone. The American conventional and nuclear military presence provided South Korea with security against a possible North Korean invasion.

However, two events aroused South Korean interest in nuclear weapons in the 1970s. The first was the Nixon Doctrine of July 1970, during the Vietnam War, under which the United States reduced its military presence in Asia. The plan was to reduce the 70,000-strong U.S. forces stationed in South Korea to 44,000, which gave incentives to South Korea to look for alternative security arrangements. President Chung Hee Park stated that if the United States were to withdraw its nuclear umbrella, South Korea would develop its own nuclear weapons.[37] In 1974, Seoul requested a bigger role in nuclear war planning, which the United States rejected. During 1974–75, the United States discovered the secret nuclear weapons project.[38] In response to Secretary of State Henry Kissinger's threat to cancel U.S. security commitments and withdraw all forces from Korea, Seoul decided to abandon the weapons project, and in April 1975 it ratified the NPT.[39] Despite the ratification, South Korea continued to seek a plutonium-reprocessing facility from France, showing its lingering interest in nuclear weapons. The Ford administration threatened to withhold U.S. Export–Import Bank credits worth $275 million in direct low-interest loans and another $227 million in loan guarantees for South Korea's nuclear energy program, and it warned that the proposed deal would jeopardize U.S.–South Korean security relations, and so Seoul cancelled the order in 1976.[40]

The second event that provoked South Korea to consider nuclear acquisition was the proposal by President Jimmy Carter in 1977 to withdraw American troops and about 1,000 tactical nuclear weapons from South Korea. South Korea greeted this announcement with considerable alarm and sent reports that it might develop its own nuclear weapons.[41] In 1993 Sunu Ryun, a legislator who had been an aide to President Park, revealed the existence of a report from the Defence Ministry that South Korea could develop a nuclear weapon by the first half of 1981 and reveal the weapon's existence during the Armed Forces Day ceremony in October 1981.[42] This report was prepared in response to Carter's plan. American diplomatic pressures, threats of economic sanctions, and willingness to cancel the withdrawal plans forced Seoul to back off from nuclear acquisition.[43] The assassination of Park in 1979 put an end to the program, as his successor, Chun Doohwan, is believed to have canceled it altogether. Some reports also indicated that South Korea responded to North Korea's nuclear development by reviving the weapons program under President Tae Woo Roh in 1991 but discontinued it following intense U.S. pressure.[44]

Debate among strategic analysts and officials continues on the need for South Korea to adopt a Japanese model of "asymptomatic nuclearization" – i.e., "climbing the nuclear ladder without emitting the 'symptoms' normally associated with the production of nuclear weapons and, until cooperation becomes necessary, stopping just below the last rung."[45] This would, however, entail South Korea's resuming uranium enrichment and plutonium reprocessing, which it had forgone under the 1992 agreement. The demand for such a move is likely to intensify, especially if there is proof that North Korea has developed a few crude bombs and a simultaneous weakening of the u.s. nuclear umbrella. Anticipated negative responses by the United States and other neighbouring countries, especially Japan, prevent South Korea from adopting a latent nuclear route.[46]

South Korea has been engaged in one of the most active and successful nuclear energy programs in the world. It runs fifteen power reactors, all safeguarded by the IAEA and bilateral agreements with supplier countries, producing over 34 per cent of its energy. In addition, it has plans for building three new reactors.[47] Seoul does not possess any reprocessing or enrichment facilities and acquires plutonium and enriched uranium from the United States for energy programs. Being a scientifically advanced and economically prosperous nation, it could have started a small nuclear weapons program without much difficulty, and such a force could have deterred a North Korean attack. Under certain strategic conditions, the threat of nuclear attack on amassed North Korean troops passing through concentrated areas of the mountainous terrain could have helped to deter such an offensive.[48] Moreover, since Seoul is only thirty miles from the demilitarized zone and is extremely vulnerable to surprise attack, a nuclear capability would have helped South Korea to deter such an attack, and if deterrence failed, to engage in crisis bargaining or compellence vis-à-vis North Korea.[49]

During the early 1990s South Korea was threatened by North Korea's nuclear weapons program. Despite signing the NPT in 1985, Pyongyang refused to conclude a full-scale agreement on safeguards with the IAEA. Although it made such an arrangement in January 1992, it rejected intrusive verification of suspect sites, raising fears that its beleaguered regime was engaging in an intense nuclear program. American and French reconnaissance satellite pictures showed that North Korea was developing nuclear weapons at its Yongbyun facilities. The collapse of the Soviet Union and the loss of alliance support from Russia and China increased North Korea's isolation and its temptation to acquire nuclear weapons as a security guarantee as well as a bargaining chip.[50] This, however, caused a flurry of diplomatic activity involving offers of "carrots and sticks" by the United States, South Korea, and Japan. The u.s. proposal to withdraw tactical nuclear weapons from South Korea also could have, as in the past, been a matter of serious concern to South Korea.[51] Despite its threat of reviving its nuclear weapons program, Seoul sought a diplomatic solution to the problem.[52]

On 8 November 1991 South Korea declared that it would not manufacture, possess, store, deploy, or use nuclear weapons and that it would not acquire enrichment or reprocessing facilities. The declaration on denuclearization of the Korean peninsula by President Tae-Woo Roh that contained this commitment thus reaffirmed the non-nuclear policy.[53] The pledge not to acquire enrichment or reprocessing facilities was a major step. Bilateral efforts with North Korea were also significant indicators of non-nuclear intent. In the adoption of the Joint Declaration on Denuclearization in 1991, both countries promised not to manufacture or produce, deploy, store, or use nuclear weapons or to possess reprocessing and enrichment facilities, and in March 1992 they set up a Joint Nuclear Control Commission (JNCC) to conduct reciprocal inspections of each other's nuclear facilities. Despite these bilateral efforts, North Korea continued its opposition to full inspection by the IAEA, and it took a considerable diplomatic campaign to conclude the tripartite "Agreed Framework" with the United States in October 1994. The North agreed to freeze its nuclear program and by 2003 to dismantle its nuclear reactors in return for receiving technology and energy supplies worth $4 billion over five years. The crucial element of the agreement has been construction of two light-water reactors in the North by the consortium Korean Peninsula Energy Development Organisation (KEDO), funded largely by South Korea and Japan.[54]

Why did South Korea give up its nuclear weapons option? A regime-based explanation would suggest that the NPT and the IAEA safeguards acted as major constraints on Seoul. However, this explanation has problems. Although South Korea signed the NPT in April 1975, it ratified the treaty seven years later, and only after intense American pressure. When in 1977 the South threatened to "go nuclear" it was indeed a party to the NPT and had an IAEA safeguards agreement in place. It was using the NPT as camouflage for its planned clandestine nuclear weapons program. The NPT regime put constraints on the South from openly pursuing a nuclear route but did not determine its nuclear forbearance.

A power-based explanation would contend that American hegemony was the main factor.[55] According to one South Korean analyst, "Seoul's lack of independent means to respond in kind to or even deter a possible North Korean nuclear threat results from American hegemonic interests outweighing South Korean security interests."[56] The most visible U.S. pressures were those exerted in 1975 by Henry Kissinger to cut off security ties and the Ford administration's threat to bring the South's civilian nuclear programs to a halt by blocking the sales of reactors from Westinghouse and Canada, as well as the reprocessing facilities from France.[57] In fact, the United States also offered positive reassurances of continued security guarantees. Since then, Washington has annually declared its strong commitment to

South Korea's security, implemented through joint military exercises and an active military presence in the country.[58] The cancellation of Carter's plans to pull out tactical weapons was another inducement. Thus the hegemony-based argument has more validity than a regime-based argument. However, even under hegemony, Seoul's repeated threats to build nuclear weapons had the desired effect on the United States, to the extent that Washington often conceded to South Korea's demands for continued military presence and closer economic ties.[59]

It is indeed the active U.S. military presence and security guarantees, rather than simple hegemonic control, that obviate the need for a nuclear capability by this enduring-rival state. However, the U.S. nuclear presence alone is not critical in this case. It is instead the American conventional military presence that guarantees South Korean nuclear abstinence, because it is politically and logistically difficult to use nuclear weapons against North Korea.[60] The closeness of the two Koreas makes a nuclear attack on invading forces illogical. A nuclear attack on Pyongyang may not be enough to compensate for the damage done to South Korea by a North Korean invasion.[61] Indeed, after President Bush's decision in 1991 to pull out tactical nuclear weapons worldwide, including from Korea, the United States apparently removed 600 or so such weapons from South Korea. Seoul is still arguably under the U.S. nuclear umbrella, as the United States can send in nuclear weapons at any time from its forces in the Pacific.

CONCLUSIONS

The three cases of nuclear forbearance in this chapter support the theoretical framework presented in this study. Two of these states, South Africa and Ukraine, gave up nuclear weapons even without having a great-power protector. Maintenance of the capabilities would have created powerful negative security externalities for their neighbours and other significant actors with which they want to maintain friendly relations. South Africa developed nuclear weapons during a period when Southern Africa was a theatre of high conflict and gave up that capability when events transformed it to a zone of moderate conflict. Ukraine inherited its weapons and gave them up to avoid generating hostile relations with Russia and the West. The absence of an intense, enduring rivalry characterized by militarized inter-state disputes allowed Ukraine to forgo its nuclear capability. South Korea would have been a powerful candidate for nuclear acquisition, because of its ongoing enduring rivalry/protracted conflict with the North, but for U.S. protection and hegemonic persuasion, as evident in its past unsuccessful efforts to acquire nuclear weapons.

CHAPTER EIGHT

New Nuclear States:
India, Pakistan, and Israel

Although the main focus of this study has been on national decisions to forgo nuclear weapons, we should look at new nuclear states in order to establish or refute the arguments presented in chapter 2. In this chapter, I analyse three cases of nuclear acquisition – India, Pakistan, and Israel – to see why these countries decided to obtain nuclear arms even when most technologically capable states have forgone nuclear weapons. India and Pakistan openly declared their capabilities in May 1998 by conducting several nuclear tests, even though they had been known to possess nuclear weapons for over a decade. Although Israel has not conducted any open tests, observers commonly agree that it has a medium-sized nuclear arsenal. These three countries see major strategic utility in nuclear possession – mostly prevention of large-scale war involving their adversaries. While the main concerns of Pakistan and Israel have been regional security threats, India's nuclear policies are determined by both regional and global considerations, as it hopes to become a major power in the twenty-first century. This chapter focuses first on the two South Asian states before looking at Israeli nuclear policy.

INDIA

India became the sixth declared nuclear state in May 1998 when it conducted five nuclear tests, which included a hydrogen bomb.[1] India has consistently maintained its opposition to the nuclear non-proliferation regime from its very inception. The 1998 tests were its most direct challenge to that regime, which it views as "discriminatory." An original supporter of the Nuclear Non-proliferation Treaty (NPT), India changed its position when it concluded that the nuclear states wished to maintain their monopoly. India refused to sign the treaty and initiated a strong campaign against it. A strident manifestation of its opposition occurred in 1974 when it exploded a nuclear device in the Rajasthan desert. Afterwards, for twenty-four years, India maintained a policy of deliberate ambiguity – i.e., no further tests and no open acquisition of nuclear arms. This posture changed dramatically with the nuclear tests in May 1998. Despite their success, the precise number of weapons that India holds is still not known. According to one study, at the end of 1997, India should have in its inventory sufficient weapons-grade plutonium to make seventy-four nuclear devices.[2]

India is a state with a high level of insecurity that also wishes to pursue an autonomous foreign policy. The latter goal springs from India's historical experience of domination by foreign countries, especially by Muslim invaders and the British in the modern era. However, a major source of India's autonomous defence and foreign polices is its perception of itself as a rising major power.[3] Though not stated by the Indian elite in clear-cut terms, this aspiration is the reason why India remains the most consistent opponent of the non-proliferation regime, even when the restrictive regime has become acceptable to a number of erstwhile opponents. In this respect, the non-proliferation policies and military/security interactions of the five declared nuclear states, especially the United States and China, heavily influence India's nuclear policy.[4]

Thus, unlike strictly regional states, including Pakistan and Israel, India's nuclear policies have their roots in global and regional processes simultaneously. India is situated in a high-conflict zone, South Asia, and has a history of fighting four major wars since 1947, one of them in 1962 with China, which acquired nuclear weapons two years later. The nuclear choices of India evolved in response to largely external security challenges. From 1947 to 1964, it maintained a lofty position of demanding universal nuclear disarmament. It was an active member of the United Nations Eighteen-Nation Disarmament Committee and other forums dealing with disarmament. India's first prime minister, Jawaharlal Nehru, presented many proposals on disarmament, including a nuclear test ban in the form of a "standstill" arrangement and an early version of the nuclear non-proliferation treaty.[5] Nehru believed that nuclear possession was immoral and that the superpower conflict was driving the world towards total annihilation. This outlook was markedly present in his campaign for nuclear disarmament and the launching of the non-aligned movement.[6] However, Nehru unwittingly laid the groundwork for future nuclear weapons in India when he initiated a peaceful nuclear energy program to harness the atom for the country's development. Homi Bhabha, who as chairman of the Atomic Energy Commission helped to set up several nuclear research centres, headed the program.[7] The key development was construction in 1955 of the Canadian-supplied 40-mW Cirus research reactor in Trombay, near Bombay. This reactor "went critical" in 1960, and the plutonium produced from it went into the first nuclear device, tested in 1974. Although India lost the war with China in 1962, nuclear acquisition was not yet in the cards, as Nehru resisted demands for changing his peaceful course. The precipitating event occurred after Nehru's death in May 1964 – the first test explosion of a nuclear weapon by China, in October 1964.

Nehru's successor, Lal Bahdur Shastri, was confronted with the implications of the Chinese test for India's security. Shastri, a follower of Nehru's foreign policy guidelines, had great difficulty agreeing to demands from within the political and scientific elite for India to acquire a nuclear capability. China's continued testing of weapons and its support for Pakistan, however, somewhat changed Shastri's policy. In order to avoid a national nuclear weapons program, Shastri sought nuclear protection from the United Kingdom and other great powers in the event of a Chinese nuclear attack, but he was rebuffed.[8] Shastri approved plans for a subterranean nuclear explosion project (SNEP), apparently for industrial purposes, with the condition that the policy would be changed so as to include a military option if the situation warranted. According to this plan, India would exercise its nuclear option and conduct a test if and when it deemed it to be necessary. This was the minimum response devised to respond to China's nuclear test.[9] The deaths of Shastri and Bhabha in 1966 temporarily delayed the nuclear weapons program.

The first four years of Shastri's successor, Indira Gandhi, saw very limited nuclear activism, although Gandhi did not oppose the PNE option. In 1970, the head of the Atomic Energy Commission, Vikram Sarabhai, made a ten-point proposal for developing nuclear and space capabilities.[10] The war with Pakistan in 1971 was a turning point in India's nuclear policy. The entry of the u.s. 7th Fleet into the Bay of Bengal with a veiled threat from President Nixon of intervention in the conflict seemed an extreme provocation to the Indian leadership. The larger systemic context, especially the u.s. tilt in the war in favour of Pakistan, influenced India's nuclear policy, as did the regional processes resulting from India's enduring conflicts with China and Pakistan. In October 1972 Gandhi authorized scientists to prepare for a nuclear test.[11] The preparations took place under the supervision of Raja Ramanna, director of the Bhabha Atomic Research Centre (BARC), and it was kept as a tightly held secret among the core scientists and the prime minister. In 1974, India conducted an underground nuclear test of a 15-kilotonne device at Pokhran in Rajasthan, and its leadership called the implosive test a peaceful nuclear explosion and refused to conduct further tests or openly develop an atomic arsenal until 1998.[12]

The Indian test galvanized international efforts at non-proliferation and the imposition of stringent restrictions by supplier countries on the transfer of nuclear materials to developing states. From 1974 till 1998, India followed an ambiguous nuclear posture and for a period did not keep any assembled weapons, but it had the capacity to fabricate a weapon rapidly in a crisis, calling it a "recessed deterrent capability."[13] In the 1990s, India also acquired a missile capability with the launching of the short-range Prithvi and the intermediate-range Agni. Prithvi, with a range of 150–250 kilometres and a payload of 500–1,000 kilograms, could reach most Pakistani cities, while Agni, with a range between 1,000 and 2,500 kilometres and with a payload of 1,000 kilograms, could reach key centres of southern China and the Persian Gulf. The Agni II, which India test fired in April 1999, is expected to have a range of 2,500 kilometres. In 1999 India was also developing the Agni III missile, with a range of 3,500 kilometres, bringing several population centres of the Middle East and China within its reach.[14] India's missile program paralleled its space program and has increasingly come under sanctions by the United States and its allies.

The Indian nuclear test and proven weapons capability accelerated a response from Pakistan, which, under Prime Minister Zulfikar Ali Bhutto, had already begun a nuclear program in 1972, following its defeat in the Bangladesh War of 1971. Once Pakistan launched its quest for nuclear weapons, the Indian nuclear dilemma became more vivid. With the Soviet intervention in Afghanistan in 1979, the United States adopted Pakistan as a "frontline" state and supplied it with sophisti- cated arms, including nuclear-capable delivery systems such as the F-16 deep-penetration aircraft.[15] During the 1980s, Pakistan stepped up its nuclear quest, leading to growing Indian fears of a reduction in its military and strategic superiority and that Pakistan was catching up with it.[16] The rivalry increased in the 1990s, with India successfully test-firing its medium- and short-range missiles and Pakistan acquiring missiles from China and through indigenous efforts. On 6 April 1998, Pakistan test-fired an IRBM, called Ghauri, which, with a range of 1,500 kilometres, could reach many Indian cities.

Chinese nuclear activities and support for Pakistan have further increased the Indian perceptions of threat, despite the warming of relations between India and China since 1988. New Delhi has viewed China's deployment in the 1980s of nuclear missiles in Tibet, capable of hitting targets in India, as a direct security threat. Moreover, China has reportedly supplied Pakistan with weapons-grade uranium, designs of a weapon system, and M-11 mobile missiles suitable for nuclear delivery.[17] China's effort has been to contain India and keep its power aspirations confined to South Asia by continuing to help Pakistan in its conflict with India. In the early 1990s, China began to support the NPT and the non-proliferation regime, after being a strong opponent for over three decades, with the hope of remaining the only nuclear power of Asia.[18] Thus the arms race in the sub-continent follows a familiar pattern, with India obtaining capabilities largely to catch up with China, while Pakistan attempts to balance India's nuclear and space capabilities. The triangular nature of proliferation corresponds to the triangular nature of enduring rivalries and balance-of-power activities of the major states in the region.

The nuclear policy of India came into sharper international focus in May 1998 when the newly elected coalition government led by the Bharatiya Janata Party (BJP) conducted five nuclear tests in Pokhran, Rajasthan. With this act, India declared itself a nuclear state, although the established nuclear states have declined to confer such recognition on it. Instead, they imposed a series of sanctions.[19] The tests also made a qualitative difference in India's security relationship with China and Pakistan, as deterrence is no longer implied but explicit. The government of Atal Behari Vajpayee was able to implement its party's long-held policy within one month of assuming power, because five previous governments since 1988, led by different political parties, had maintained nuclear devices and the Pokharan range ready for a test explosion on short notice. It was Prime Minister Rajiv Gandhi who began the program to build a nuclear arsenal after Pakistan gained nuclear enrichment and the failure of his 1988 Action Plan for achieving global nuclear disarmament in a time-bound fashion.[20]

The BJP has been determined to make India nuclear from its period as the Jan Sangh Party from 1964 onwards. Although all major parties would like to see India become a great power, the BJP covets this status most ardently. First, the nuclear states' determination to maintain their monopoly and the pressures that they and their allies exerted on India to sign the non-proliferation instruments during the 1990s played well into the BJP's pro-nuclear posture. The extension of the NPT in perpetuity in 1995 without any concrete commitment by the nuclear weapon states (NWSs) to disarm strengthened opposition to the treaty in India, which came to the conclusion that the NWSs wanted to preserve their nuclear monopoly for all times. Second, the negotiations that led to the Comprehensive Test Ban Treaty (CTBT) in 1996 increased Indian concerns about the unequal nature of the non-proliferation regime: the treaty neither envisioned time bound global disarmament nor prohibited laboratory-level, sub-critical tests and thereby allowed the nuclear powers to perfect weapons. Furthermore, the provision that the treaty would come into force only when all forty-four states with at least one reactor signed and ratified it indicated that the NWSS and their allies wanted to force disarmament on India.[21] The 1999 review conference of the CTBT would have resulted in economic sanctions on non-signatory states. Indian defence scientists feared that once India signed the treaty they would not be able to conduct a test to verify their nuclear capability, especially the hydrogen bomb. They saw "hot tests" as necessary to derive data for a credible deterrent as well as for conducting future "cold tests," not prohibited by the CTBT.[22]

Some scholars argue that Indian leaders, especially Indira Gandhi, may have maintained a nuclear option and tested weapons for domestic political power and prestige.[23] The 1998 tests were perhaps conducted to increase support for the BJP. Although both suggestions are credible, I argue that they may help explain the timing of the tests, but not the underlying causes of India's nuclear policy. During the last three decades, governments of different ideological leanings have supported nuclear capability. National security reasons arising from systemic and sub-systemic processes are the primary source of such behaviour. Moreover, the electorate's support for a party or government rarely changed because of its position on nuclear weapons. Soon after the 1974 test massive protests led by opposition parties forced Indira Gandhi to impose unpopular emergency measures in 1975. In 1977, she lost power in a national election. Later governments maintained the nuclear option, but hardly because of electoral considerations. In a survey of elites in 1994, 57 per cent of those polled supported continuation of strategic ambiguity, and 33 per cent, open weaponization.[24] An opinion poll conducted after the first round of tests on 11 May 1998 found that 91 per cent of those polled supported the tests, while 82 per cent wanted India to build a nuclear arsenal.[25] But support for the test did not translate into electoral support for the BJP. In state assembly by-elections, it did not make much headway.[26]

Governments since 1988 have kept a nuclear bomb and a testing range ready for a test on short notice. None of the six governments, headed by V.P. Singh, Chandra Shekhar, P.V. Narasimha Rao, H.D. Deve Gowda, I.K. Gujral, and A.B. Vajpayee, rejected the nuclear option. India was on the verge of testing a device in December 1995 under Rao's Congress government,[27] but the test was called off after U.S. pressures. Rao, however, left instructions with his defence scientists to be prepared for a test within one month of receiving the order,[28] and none of his successors abandoned the testing preparations. Non-Congress coalition governments under Gowda and Gujral had continued the plans for testing and were waiting for the opportune moment. Gujral, in interviews after the 1998 tests, said that, since Rao's time, the nuclear file has been on the prime minister's table all the time.[29] Without powerful compulsions from outside, Gandhi and her successors could not have accelerated a costly program opposed by the major powers. The Indian civilian nuclear and space programs have suffered heavily as a result of restrictions by supplier countries. Conflict with nuclear neighbours and restrictive non-proliferation policies transformed an idealistic anti-nuclear state into a *realpolitik*-oriented nuclear state.

In the aftermath of the May 1998 tests, Indian leaders have begun to articulate the country's nuclear strategy and doctrine. They base it on a no-first-use, defensive-deterrent logic – i.e., India will not initiate a nuclear attack, but will retaliate if an adversary uses its nuclear weapons. Before the tests, a former chief of the Indian army, General K. Sundarji, had argued that, given the deep-rooted distrust between India and Pakistan, a minimum mutual-deterrent strategy by the two countries would ensure stability in the sub-continent. Such a strategy would include declaring no first use, avoiding an arms race, targeting a small number of cities, avoiding a hair-trigger response, and eschewing a high state of weapons reliability.[30] The leading Indian strategic analyst, K. Subhramanyam, had proposed creation of a minimum deterrent force comprising sixty warheads, mounted on aircraft, and missiles such as Prithvi and Agni, as a mobile strike force. In his assessment, India does not need a larger force if it declares a no-first-use policy, thereby rejecting a war-fighting strategy but maintaining a retaliatory strike policy. Such a strategy would convince even a superior nuclear power such as China of the futility of starting a war with India.[31] The BJP government's declarations since the May tests reveal that it was following most of these proposals. Although initially it proposed a bilateral no-first-use agreement with Pakistan, in August 1998 it offered a unilateral no-first-use pledge and no use against non-nuclear states and expressed the determination to maintain a "minimum but credible nuclear deterrent" and to sign disarmament treaties that are non-discriminatory.[32] In August 1999 a government-appointed twenty-seven-member National Security Advisory Board released a draft nuclear doctrine for public debate; it proposed a minimum nuclear deterrent based on a "survivable triad of land, air and sea-based systems" meant to deter nuclear attacks by inflicting unacceptable damage on the aggressor. The draft reiterated India's no-first-use policy and no use or threat of use against non-nuclear states.[33]

The nuclear non-proliferation regime – especially the NPT – has accentuated India's determination to develop nuclear capabilities. The supplier restrictions have slowed down its nuclear and space programs, but the regime restrictions have galvanized elite and public opinion in favour of nuclear arms. Ironically, "in periods when the regime has been undergoing strong development, India's attachment to nuclear weapons has tended to increase rather than decrease ... Especially in the 1990s, the intensification of international pressures against nuclear weapons has paradoxically led to the intensification for political support for nuclear weapons within India."[34] The extension of the NPT in perpetuity and the conclusion of the CTBT contributed to the timing of India's 1998 tests and strengthened public opinion in favour of openly displaying nuclear capability.

Most factors identified in this study for nuclear forbearance are absent in the Indian case. India is situated in a zone of high conflict, with two ongoing enduring rivalries, one with a declared and the other with a newly declared nuclear state. By the model presented in chapter 2, India is indeed a powerful candidate for nuclear acquisition. Moreover, it aspires to becoming a major power and challenges the non-proliferation regime because it privileges the five declared states while arresting India's "progress." Indian leaders have perceived that their country is the leading candidate for major power status in the twenty-first century, despite all the current economic and political constraints.[35] The hard-realist considerations of security dilemma, anarchy, lack of alliance support, and concerns about relative gains are all powerfully present in India's security environment. A security-first approach arises from the territorial nature of its conflicts; the lack of economic co-operation with its regional rivals, Pakistan and China; the limited economic integration of South Asia; and the absence of a credible nuclear ally. These factors are likely to persist, forcing India to continue its nuclear program for the foreseeable future.[36] Earlier concerns over adverse regional and international reactions if India went nuclear declined as China's tests and subsequent nuclear build-up augmented India's desire for a minimum deterrent capability. Pakistan's acquisition of nuclear capability during the 1980s increased the immediate perceived need for India to build a nuclear deterrent. Finally, the entrenchment of a restrictive non-proliferation regime and the continued possession of weapons by NWSs increased Indian determination to build an arsenal. Thus the worry about generating negative security externalities declined as rivalries became chronic and a principal adversary acquired a nuclear capability, and the ambition for power and influence increased concomitantly.

PAKISTAN

Pakistan is another state that has acquired an independent nuclear capability. Although it was reported to have developed nuclear weapons as early as 1987, on 28 and 30 May 1998 it conducted six nuclear tests in the Chagai Hills of Baluchisthan, following India's five tests two weeks earlier. In a television address, Prime Minister Nawaz Sharif declared: "today, we have evened the score with India."[37] Pakistan's tests clearly suggest that its main security concern is regional and that achieving nuclear parity with India is a paramount goal.

Pakistan began nuclear energy research in 1955 with the establishment of the Pakistan Atomic Energy Commission. It purchased a U.S. research reactor and a small power reactor from Canada, which were set up in Karachi, both under IAEA safeguards. Up to the early 1970s, the United States also provided training to Pakistani scientists. Until 1971, the nuclear program was largely for peaceful purposes, although Zulfikar Ali Bhutto, foreign minister under the military regime of Ayub Khan, had advocated a weapons program during the 1960s. Bhutto had warned in 1960 that if Pakistan suspended its nuclear program it would allow India to blackmail his country. He believed that since all wars were now total wars, any waged against Pakistan could also become total and that therefore Pakistani military capability and planning should include a nuclear deterrent.[38] However, Ayub was more interested in acquiring conventional weapons from the United States and China. The absence of an imminent nuclear threat from India; Pakistan's alliance with the United States, especially through CENTO and SEATO; the dearth of strong scientific leadership; and financial and technological constraints discouraged Ayub Khan's interest in nuclear weapons.[39]

The defeat in the 1971 war with India and Bhutto's rise to prime minister in December 1971 set in motion weaponization of Pakistan's nuclear program. In the 1971 war, none of Pakistan's great-power allies, especially the United States and China, provided timely support to avert a military defeat. Bhutto apparently held a meeting of top officials and scientists in January 1972 in Multan, where they decided on a crash program, through reprocessing of plutonium.[40]

The Indian nuclear test in 1974 increased pressure on Bhutto, who did not accept India's contentions that the test was peaceful and that India did not plan a nuclear arsenal. Pakistan's nuclear plans became more intense when it failed to obtain security guarantees from major powers.[41] It viewed India's nuclear capability as augmenting New Delhi's already considerable lead in conventional capability and economic and industrial assets. Moreover, the Indian explosion came only three years after India dismembered Pakistan by its military intervention in East Pakistan, now Bangladesh. Acquiring an independent nuclear capability also seemed essential for dealing with India as an equal on Kashmir.[42] Bhutto received assistance in his nuclear plans from Munir Ahmed Khan, chairman of the Pakistan Atomic Energy Commission, a staunch proponent of acquisition, and S.A. Butt, who ran an office in Paris to purchase components for making nuclear weapons clandestinely.[43]

When General Zia Ul Haq overthrew Bhutto in 1977, he focused the nuclear program more on uranium enrichment, although plutonium-reprocessing also continued.[44] Plutonium had been reprocessed at the Karachi Nuclear Power Plant (KANUPP) since the 1980s. In addition, Pakistan also attempted to smuggle plutonium from foreign countries. In uranium enrichment, by the mid-1980s Pakistan reportedly had some successes. In February 1984, Abdul Qadeer Khan, head of the Kahuta centrifuge facility and "father" of the Pakistani bomb, announced commendable progress in enriching weapons-grade uranium and that making a nuclear bomb required only a political decision.[45] In 1987, the army chief, General Mirza Aslam Beg, declared that Pakistan possessed nuclear capability. Beg later revealed that Pakistan had acquired such capability in 1987 by enriching uranium up to 95 per cent and had integrated elements of a nuclear device and conducted laboratory tests as well as developing delivery systems.[46]

The Soviet invasion of Afghanistan in 1979 strengthened Pakistan's alliance with the United States, which substantially helped its nuclear weapons program. Pakistan became a "frontline" state and a conduit for American supplies to the Afghan resistance. Ronald Reagan subordinated the U.S. non-proliferation policy to its anti-Soviet crusade and left Pakistan's nuclear efforts unchecked. Washington attempted to make economic and military aid conditional on Pakistan's forgoing nuclear weapons, but those efforts failed.[47] Secret U.S. State Department documents showed in 1983 that the United States had "unambiguous evidence that Pakistan was actively pursuing a nuclear weapons program," and the evidence revealed a secret nuclear bomb obtained from China. When U.S. officials confronted Zia Ul Haq, he reportedly stated that Reagan and CIA Director William Casey had given the go-ahead for Pakistan to build the bomb. From 1985 to 1990, both Reagan and George Bush certified, as required by law, that Pakistan did not possess nuclear weapons in order to qualify it for continued military and economic aid.[48]

With the Soviet withdrawal from Afghanistan in 1989, the United States curtailed its ties with Pakistan and increased pressure on it to stop its nuclear program. The loss of U.S. support has increased Pakistan's desire for nuclear weapons, helped considerably by China, which is believed to have transferred blueprints, enriched uranium, and ring magnets for uranium processing and trained Pakistani nuclear engineers. In addition, China has also delivered nuclear-capable M-11 missiles and technology and materials for other missiles, including IRBMS.[49]

Some in the Pakistani elite believe that nuclear possession averted wars in the 1987 and 1990 crises involving India.[50] The crisis of January 1987 arose as a result of India's "Operation Brasstacks" military exercise, and the one in 1990 from the intensification of operations by Pakistani-supported guerrillas within Indian Kashmir. "Operation Brasstacks" took place near Pakistan's southeastern boarder, provoking a Pakistani military alert and counter-deployment. Although there is no strong evidence that the Indian military was planning to launch an attack, Pakistani leaders took the exercise as a provocative step. A.Q. Khan warned that Pakistan was capable of producing nuclear weapons and would use the bomb if its existence were threatened.[51] During the 1990 crisis, Pakistan, according to an account by American journalist Semour Hersh, deployed its main armoured tank units on the border and secretly placed nuclear weapons on alert. This prompted India to deploy its nuclear forces. Realizing the possibility of a nuclear war, the u.s. administration dispatched Deputy National Security Advisor Robert Gates to mediate, although there has been little evidence to prove that either side was about to launch a nuclear attack.[52] By 1996, Pakistan had completed preparations for a nuclear test in the Chagai hills of southwest Baluchistan in response to reports that India was preparing for tests.[53]

The Pakistani nuclear tests on 28 May 1998 followed India's tests seventeen days earlier. Pakistan, like India, had been maintaining a test site and weapons ready to conduct the tests on short notice; otherwise it would not have been able to achieve such a feat in less than three weeks. Prime Minister Nawaz Sharif initially gave the impression that he was willing to forgo testing in return for substantial economic and military aid and security guarantees from the West. When those failed to materialize, Sharif, under pressure from his army and his own and opposition parties, ordered the tests. In subsequent diplomatic efforts, Pakistan attempted to bring the Kashmir issue to international attention, but despite increased media attention, no active intervention has taken place.[54] Continued cross-border shelling in the 550-mile-long border in Kashmir has increased tensions. In May 1999, Pakistan fomented a serious crisis with India by sending Islamic guerrillas to the Kargil sector of India's Kashmir. Although Western intelligence confirmed the Indian contention that the guerrillas included Pakistani regular soldiers, Pakistan kept denying it. The crisis ended in July when Sharif visited Washington and agreed to a pullout. During the crisis, several members of the Pakistani elite raised the nuclear threat in order to prevent India from escalating the conflict beyond Kashmir. India's decision not to widen the war or cross the line of control contained the crisis, but relations between the nuclear rivals deteriorated further when the composite negotiations begun in Lahore in February 1999 suffered a severe setback.[55]

In terms of delivery systems, Pakistan possesses several U.S.-supplied F-16 fighter aircraft, which could be configured for nuclear strikes. It also has made strides in missile development, largely with China's assistance. It has acquired 300-kilometre-range M-11 missiles from China and has developed short-range missiles, the Hatf-I and the Hatf-II. The Hatf-I, with a range of 80 kilometres and a 500-kilogram payload, and the Hatf-II, with a 300-kilometre range and a payload of 500 kilograms, can reach many Indian cities near the border. In July 1997, Pakistan was believed to have tested a Hatf-III missile, which, with an estimated range of 600 to 800 kilometres and a payload of 250 to 900 kilograms, can reach targets in most of northern India, including New Delhi.[56] Pakistan's most significant delivery system is the Hatf-V, or the Ghauri missile, which can reach all major urban centres in India. It successfully test-fired the missile, with a range of 1,500 kilometres and a payload of 700 kilograms, on 6 April 1998.[57]

Nuclear weapons have been believed to be part of the Pakistani military strategy and doctrine since the late 1980s. They are perceived as weapons capable of "striking terror into the hearts of the enemy" and would act as a deterrent against an attack by the opponent – i.e., India.[58] Pakistani military doctrine, according to General Beg, has been based on offensive defence, which calls for the army taking "war into India" by "launching a sizable offensive on Indian territory," in the opening rounds of a war. Pakistan's retaliatory nuclear capability would deter India from launching a conventional or nuclear strike and would thereby contribute to the total fighting ability of the Pakistani army.[59] However, after the 1998 tests, Pakistan rejected India's offer of a no-first-use agreement, contending that it needed the first-use threat to prevent a conventional war initiated by India and to avoid defeat in case war broke out, given India's lead in conventional and nuclear capability.[60] Pakistan attempted to practise a high-risk strategy of mixing nuclear deterrence, compellence, and conventional conflict in Kashmir during the Kargil crisis in 1999.

Pakistan's nuclear choices have been heavily determined by its enduring rivalry/protracted conflict with India. In this sense, Pakistan's concerns are largely regional, as it is not worried about the nuclear weapons of either China or other declared weapon states as India is. Pakistan's nuclear and arms-control policies attest to this argument. Pakistan tested the devices to match India's, and it will not sign any treaties that India has not. The nuclear behaviour of other states, especially the five declared powers, has little relevance to Pakistan. This sub-systemic focus is a function of Pakistan's historical rivalry with India, largely over Kashmir, and the fact that it is a regional power, unlikely to achieve major-power status.

Pakistani military thinkers see nuclear capability as a powerful deterrent against India's nuclear and conventional superiority. They view it as a great equalizer in this otherwise-asymmetrical power relationship.[61] It may help prevent a large-scale war while Pakistan continues low-level military support to the insurgents in Kashmir. Pakistan's nuclear choices corroborate the expectations of the model presented in chapter 2. The country is situated in a high-conflict zone, has an active, protracted conflict with a more powerful neighbour, has weak or unreliable alliance support, and has a security-first approach in its national strategy. Pakistan, like India, is a powerful candidate for nuclear acquisition. The transformation of the India–Pakistani enduring rivalry into peaceful relations is the most likely precursor to a non-nuclear Pakistan.

ISRAEL

From its inception in 1948, Israel has been in a constant conflict with its Arab neighbours, and its leaders have viewed nuclear acquisition as a way to deter a large-scale invasion.[62] The first prime minister, David Ben-Gurion, laid the foundations of the nuclear program, which began with establishment of the Israel Atomic Energy Commission (IAEC) in June 1952. In 1955, the United States signed a contract to supply Israel with a 5-mW reactor, which began operating in 1960 at Nahal Soreq, fuelled by 90 per cent highly enriched uranium.[63] The main source of support for the Israeli nuclear program was France, which supplied the first major power reactor in 1957. Construction of the 24-mW Dimona reactor in the Negev desert began in 1958, and it was commissioned in 1963.

Collaboration with France allowed Israel to obtain technical data, train scientists in French facilities, and work swiftly on the reactor program, drawing on French experience. Israeli–French co-operation began with the 1956 Suez crisis, in which both countries, along with Britain, attempted to force Egypt to abandon its nationalization of the Suez Canal. The failure of this military operation, and the U.S. opposition to it, convinced France to accelerate its own nuclearization and help its ally Israel to build an independent capability. Despite claims to the contrary, the Dimona reactor was from the start meant to develop nuclear weapons – when the reactor was placed under the control of the Ministry of Defence, all members of the IAEC except its chairman, Ernst Bergmann, resigned in apparent protest against military uses of nuclear technology.[64]

In 1986, Mordechai Vanunu, a former technician working at Dimona, revealed that the reactor's power-generating capability had expanded to 150 mW, enabling it to produce sufficient plutonium for nuclear weapons. The Dimona complex contains six stories of building, and the u.s. inspectors were allowed only on the first. The other floors were used to develop materials for nuclear weapons.[65] According to Vanunu, up to 1985 Israel had produced about 600 kilograms of plutonium; at this rate of production, by 1994 Israel may have acquired about 900 kilograms of plutonium, enough to make 200 nuclear weapons. The photographs taken by Vanunu also showed that Israel was able to make thermonuclear devices, including hydrogen bombs.[66] Israel has limited uranium reserves and has been able to extract 100 tonnes of uranium annually. In 1968, Israel was reported to have obtained 200 tonnes of yellowcake by diverting a cargo ship chartered by a West German chemical company and another 100 kilograms covertly from the United States.[67]

Israel is believed to have accelerated its nuclear weapons program after the 1973 Middle East War. The near-breakthrough by the Syrian forces in the Golan Heights and the Soviet nuclear alert gave incentives to Israeli leaders to speed up development of nuclear weapons, including hydrogen bombs.[68] In delivery systems, Israel possesses advanced aircraft and Jericho I and II surface-to-surface intermediate-range missiles. Its 650-odd combat aircraft include u.s.-supplied F-4Es, A-4s, F-15s, and F-16s. It has deployed the Jericho missiles, with a maximum range of 1,500 kilometres, in the Negev desert since 1981.[69] It could equip these missiles with nuclear warheads during a crisis.

The stated rationale for the Israeli nuclear program is to prevent an all-out Arab assault that would destroy the Jewish state. Since Israel has limited strategic depth to absorb a combined armoured and air attack, it has seen nuclear capability as providing the ultimate guarantee for the state's survival. Ben Gurion and his successors feared that Israel could mitigate the structural asymmetry caused by "the preponderance of men and equipment" held by Arab states only through nuclear capability.[70]

Israel shrouds its nuclear strategy in what is known as "deliberate ambiguity." However, Israel is willing to use these weapons as a last resort against several Arab capitals and cities in the hope that the potential for such an assault will deter an Arab onslaught. The undeclared nature of its weapons is also meant to create ambiguity about its capability and intentions among potential adversaries.[71] Israeli policy on arms control reflects this ambiguity; while Israel has signed the Partial Test Ban Treaty (PTBT) and plans to accede to the CTBT, it has not agreed to sign the NPT or accept full-scope IAEA safeguards on its nuclear facilities. Moreover, it has consistently opposed Arab proposals for a nuclear weapon–free zone in the Middle East, except for making a declaratory position that Israel will not be the first to introduce nuclear weapons in the region, implying that it will not openly test or deploy nuclear arms unless some other country does so. Israel retains a virtual monopoly in nuclear capability in the region, and this asymmetry vis-à-vis its Arab neighbours means that Israel has very little incentive to reach a meaningful agreement on controlling nuclear arms with other states with which it has enduring rivalries.

A prominent aim of Israeli security policy has been to prevent Arab states from acquiring nuclear weapons. Several actions – Israeli complicity in the destruction in Paris in April 1979 of the core of a nuclear reactor meant for export to Iraq, the killing of the chief of the Iraqi atomic energy authority in Paris in 1980, and, most prominently, the attack on Iraq's Osiraq nuclear facility in June 1981 – demonstrated Israeli determination to prevent the rise of a nuclear challenger in the Middle East.[72] Israel does not subscribe to theories of mutually assured destruction, or "balance of terror," with Arab states as a condition for regional stability and security.[73] However, the Gulf War and Iraqi progress in nuclear acquisition raise considerable doubts about the efficacy of Israel's nuclear strategy. The Israeli attack in 1981 temporarily slowed Iraqi nuclearization but probably increased Iraqi leader Saddam Hussein's determination to acquire nuclear weapons. Israeli diplomatic initiatives since 1991 by Prime Minister Yitzhak Rabin and Foreign Minister Shimon Peres were part of a new strategy to make use of the short-term window of opportunity to achieve peace with the Arab states while they were not in possession of nuclear weapons.[74]

The Arab countries have not made serious efforts to counter the Israeli capability and have designed their military strategies to circumvent it. The number of wars and crises with Israel since 1970 attest to this contention.[75] In any event, their efforts to acquire nuclear weapons have not succeeded so far. Egypt was the most likely candidate, but its technological capacity remained very weak. Despite threats by Presidents Abdel Gamal Nasser and Anwar Sadat and efforts to acquire reactors and bombs from the Soviet Union and China, Egypt did not develop even a civilian nuclear energy program, let alone a rudimentary nuclear weapons capability.[76] The Camp David Accords of 1978 decreased considerably Egypt's need for a nuclear deterrent, returning to it the lost Sinai territory and thereby ending its long-lasting conflict with Israel. Still, the Egyptian inability to acquire a rudimentary nuclear capability in the face of active Israeli nuclear pursuits remains a puzzle for proliferation analysis.

The Egyptian–Syrian offensive of 1973 and the Iraqi attack on Israel in 1991 suggest that Israel's nuclear capability did not have much effect on the calculations of its adversaries. The Egyptians were aware of the

Israeli capability in the War of Attrition (1969–70) and the Sinai operations of 1973. The nuclear capability, however, probably was one reason why Egypt devised a limited-aims strategy for regaining the territory.[77] Some Israeli analysts also claim that Egypt decided to conclude peace because of Israeli nuclear capability.[78] If this is the case, one wonders why Syria, Iraq, Iran, and the Palestinians have not come to the same conclusions. The Arabs have relied mostly on conventional, chemical, and biological weapons and guerrilla strategy to counter Israeli nuclear dominance. In recent years, however, Iraq and Iran have engaged in efforts at nuclear acquisition partially in response to the Israeli nuclear build-up.

Israel is in a high-conflict zone and has several enduring rivalries and protracted conflicts with its Arab neighbours. Since its foundation in 1948, it has engaged in six wars and had several military crises with its neighbours.[79] The high frequency of crises and wars makes the Middle East a zone of extraordinarily high conflict. Worst-case assumptions dominate Israeli strategic thinking, and its search for security has led to the acquisition of high-tech weaponry and the creation of a powerful domestic defence infrastructure. Successive governments have viewed nuclear capability as a way to offset the numerical superiority of the Arab states. In many respects, the Israelis perceive their nuclear capability as a "great equalizer" vis-à-vis their neighbours. Israel's technological superiority in terms of conventional capability may deter any offensive by one or two Arab states, but only nuclear arms could prevent an offensive by a grand coalition or an attack with weapons of mass destruction by Iraq.

The forbearance of nuclear weapons by Israel is an unlikely, but not impossible prospect. The major precursor could be an effective and comprehensive peace agreement between Israel, the Palestinians, and all Arab states, including Iran and Iraq. The latter two have their own enduring rivalry that could still motivate them to acquire nuclear capabilities. Their nuclear programs further complicate Israeli nuclear policy. Even under these circumstances, Israel may still maintain virtual nuclear capability with the aim of reactivating it should the security threat resurface. Confidence-building measures to prevent surprise attacks could reduce Israeli perceptions of threat.

CONCLUSIONS

As presented in the model, the key explanation for nuclear acquisition by India, Pakistan, and Israel lies in their strategic situations – i.e., high-conflict regions, protracted conflicts, and lack of credible alliance support.[80] Bureaucratic politics, domestic politics, and dispositions of individual decision-makers explain little, as these countries followed more or less the same kind of policies under different governments, right wing or left wing. The high level of consensus on nuclear weapons among the elite and the public points to the fact that security choices involving nuclear weapons often derive from circumstances rather than from internal political dynamics. These three cases provide compelling support for the hard-realist explanation for nuclear acquisition. They also point to the strength of the model proposed in this study – i.e., situational variables are the key determinants of national nuclear choices.

CHAPTER NINE

Conclusions

Several theoretical and policy conclusions emerge from this study with regard to the nuclear choices of nation-states. Here I provide a brief discussion on whether the case studies corroborate or refute the model presented in chapter 2. I argued above that the nuclear choices of non–great power states depend on the degree of security interdependence they experience vis-à-vis allies and adversaries and the level and type of conflict in the region where they are situated. Those technologically capable non–great power states not engaging in protracted conflicts and/or enduring rivalries, being aware of the consequences of arming with nuclear weapons, may prudently avoid their acquisition. They may do so knowing that these weapons cause intense negative security externalities for their neighbours, who may take countervailing measures, including diminution of politico-economic ties and seeking the aid of extra-regional powers. In some cases, this fear may pertain to intensification of conflict with neighbours; in others, it may concern the targeting of their population and industrial centres by nuclear powers. Allied states may also lose their alliance support and economic markets if they nuclearize. Nuclear acquisitions can generate higher levels of negative security externalities for other states than conventional weapons, partly because of the dearth of defences against a nuclear attack. Moreover, the speed and intensity of destruction are much greater in a nuclear attack than in a conventional offensive.

I argued above that the nuclear policies of a non–great power state are determined by the degree of conflict in its regional environment. I proposed three analytical types of regions – zones of high, moderate, and low conflict – in addition to three subsets – zones of high/moderate, high/low, and moderate/low conflict. The conflict level in each type of region depends on the number, scope, and intensity of militarized inter-state disputes. Zones of high conflict have protracted, active conflicts. In moderate zones, rivalries tend to be episodic, rather than protracted or enduring. In low-conflict zones, states enjoy high levels of economic and security interdependence. According to this categorization, the most likely candidates for nuclear forbearance are states in low- and moderate-conflict zones with extensive security interdependence. Such states avoid risky actions that upset economic and political co-operation with neighbours. The states that are most likely to acquire nuclear capabilities lie in zones of high conflict, especially those engaged in an ongoing, protracted conflict or enduring rivalry. If technologically capable states in these zones forgo nuclear weapons, it would be the result of credible security guarantees provided by an ally or their possession of countervailing capabilities, such as chemical or biological weapons or superior conventional arms. The transformation of such regions into moderate- or low-conflict zones could herald nuclear forbearance by non–great power states.

The case studies support strongly the analytical framework and the arguments presented in chapter 2. Security interdependence powerfully helps to explain the German and Japanese cases. Germany's nuclear options are constrained by its historical and current interaction with allies and adversaries and its alliance relationship with the United States. During the Cold War era, West Germany was in a zone of high/low conflict (Soviet bloc/Western Europe). The alliance factor was critical during the 1950s and 1960s, and security interdependence since then. With the end of the Cold War, Germany's security environment has improved considerably, making its asymmetrical security interdependence even more determinative of continued nuclear abstinence. The surrounding region has become a zone of low/moderate conflict, and so Germany will probably remain non-nuclear unless Russo–German relations deteriorate and NATO collapses simultaneously or Germany decides to become a great power – i.e., an independent centre of power in the international system.

Japan is another case that the model can explain well. During the Cold War era, Japan was situated in a high/moderate–conflict zone. Japan and the Soviet Union had a high-conflict relationship, while Japan was in a moderate-conflict zone vis-à-vis East Asia. The American nuclear umbrella appears to many a major constraint on Japanese nuclearization. However, Tokyo's asymmetric security interdependence vis-à-vis neighbouring states is also a critical factor. Nuclear acquisition would have provoked hostile responses from allies and adversaries, hurting Japan's economics-first foreign policy. Japan had to tread a cautious path, which meant a low-profile defence policy. The end of the Cold War has moderately improved Japan's security environment. The Russian threat has decreased, but nuclear acquisition by regional states such as North Korea could compel Japan to respond. The U.S. security assurances are critical in this case. If the United States withdraws completely from the Pacific, Japan may upgrade its latent capabilities to virtual nuclear capability. But conversion to a declared weapon force is likely only if enduring rivalries develop vis-à-vis China or Korea or if Japan decides to become a great military power concomitant with its economic clout. Regional constraints are still valid in this case, as such a course of action would inevitably affect Japan's relations with its Asian neighbours and trading partners.[1]

The cases of two allied middle powers, Canada and Australia, strongly uphold the model. They belong to zones of low conflict, although during the Cold war era their participation in the Western alliance forced them into a collective, enduring rivalry with the Soviet Union. Even at the height of Cold War tensions, they attempted individually to reduce Soviet hostility and to become examples of non-proliferation in order to safeguard their foreign policy framework of middle-power internationalism. While the Canadians assumed early on that nuclear acquisition was not in their interests as a middle power, there were voices within Australia favouring nuclear acquisition in the 1950s and 1960s. The regional dynamics – i.e., fear of provoking an arms race in Asia and setting a bad example for non-proliferation – encouraged Australia not to exercise its nuclear option.

The cases of neutral states – Sweden and Switzerland – also support the model. Neutral states especially worry about the image that they create among other states. By acquiring nuclear weapons, Sweden and Switzerland would have invited hostile attention from the Soviet Union, with the possibility of their becoming involved early on in a European war. Security interdependence vis-à-vis their European neighbours has been high for these states. Moreover, these countries belonged to zones of low/moderate conflict (Europe/Soviet bloc). An idiosyncratic problem for the neutral states has been the simultaneously offensive and deterrent characteristic of nuclear weapons. Neutral countries' acquiring tactical nuclear weapons would have increased their deterrent capabilities, but the Soviet Union would have seen that as offensive capability. In the event of a military conflict, Moscow would have been tempted to resort to a nuclear first strike to get rid of their nuclear capability, provoking early involvement in a possible European war – a situation the neutrals very much wanted to avoid.

The nuclear choices of Argentina and Brazil strongly uphold the model. However, in this case, a comprehensive explanation should include domestic-level variables in addition to regional security interdependence. Latin America, especially its Southern Cone region, has been a zone of moderate conflict, which has managed to transform itself into a low-conflict, economically interdependent region since the early 1990s. The transition to democracy helped the process tremendously, but the ending of the Brazilian–Argentine limited, enduring rivalry – a development that had begun with military regimes and intensified under civilian governments – allowed denuclearization. Brazil's ending of its historic ambition to become a great military power, focusing instead on economic development, also seems to have influenced its decision to forgo nuclear weapons. The bilateral regime for denuclearization that Argentina and Brazil have created attests to the argument that nuclear choices of non–great power regional states depend on anticipated responses by neighbouring states and the desire to avoid an arms race. This is especially important for countries attempting to transform their regions into low-conflict zones so as to further economic co-operation.

The decisions on nuclear forbearance of South Africa, Ukraine, and South Korea are also consistent with the model. Apartheid-era South Africa was a powerful case of an isolated state in a high-conflict region caught in enduring rivalries and protracted conflicts. Its decision to acquire nuclear weapons was influenced heavily by the intensification of conflict in Southern Africa in the 1970s and 1980s. With the end of these conflicts and the demise of apartheid, South Africa's nuclear propensity evaporated. The ANC government professes a non-nuclear policy, signifying that regional-security and political constraints still exist in the South African case. This case also points out that domestic changes as well as changes in regional conflict profoundly affect nuclear choices. The Ukrainian case is somewhat unique, as Kiev inherited nuclear weapons rather than building them. It could have maintained its tactical nuclear capability for deterrence purposes. Security and economic interdependence with Russia and the desire to move closer to the United States and Western Europe prompted nuclear forbearance. Maintenance of nuclear weapons would have increased conflict with Russia and the West. The Ukrainians effectively used their nuclear capability for gaining economic aid and security assurances from the United States and Russia. The South Korean nuclear choice has been heavily determined by U.S. policy. The security umbrella explains much in this case, as without the U.S. presence and threat of economic sanctions South Korea would probably have gone nuclear. However, the ending of the protracted Korean conflict and peaceful reunification would eliminate its nuclear propensity.

The three cases of nuclear acquisition – India, Pakistan, and Israel – strongly uphold the model. All three states are involved in protracted conflicts and enduring rivalries and have no clear security commitment from any major nuclear power. Although Israel has U.S. security assistance, this still is not equivalent to membership in an alliance similar to NATO. The three states belong to zones of high conflict where relative gains matter immensely and zero–sum perspectives abound. Security and economic co-operation has been extremely difficult to develop, largely because of the existential and territorial nature of the conflicts. Among the three states, India holds great-power ambitions and has the potential to achieve major-power capabilities in the twenty-first century. Denuclearization of Pakistan and Israel will depend heavily on when and how the enduring rivalries/protracted conflicts end in their regions. However, India's choice will be determined by regional and global changes. The end of the enduring rivalries with Pakistan and China may facilitate India's nuclear disarmament, but as long as major powers, especially China, possess nuclear weapons, India is unlikely to forgo them unilaterally.

The argument advanced in this study – that security strategies depend on where states are situated – is generally upheld by the case studies. The nuclear policies of the aligned, non-aligned, and neutral states discussed in this book reveal that their nuclear choices derive largely from their security environments and strategic contexts. The framework is sufficiently dynamic, as it takes into account the changing security environments of states. The options for nuclear acquisition or non-acquisition could shift as and when regional conflicts change. Nuclear choices are not permanent, as a nation in a high-conflict region could opt for nuclear-free policies as and when its security environment changes. Similarly, a zone with moderate conflict could become one of high conflict, raising the prospects of states' acquiring nuclear weapons.

THEORETICAL IMPLICATIONS

The theoretical conclusions are relevant mostly to hard realism, of both classical and structural varieties, and to liberal institutionalism.

Realism and the Understanding of Nuclear Choices

The hard-realist concerns about tendencies in national arms acquisition and the larger problem of security dilemma are only partially endorsed by the case studies. Although security is a paramount goal of all states, it does not necessarily follow that arming with the most lethal weapon ever invented is the dominant approach of most of them. A number of states have forsworn nuclear weapons even when they could have acquired (or in some cases after acquiring) them, realizing that nuclear possession may indeed decrease their security by magnifying the condition of anarchy, creating arms races, and thereby turning their benign security surroundings into conflict-prone environments. The important finding is that states follow diverse security strategies in order to deal with the consequences of anarchy in the international system.[2] Some attempt to ameliorate the effects of anarchy by consciously avoiding provocative actions, including nuclear weapons programs. Some are content with alliances, while others forgo nuclear weapons, believing that new and established nuclear states will not use their weapons against them, as they would be breaking the tradition of non-use. States are security maximizers, but that does not automatically entail their arming themselves with the most lethal weapon, even if they possess the potential capability to do so.

National security is a much more eclectic concept than the military security presented in hard-realist accounts. Nations may engage in sovereignty-sacrificing behaviour in order to improve their security. Attempts to avoid an intense security dilemma could be based on a state's recognition that the actions of one country, in seeking military security unilaterally through nuclear acquisition, can be threatening to another state. Nations may follow policies that seek to protect their vital interests in a manner that avoids treating security as a zero–sum game. Balancing against threats militarily may depend on the nature of the threats.[3] It is true that no nation can fully transcend anarchy, but it can ameliorate the effects through policies that do not increase the insecurity of others, which in turn causes the security dilemma. The effects of anarchy are mitigated in regions of high-level security interdependence, where states choose less threatening security policies. Thus a problem with the hard-realist conception is the deterministic nature of its precepts about security strategies under anarchy. Even under enormous constraints, states do have choices and non-military ways to ameliorate the harmful effects of anarchy.[4]

The debate between proponents of realism and liberal institutionalism has created overly dismissive arguments. Each paradigm by itself serves to explain state behaviour in some contexts more than others. This book shows that the main tenets of these paradigms are useful in explaining state security policies in different contexts. Level of conflict and security interdependence with allies and adversaries powerfully explain the arms acquisition or dis-arming propensity of a state, especially in nuclear weapons. Thus this book aims to bridge the gap between the central realist insight about anarchy and states' acquisition of arms and the liberal insight that anarchy can be ameliorated through norms that reinforce conscious acts such as non-acquisition.

In presenting an eclectic model, I have developed an essentially soft-realist approach called "prudential realism." Nations prudently balance their capabilities and interests in accordance with their security environment, and they try not to create intense insecurity for other states. Nation-states are self-interested yet cautious actors, and they assess threats on the basis of most-probable assumptions, not worst-case assessments, if they are in a benign strategic environment. Enlightened self-interest is thus the core of a prudential realist understanding of states' behaviour. Prudential realism does not reject anarchy but postulates that benign and cautious strategies other than arming can lessen its effects. Prudential realism views security polices of states as mutually interdependent and less unilateral than hard realism would expect. Hard-realist accounts have relegated prudence to a secondary role, but I contend that prudence is critical to the security choices of many states in the nuclear age.

Hard realists might suggest that non-nuclear decisions could be reversed. Reversal, however, involves much higher costs than is generally assumed. In fact, the exit costs have increased, largely because of the entrenchment of norms and principles in non-proliferation. During the 1950s and 1960s, the exit costs were less, which explains why most proliferation occurred before 1980. The hard-realist argument that the end of the Cold War has unleashed forces that would result in more and more countries acquiring nuclear weapons may not be accurate; trends so far do not seem consistent with this prediction. Changing security policies from a benign to an offensive mode is more costly than ever. Further, all the goals identified in the study – attracting less hostile attention, keeping one's region militarily benign, and achieving economic integration – will suffer under unilateral nuclearization.

Power, Norms, and Interests

According to hard-realist frameworks, maximization of power is a key interest of states. However, not all nations maximize power in the way that hard realists predict. Circumstances determine whether a country seeks to maximize power or not. Maximizing power can be costly, inhibiting pursuit of other goals. Friends could become enemies, and moderate opponents, bitter adversaries. The case studies show that considerations of power, norms, and prudence may govern states' behaviour, and the values that a given state attaches to each of these factors may vary with circumstances. The treatment of interests defined in terms of power – i.e., military power – and the argument that states have an insatiable propensity to acquire more and more military power (eloquently portrayed by Morgenthau) often fail to acknowledge that not every state is predisposed to seeking military dominance even if it could. Morgenthau argues further that the struggle for power is universal in time and space and that states, regardless of their socio-economic and political conditions, "have met each other in contest for power."[5] Despite the many strengths of classical realism, this seems an exaggerated position that is challenged by the behaviour of several states studied in this book.

A state's experience with the acquisition and use of military power resources and its environment determine whether it follows the path of military dominance or not. Japan and Germany's failure to achieve military objectives through war has given them a powerful lesson to restrain from acquiring threatening weapon systems or from pursuing highly autarkic military policies. To some extent, Brazil's choice to forgo nuclear weapons also points out that sometimes states that have the potential to achieve great-power status need not pursue that route vigorously. A country of enormous size, population, and economic wealth, Brazil has often been portrayed as a great power in the making. The country's elite, especially the military, had viewed Brazil as an emerging great power in Latin America, and they maintained the nuclear option with that objective in mind. Civilian regimes decided to change that course and pursue an economics-first policy. The Argentine and the Ukrainian decisions to forgo nuclear weapons also pose some problems for hard realism. Being relatively weaker powers, they could have used nuclear capability to deter potential military threats from their larger neighbours, Brazil and Russia, respectively. According to the conventional wisdom, nuclear capability would have been a great equalizer for these states.

Interest defined in terms of power – i.e., military power – is overly restrictive and cannot adequately explain choices for the forbearance of a capability that would supposedly increase the measurable and tangible deterrent power of a state. Moreover, power, interests, and norms may not be completely on opposite poles, as hard realism often portrays them. Nuclear forbearance could be in a state's interest and may indeed increase its ability to manage its security environment effectively. The norm of non-proliferation would be in the interests of a state as well if it reduced proliferation internationally and regionally. Similarly, a state's power is not always equivalent to how much "threat power" it holds. Under some circumstances, a policy of non-acquisition of threatening agents could increase power. Once a nation acquires nuclear capability, it may experience a decrease in its power capability in other domains, as it may be isolated by other states, thereby losing influence over these states. Effective power, in this sense, arises from a state's capacity to control its environment, reduce threats to its survival, and influence the choices of allies and adversaries by not giving them cause to arm against it.

Neo-realists have identified concerns about relative gains as a main obstacle to co-operation among states, especially if the co-operation involves defensive capabilities and makes a state dependent on others for security.[6] As these cases of nuclear forbearance point out, relative gains do not seem to matter as much in national policies as neo-realists suggest. States in low-conflict, economically interdependent zones worry less about relative gains than do states in high-conflict regions. However, the latter states tend to be highly concerned about relative gains. Moreover, states in low- and medium-conflict zones often deliberately avoid getting entrapped in a relative-gains situation. Thus national contexts determine whether relative gains become a problem. All these points reveal the need for greater specification and context-dependent analysis to make the theoretical framework more powerful.

Liberal Institutionalism and Nuclear Decisions

The main factor presented by liberal institutionalists as dissuading nuclear forbearance, the non-proliferation regime, and the norms inherent in it has a modest constraining effect on adherents of the regime, especially in low- and moderate-conflict zones. The regime has created certain stable expectations regarding states' behaviour in this realm. The case studies show that the regime is more of a facilitator than a determinant in this respect. In most of the cases studied in this book, states had chosen to give up their nuclear options prior to joining the Nuclear Non-Proliferation Treaty (NPT). Adherence to the treaty, however, formalized their choices. Germany and Japan had already forsaken their nuclear options when they joined the NPT. But they were initially reluctant to sign and ratify the treaty. As their principal objections, based on fear of harm to civilian nuclear exports and imports and inadequate security guarantees, evaporated, their opposition waned. In the case of Canada, the NPT hardly played any role. Canada was already a non-nuclear state (barring the U.S. weapons under dual control) when it signed the NPT. The treaty somewhat influenced Australian choices, as the final decision on nuclear weapons coincided with the NPT signature. Over time, both Canada and Australia have emerged as major defenders of the NPT, as evident in their leadership in gaining the extension of the treaty in perpetuity.

Sweden and Switzerland were also influenced by the treaty, although Sweden was moving towards a non-nuclear posture by the time it came into force. The treaty helped to codify and legalize their non-nuclear policies. The non-proliferation regime and the NPT had very little effect on Argentina and Brazil's forgoing of nuclear weapons, as is evident in their creation of a regional approach for non-proliferation. The discriminatory nature of the regime dissuaded these states from joining it earlier. Ukraine, South Africa, and South Korea all have signed the NPT, mostly as a way to legalize their non-nuclear status, and the treaty had no causal effect on their non-nuclear policies.

As for the new nuclear states, the non-proliferation regime has probably put pressure on them to go underground with their nuclear programs. At least in one of the cases, India, the regime exerted a reverse effect; it reinforced India's pro-nuclear policy and solidified public opinion in support of maintaining the nuclear option. India's nuclear tests in May 1998 were aimed at challenging the regime, especially in view of the 1995 extension of the NPT in perpetuity and the conclusion of the CTBT – two measures that solidified the nuclear monopoly of the five nuclear states. These three cases show that multilateral treaties on arms control have little effect if they totally ignore regional security realities. The exclusive focus of the regime on technical approaches and its disregard of political factors that underlie nuclear choices explain why it has not been fully successful as a non-proliferation instrument. The narrow technical approach has permitted states in regions with protracted conflicts, such as Iraq, Iran, and North Korea, to use the regime as a cover to acquire nuclear materials for obtaining a weapons capability.

One of the deficiencies of the liberal-institutionalist literature is its inability to provide a clear-cut statement as to when and how institutions matter in national security choices – specifically in this case, the decision to forgo nuclear weapons. The non-proliferation regime indeed facilitates exchange of ideas, builds confidence through safe-guards, and educates nations on the virtues of non-acquisition. It is also an arena where non-nuclear states can encourage further disar-mament by the nuclear states, although these efforts have not produced sufficient results as yet. All these factors do not explain the causal impact that the regime exerts on nuclear choices. Moreover, the fact that some national actors perceive it as discriminatory undermines its vitality and universal applicability.

POLICY IMPLICATIONS

The case studies point out that the currently fashionable supply-side approaches have only limited utility in achieving non-proliferation.[7] The key to non-proliferation lies in resolving regional conflicts, espe-cially protracted ones. All major reverses in proliferation since 1990 have occurred in regions where rivalries have ended. South Africa,

Argentina, and Brazil changed course because their regional conflicts ended. The evidence in the case studies strongly supports the proposition that the nuclear choice of a non–great power state depends heavily on its regional security environment. The security situation of a state in an enduring conflict is dominated by concerns of self-help and relative gains much more than is that of a state without such a conflict. Technologically capable states that have an enduring rival and no strong alliance partner, or those that are isolated from the international community, have the highest tendency to acquire nuclear armaments. Security threats multiply when a state is in an enduring rivalry and is simultaneously isolated: examples include South Africa before 1991 and North Korea. Even India, Pakistan, and Israel are not fully integrated into the international system, and so economic, political, and military sanctions are unlikely to take away their proliferation propensities. Iraq and North Korea have not become non-nuclear; this is true especially of the former, despite military defeat, near-universal economic sanctions, and the unprecedented intrusive UN inspections of its weapons facilities. The policy implication here is that the economic and political integration of these states into the international community is likely to have a greater effect on their nuclear choices than coercive sanctions.[8]

Economic and technical sanctions can constrain a nuclear aspirant and delay weapons programs, but again they may not resolve the fundamental reasons for nuclearization.[9] States in moderate-conflict zones with nuclear tendencies may be more susceptible to sanctions than states in high-conflict zones. Fence-sitters in high-conflict regions are less prone to external manipulation,[10] as we see in India, Pakistan, and Israel. These states in the 1990s embarked on economic liberalization and stepped up their nuclear activities substantially, as evident in the 1998 tests by the two South Asian states. Although state policies affect how co-operation or conflict develops, any non-proliferation policy that does not acknowledge the underlying conflict dynamics of a region is bound to fail.[11] They may undermine the same liberal societal forces that external actors are trying to influence while allowing pro-nuclear groups to emerge as even more powerful. Positive and negative economic sanctions may have a greater effect on states in zones of low and moderate conflict. Such states are especially sensitive to the economic policies of their major trading partners.

The role of alliances and nuclear umbrellas as inhibitors of nuclear proliferation needs further exploration. This study points out that alliances can serve both negative and positive functions.[12] Alliances contributed to Germany's nuclear non-proliferation. The U.S.–Japanese military alliance has been a powerful element in Japan's continued restraint in this realm. In South Korea also, the alliance encouraged nuclear non-acquisition. However, the u.s. alliance and nuclear presence in South Korea have caused North Korea to pursue the nuclear route. Alliances were a factor in the Canadian and Australian cases, but there is no compelling evidence that, in the absence of alliances, these states would otherwise have acquired nuclear arms. In fact, throughout the Cold War era they sought to reduce the alliance dilemma problem and avoid nuclear entrapment. Alliances played no role in the Argentine and Brazilian cases, while (in the form of the presence nearby of NATO) they may have played an indirect role in the Swedish and Swiss cases. Israel and Pakistan's tacit alliances with the United States and India's with the USSR (1971–90) had the reverse effect. These nations used their friendships as camouflage for their secret development of nuclear weapons. Security imperatives are so powerful in these cases that limited alliance support had no impact on their nuclear choices.

Not all alliances reduce nuclear propensities. Thus the alliance relationship of India with the USSR, Pakistan with the United States and China, and Israel with the United States did not obviate their desire for nuclear weapons. These states did not receive credible security guarantees similar to what the United States had provided to Japan, West Germany, and South Korea. The presence of allied troops and conventional and nuclear weapons on the ally's territory and explicit commitments in the event of attack help determine the credibility of an alliance relationship. Credibility may also depend on how well integrated are the allies' armed forces, military doctrines, strategies, and operational plans and on their overall politico-economic relationship. States in enduring rivalries tend to be sceptical about the strength and credibility of an alliance versus reliance on their military capability.

Is Nuclear Forbearance Reversible?

Hard-realist scepticism about nuclear forbearance rests on the belief that such choices are reversible and that constraints in this regard have only limited value. According to the model presented in this study, decisions not to acquire nuclear weapons could be reversed only when a zone of low or medium conflict becomes one of high conflict and when states in such a region lose the protection of their allies. The probability of such reversals is high for states engaged in protracted conflicts and enduring rivalries or those likely to enter them.

Under what conditions could countries that have forgone their nuclear options revert to nuclear acquisition? A major deterioration in the international order similar to that in pre-1914 Europe could compel several states to rethink their nuclear policies. States in protracted-conflict zones that lack adequate conventional capability to deter their adversaries are the most likely candidates. Power transitions could be another circumstance, where rising great-power states (today's regional powers) perceive that they have no effective means to achieve global leadership without possessing an effective deterrent capability. Proliferation would, however, occur only if nuclear weapons remain the ultimate source of coercive power in the future international system. Such power transitions follow enduring rivalries among major powers.[13] Further, middle powers that are targets of great-power intervention and military conflict also have high potential for nuclear acquisition. What is remarkable, however, is the near-absence of revocation by technologically capable states that have forsworn nuclear weapons during the past thirty years or so and the increase in the number of such states in each decade.

Indeed, many political phenomena of substantial interest to political scientists are not permanent in nature. An example is the democratization of states. Democratization and sustenance of democracy in new democracies are major topics of research in comparative politics because of the ever-present possibility of reversion to authoritarian rule. But this possibility does not prevent scholars from studying democratization, as it is important that we understand what sustains and nourishes a new democracy. Similarly, what sustains a nation's non-nuclear status should be a subject of scholarly and policy interest. Another issue in which national policies are susceptible to change is free trade. Countries could revert to protectionist policies under certain conditions. Yet it is still useful to study how free trade is sustained and under what conditions a state would change its policies. Similarly, in security, it is important to study when and why states pursue autarkic policies of arms acquisition, especially relating to nuclear weapons, so as to develop ways and means to sustain disarmament and arms control.

Notes

1 Amplifying this puzzle is the fact that almost all states obtain and maintain conventional forces, but the picture is quite different for nuclear weapons. In addition, nuclear weaponry may provide an effective deterrent in the hands of smaller powers vis-à-vis their larger neighbours and great-power adversaries and thereby serve as "great equalizers" in relations between small and big powers. Yet almost all smaller powers have chosen not to seek nuclear weapons.

2 Dunn, "The Common Problem," and Bernard Brodie, "War in the Atomic Age."

3 *Public Papers: Eisenhower, 1953*, 816.

4 *Public Papers: Kennedy, 1963*, 280.

5 Philosophers such as Aristotle and St Thomas Acquinas consider prudence a cardinal virtue. For the moral and philosophical bases of prudence, see Den Uyl, *The Virtue of Prudence*. However, I do not use the term in the moral sense.

6 Elements of prudential realism can be gleaned from the works of Hans Morgenthau, Raymond Aron, E.H. Carr, and Reinhold Niebuhr, even though the main thrust of their writings falls under hard realism. See Kaufman, "E.H. Carr ... ." Morgenthau in his classic book devotes only a few sentences to prudence. He contends (without much elaboration) that realism "considers prudence – the weighing of the consequences of alternative political actions – to be the supreme virtue in politics." Morgenthau, *Politics among Nations*, 10. However, his nine rules of diplomacy contain several points relevant to prudential conduct of statecraft.

7 I do not cover all prevailing explanations for nuclear choices, such as domestic politics, bureaucratic politics, and dispositions of decision-

makers. Some such explanations appear, however, in the case studies below.

8 Some scholars have characterized hard realism as "offensive realism" or "aggressive realism" and soft realism as "defensive realism." Parts of the writings of classical realists, including Morgenthau and neo-realists such as Mearsheimer, are hard realism. Offensive realism highlights the systemic causes of conflict, while defensive realism looks more closely at domestic politics of countries to explain why some states act aggressively while others do not even when they all face the same systemic conditions. Accordingly, offensive realism posits that states exploit their opportunities to maximize their power and influence relative to others in order to attain security, while defensive realism contends that systemic pressures would make states want to preserve the status quo. On defensive realism, see Jack Snyder, *Myths of Empire*; Zakaria, "Realism"; Rose, "Neoclassical Realism"; Labs, "Beyond Victory." For various realist approaches, see Mastanduno, "A Realist View."

9 Michael Mandelbaum, *The Nuclear Future*, 19–20. To structural realists, co-operation is limited because of the problem of relative gains – i.e., a state is constantly afraid of others' gaining more than itself. Grieco, "Anarchy"; see also Waltz, "More May Be Better"; and Lynn-Jones, "Offense–Defense Theory."

10 On the security dilemma, see Herz, *International Politics*, 231; and Jervis, "Cooperation."

11 Dunn, "The Common Problem," 12. On problems with security regimes, see Jervis, "Security Regimes," 175–6.

12 Kenneth Waltz, *Theory*, 194. Waltz also argues that states tend to imitate the capabilities of others. See also Morgenthau, *Politics among Nations*, 114–16; and Freedman, "Great Powers."

13 Waltz, *Theory*, 118; Reiss, *Without the Bomb*, xxi.

14 Frankel, "The Brooding Shadow"; Mearsheimer, "Back to the Future."

15 Olson and Zeckhauser, "Economic Theory." For the European case of nuclear protection, see Joffe, "Europe's American Pacifier."

16 On coercive versions of the theory, see Gilpin, *U.S. Power*; Muller, "Role," 228. In addition, a hegemon can help socialize elites in other countries to embrace a set of normative ideals articulated by it in order to create a particular international order. Ikenberry and Kupchan, "Socialization.

17 Strange, "Cave!," 345; see also Nayar, "International Regimes."

18 On the need for co-operation by subordinate states for the hegemon's success, see Brawley, *Liberal Leadership*, 14.

19 Israeli, Pakistani, and Indian nuclear programs speeded up during periods when these states were very close to their superpower patron. The alliance relationship was a cover for them to acquire nuclear weapons,

as they anticipated less hostile reaction from their superpower ally and diplomatic support to lessen adverse international reactions. Additionally, some nuclear umbrellas have in fact encouraged proliferation. The u.s. alliance with South Korea, especially the nuclear umbrella, helped bring about the North Korean decision to acquire nuclear weapons.

20 The nuclear tests by India and Pakistan could be posited as a challenge to this argument. But these two states had already acquired nuclear weapons during the Cold War period itself. In May 1998, they declared their nuclear status openly. Indeed, the largest number of technologically capable states giving up their nuclear options at once occurred after the end of the Cold War and included Argentina, Brazil, and South Africa, as well as Belarus, Kazakhstan, and Ukraine, which had lost their Soviet nuclear umbrellas.

21 Waltz, "The Emerging Structure." In fact, nuclear weapons may be of diminished value in meeting many security threats in the post–Cold War era. John E. Mueller, "Escalating Irrelevance," and Paul, "Power." Moreover, co-operation among major powers has increased since 1991. Davis, "The Realist."

22 Social constructivism is an emerging, norm-based alternative approach that could help explain nuclear forbearance. It sees national security policies as determined more by norms, culture, and identities of a state than by material circumstances. It sees national identities as socially constructed, rather than structurally determined, as envisioned by both realists and liberals. For various analyses under constructivism, see Katzenstein ed., *Culture of National Security*, especially chapters by Jepperson, Wendt, and Katzenstein, "Norms," and by Berger, "Norms." See also Wendt, "Anarchy." Constructivism offers much, but more work is needed to determine how norms, culture, and identities determine a country's nuclear policies. For a critical analysis, see Checkel, "The Constructivist Turn." It is especially crucial to know how this perspective accounts for change in security policies. More concretely, when will socially constructed ideas change and how do externally determined conflict processes affect national security policies?

23 Theorists differ on the effects that regimes can have on states' behaviour. See Krasner, ed., *International Regimes*.

24 Keohane and Nye, *Power*, 8, 25, and 27.

25 Rosecrance, "International Theory"; Keohane and Nye, *Power*, 246.

26 For these functions, see Kratochwil, *Rules*, 10–11; Stein, *Why*, 32–6. Some regime theorists contend that regimes are grounded largely in states' mutual interests. See Zacher and Sutton, *Governing*.

27 Keohane, *After Hegemony*, 57–8.

28 Young, "Effectiveness, 177; Meyer, *Dynamics*, 69.

29 This attempt to marry realist and liberal insights is prone to criticism from adherents of one perspective or the other. However, I contend that the realist/liberal divide has slowed the advancement of knowledge in international relations. Scholarly efforts to "prove" one or the other correct have often obscured diverse political phenomena that require more nuanced and context-dependent explanations. Moreover, polar conceptions of state's behaviour have difficulty accounting for changes and variations in national policies in a crucial area such as nuclear acquisition. For an attempt to link realism and liberalism by a historical sociologist, see Hall, *International Orders*. See also Hall and Paul, "Preconditions."

30 For a similar methodological perspective among comparative politics scholars, see Kohli et al., "Role." On the need for puzzle-driven international relations scholarship, see Rosenau, "Desirable."

31 For process-tracing method, see Alexander George, "Case Studies."

32 On this method, see Dogan and Kazancigil, "Introduction."

CHAPTER TWO

1 The security interdependence that I discuss refers to states in non-weaponized strategic relationships. Weaponized relationships can have a different kind of security interdependence. For instance, in mutual assured destruction (MAD), a nuclear state's security in an existential sense will depend heavily on the choices that its nuclear adversary makes. MAD creates a different kind of security and strategic interdependence. The non-nuclearized state seeks not to get into this situation so as to retain its capacity to fashion its security environment.

2 Negative externalities are defined as costs, and positive externalities as "benefits that do not accrue only to the actors that create them." Lake, "Regional," 49. Negative security externalities in this instance are costs defined in terms of depreciation of the security of external actors.

3 This is somewhat equivalent to the prisoners' dilemma outcome in game theory. Actors co-operate with each other, fearing that defection by any makes all of them vulnerable, while co-operation provides the most preferred outcome. See Axelrod, *Evolution*; Jervis, "Cooperation."

4 "Security dilemma" appears in the literature also to signify a state of affairs nations are born with, given the anarchic nature of the international system.

5 Potter, *Nuclear Power*, 138.

6 Sharp, *Making*, 19. States under a nuclear umbrella could be guided by this concern as well. Although alliances create the problem of "entrapment" – i.e., getting involved in allies' conflicts whether one likes it or not – maintaining no nuclear weapons on one's soil can mitigate such effects. The expectation could be that in a prospective nuclear war,

the ally without nuclear weapons would not be the first to be targeted and destroyed.

7 As Richard Harknett argues, "measured on a scale of contestabilty – the degree to which technical, tactical, or operational effects can impact the actual destruction to be borne in combat- the destructive potential of nuclear weapons tends to be highly resilient ... Without the ability to degrade or adapt in any significant manner, the ability to contest or believe that one can avoid significant nuclear destruction disappears. The incontestable nature of nuclear weapons creates an environment that affects state security relations in a manner indistinguishable from prenuclear security dynamics." "State Preferences," 53.

8 For a discussion of these dimensions of power, see Paul, "Power."

9 Thompson, "Regional," 101.

10 Perhaps in an era of ICBMs regions do not matter for the security of any state. For such an argument, see Wirtz, "Beyond Bipolarity." I contend that the security interests of a non–great power state are heavily concentrated in its region. For instance, the acquisition of nuclear weapons by Pakistan is unlikely to pose a big security threat for East Asian states such as South Korea and Japan, whereas North Korea's nuclear acquisition could dramatically affect their security and threat perceptions. The main security concerns of most regional powers are the capability and intentions of their significant neighbours. Moreover, ICBMs are in the possession of a small group of great powers with global interests, and they tend to have little relevance to the strategic environments of most regional states. The nuclear capability of a great power, however, matters when that capability is part of a regional security complex. For instance, U.S. tactical nuclear weapons in South Korea form a major component of the regional security complex and generate powerful negative security externalities for North Korea. Similarly, China's nuclear weapons are a critical part of the South Asian regional security complex.

11 Buzan, *People*, 106.

12 Lake and Morgan, "Regionalism," 12; Buzan, *People*, 106.

13 On the reasons why great powers strive to prevent proliferation, see Paul, "Great Equalizers."

14 The originators of the concept of complex interdependence, Keohane and Nye, look only at one type of zone – the area of low conflict where economic interdependence prevails. Keohane and Nye, *Power*.

15 Gochman and Maoz, "Militarized." An interstate crisis is a "situational change characterized by increase in the intensity of disruptive interaction between two or more adversaries, with a high probability of military hostilities." Brecher and Wilkenfeld, *Crisis*, 5.

16 Brecher, *Crises*, 5.

17 Vasquez, *The War Puzzle*, 76–7.

18 Goertz and Diehl, "Enduring Rivalries."

19 For the characteristics of interdependence, see Keohane and Nye, *Power*, 24–5.

20 On security communities, see Deutsch et al., *Political Community*, 5–6.

21 The words "independent nuclear capability" are crucial here, because countries in this zone may station nuclear weapons as part of a common alliance policy or to deter a common adversary outside the region. If the capability is generally understood to be for the sole purpose of deterring the extra-regional power, it has little relevance for relations in the zone.

22 On the European example, see Ullman, *Securing Europe*.

23 On "balancing against threats," see Walt, *Origins*.

24 As Nye argues, in an interdependent world "power is less fungible, less coercive and less tangible." "Co-optive behavioral power – getting others to do what you want – and soft power resources – cultural attraction, ideology, and international institutions" become important. Nye, *Bound*, 188–9.

25 Rosecrance, *Rise*, 30 and 174.

26 This study does not consider how and why conflict relationships change or how a region of moderate or high conflict becomes a low conflict zone or vice versa.

27 On issues that generate rivalries, see Vasquez, *The War Puzzle*, and Holsti, *Peace and War*.

28 For explanations based on domestic politics, see Solingen, "Political Economy"; and Sagan, "Why."

29 Thayer, "Causes," 78; see also Desch, "Culture Clash."

30 The cost of attack for an attacker may be higher than the benefits that it might derive from such an action. The cost could be human suffering, radioactive fallout, harm to reputation, international and domestic condemnation, and, above all, the normative and moral questions involved in using weapons of mass destruction that do not discriminate combatants from non-combatants and thereby severely violate the two key principles of a just war – proportionality and minimum civilian damage.

31 Hoffmann, "Nuclear Proliferation," 95. On "putative" and "actualized" power, see Knorr, *Military Power*, 3.

32 Nye, *Bound*, 27. Perceptions regarding the other's capabilities and intentions also matter. "B's estimates of A's capabilities and intentions do not suffice to explain the coercion of B. If B has no intention of committing murder, he will not feel coerced by his government's threat to hang murderers." Baldwin, *Paradoxes*, 50. This is a major reason why small countries are not all that afraid of the nuclear weapons of major powers. Moreover, major powers can harass or conquer them if they desire to

do so without using nuclear weapons. For small states, deterrence is often achieved through political rather than military means. For small states' deterrence strategies, see Karl Mueller, *Strategy*.

33 On the need for information to found prudential behaviour, see Sabia, "Prudence," 4.

34 Martin, "International Institutions."

35 IAEA officials whom I interviewed agreed in general that the regime is not a cause of non-proliferation, but a facilitator. Once a country makes a decision to forgo nuclear weapons, the NPT becomes a "convenient vehicle" to present its non-nuclear policy to the international community. Interviews with IAEA officials, especially Mohammed Elberradei, David Kyd, and Bruno Pellaud, Vienna, 12–13 Dec. 1994.

36 Ruggie, "International Responses." In addition, unilateral efforts such as eliminating provocative military forces would be essential for peace in the region. See, for instance, Brown, *Causes*, 190.

37 On problems with this expectation, see Paul, "The NPT."

38 For the Indian position on the regime, see Poulose, *Nuclear Proliferation*, and Subrahmanyam, *India*.

39 Paul "Systemic Bases."

40 For these national positions, see Blackaby, Goldblat and Lodgaard, "No First Use"; Gompert, Watman, and Wilkening, "Nuclear." Russia later withdrew its unilateral no-first-use pledge.

41 Prakash Nanda, "India Evolves Nuclear Doctrine," *Times of India*, 5 Aug. 1998 (http://www.timesofindia.com/today/05home1.html).

42 Schelling, *Strategy*, 260. See also Paul, "Nuclear Taboo"; Tannenwald, "The Nuclear Taboo." For discussions of a taboo in chemical weapons, see Price, "Genealogy"; Legro, *Cooperation*.

43 Schelling, "Role," 110.

44 Prospects for "spillover" effects into the U.S.–Soviet central strategic balance might have been a key factor in their restraint. Also both the superpowers needed the support of other countries. In their propaganda war to get smaller powers' allegiance, the use of nuclear weapons would have had an adverse effect, especially among developing countries. However, it could be argued that the failures in Vietnam and Afghanistan did affect American and Soviet credibility as superpowers.

45 Herz, *International Politics*, 21.

46 Gaddis, "Nuclear Weapons." See also Bundy, *Danger*, 587–8.

47 This does not imply that this trend is likely to continue in all future conflicts. Nuclear weapons could become important in conflicts involving nuclear states and regional states possessing other forms of weapons of mass destruction, primarily chemical and biological weapons.

48 On some such problems, see Feaver, "Command." For an opposite view, see Seng, "Less Is More."

49 The subject of nuclear learning by small and medium-sized states is worthy of an independent research project.

50 For this conception of learning, see Haas, "Why Collaborate?" 390. For the application of learning theory to the U.S.–Soviet nuclear context, see Nye, "Nuclear Learning."

51 According to this definition, policy changes are not automatic following learning. Levy, "Learning."

52 Bundy, *Danger*, 461. See also Harvey and James, "Nuclear Crisis."

53 Malcolmson, *Beyond Nuclear Thinking*, 89.

54 On the role of peace movements, see Knopf, *Domestic Society*.

55 Since 1945, non-nuclear states have fought limited wars with nuclear states. Four cases of wars initiated by non-nuclear states are prominent – the Chinese offensive against U.S./UN forces in Korea in 1950; the Egyptian and Syrian offensives against Israel in 1973, the Argentine invasion of the Falklands in 1982; and the Iraqi attacks on Israel during the Persian Gulf War in 1991. The initiators believed that their adversary would not use its nuclear capability, probably because they did not challenge the core interests or security of the nuclear state. For a discussion of the first three cases, see Paul, *Asymmetric Conflicts*, chaps. 5 and 7–8, and "Nuclear Taboo."

CHAPTER THREE

1 *IAEA Bulletin*, 41 no. 1 (1999): 50.

2 Reports in 1995 suggested that Germany would also acquire weapons-grade highly enriched uranium capability if the proposed 20-mW reactor were to be built in the Munich suburb of Garching. Cowell, "Germans Rebuff U.S. on Plans for Reactor," *New York Times*, 22 July 1995, 3. For the Japanese estimates, see "Japan Details Size of Plutonium Stockpile," *International Herald Tribune*, 26–7 Nov. 1994, 5.

3 Monju, Japan's first commercial fast-breeder plutonium reactor, began operations in April 1994. *Daily Telegraph*, 26 Nov. 1994, 15; see also Kitamura, "Japan's Plutonium Program."

4 *IAEA Bulletin*, 41 no. 1 (1999): 50. According to Hottori Manabu, former chief of the Institute of Atomic Energy at Tokyo's Rikkyo University, it would take only one month for Japan to produce a reliable nuclear bomb. "Thinking the Unthinkable: What would it Take for Japan to Go Nuclear?" *Asia Week*, 6 Oct. 1993, 38. At the height of the North Korean nuclear crisis in 1994, former prime minister Tsutomu Hata stated, "it is certainly the case that Japan has the capability to possess nuclear weapons, but has not made them." The Japanese Foreign Ministry later denied that this was the case. David E. Sanger, "In

Face-Saving Turn, Japan Denies Nuclear Know-how," *New York Times*, 22 June 1994, A10.

5 Andrew Pollack, "Japan Launches Rocket, Cutting Reliance on U.S.," *New York Times*, 4 Feb. 1994, A17.

6 Harrison, "Japan and Nuclear Weapons," 21.

7 Britain's Defence Ministry, in a secret report to the cabinet, warned that Japan had all the elements necessary to build a nuclear bomb and that the North Korean nuclear crisis would force Tokyo to abandon its non-nuclear stance. Nick Rufford, "Japan to 'Go Nuclear' in Asian Arms Race," *Sunday Times*, 30 Jan. 1994, 1 and 15. A Japanese government spokesman quickly denied the report by saying that "it is out of the question" for Japan to lift its restrictions on nuclear acquisition and that "the nuclear arms race option would only destabilize Japan's international environment." Quoted in David E. Sanger, "Japan Denies Any Plans to Build Nuclear Bombs," *New York Times*, 2 Feb. 1994, A9.

8 West Germany was the site of thousands of theatre nuclear weapons, such as atomic demolition munitions (ADMs), artillery pieces, and cruise missiles, as well as aircraft-based nuclear warheads. Boutwell, *German*, 14.

9 NATO *Facts and Figures* (Brussels: NATO Information Service, 1969), 287. Critics have charged that these accords did not prohibit West Germany from importing nuclear weapons, or making bilateral or multilateral co-ownership arrangements with other countries, or developing nuclear weapons outside the country. Kelleher, *Germany*, 9.

10 Schwartz, NATO's *Nuclear Dilemma*, 41.

11 Ibid., 41–2. Speier, *German Rearmament*, 231.

12 Schwartz, NATO's *Nuclear Dilemmas*, 45; Ahonen, "Franz-Josef Strauss," 31. Strauss's effort to acquire a nuclear capability through co-operation with France was viewed by some as a way to force the United States to provide more security guarantees to West Germany. Strauss was influenced by the post-Hiroshima belief that possession of nuclear weapons was essential for preventing capitulation to another nuclear power, that it would increase the credibility of the Western deterrent against the Soviet Union, and that without nuclear weapons West Germany would remain a second-ranking state. Ahonen, "Franz-Josef Strauss."

13 Blacker and Duffy, *International*, 154.

14 Horst Mendershausen, "Will West Germany?" 415. One of the coalition partners, the Social Democratic Party, did not share these fears, and Willy Brandt, then foreign minister, supported the treaty.

15 Boutwell, *The German Nuclear Dilemma*, 44–5.

16 Schwartz, NATO's *Nuclear Dilemmas*, 189.

17 Further, it was argued that the treaty would place the five nuclear states on a higher pedestal in international relations. Kelleher, "Issue."

18 Joffe, "Europe's American Pacifier." This was also somewhat consistent with NATO's "double track approach" to the USSR, which became official policy in 1967. This policy called for joint defensive efforts to deter Soviet invasion, while promising assured security through mutually agreed on treaties and economic cooperation. Schmidt, *A Grand Strategy*, 11–12.

19 Cited in Mendershausen, "Will West Germany?" 416.

20 Boutwell, *The German Nuclear Dilemma*, 45.

21 Kelleher, "Issue," 103; Boutwell, *The German Nuclear Dilemma*, 45–6.

22 Thomas Enders et. al., "The New Germany," 134.

23 Boutwell, *The German Nuclear Dilemma*, 10–11.

24 Ibid., 230.

25 Mattox, "West German Perspectives."

26 Kelleher, "The New Germany," 21; *New York Times*, 18 July 1990, A6.

27 *New York Times*, 13 Sept. 1990, A1 and A6; Linnenkamp, "Security Policy," 98.

28 For example, see Mearsheimer, "Back to the Future."

29 *Strategic Survey 1998–99* (London: International Institute for Strategic Studies, 1999), 102–3.

30 This view is also shared by a revisionist account of Germany's nuclear policy. See Kuntzel, *Bonn*.

31 The nuclear weapons deployed in West Germany included atomic mines; artillery pieces; Lance, Honest John, Nike Hercules, and Pershing missiles; and fighter-bombers carrying nuclear weapons. Bracken, *Command*, 139–55.

32 Joffe, "Europe's American Pacifier"; Art, "Why."

33 On the dual-control mechanism, see Bracken, *Command*, 139.

34 For this peculiarly German dilemma, see Bertram, "European Security."

35 Bielfeldt, "Détente."

36 Kelleher, "Issue," 96.

37 In several interviews that I conducted in Germany in December 1994, German scholars and officials reiterated this factor as critical to the nonnuclear policy. According to scholar Harald Mueller, Germany's nonnuclear policy has been part of its effort to show its neighbours that it will not acquire an independent power projection capability. Interviews by the author, Bonn, Frankfurt, and Berlin, 4–6 Dec. 1994.

38 Calleo, *German Problem*, 2.

39 Sensitivity to external opposition was reflected in the strong public opposition to West German nuclear acquisition in the 1950s and 1960s. In April 1957, eighteen prominent physicists made the "Gottingen Appeal," in which they urged their government to "promote world peace by renouncing explicitly and voluntarily the possession of atomic weapons of any kind." *Bulletin of the Atomic Scientists*, no. 13 (1957): 228.

Mass protests followed up on the scientists' initiative, with peace movements taking a leading role. Boutwell, "Politics." A poll between 1963 and 1965 found that only 5 per cent of the elite called their country a desirable possessor of nuclear arms; 84 per cent also believed that nuclear capability was not necessary for national prestige. Deutsch, *Arms Control*, 52.

40 Kelleher, *Germany*, 304–5.

41 Mendershausen, "Will West Germany?" 417; author's interview with Eckhard Lubkemeir, Bonn, 8 Dec. 1994.

42 Daalder, Kosminsky, and Garnham, "Correspondences"; Geipel, "Nature," 20.

43 Risse-Kappen, "Deja vu."

44 Schmidt, *Deterrence*, 169.

45 Rise-Kappen, "Deja vu," 333.

46 Calleo, *German Problem*, 165–6. Germany's foreign policy, according to one scholar, reflects a "culture of restraint" and is due to the "institutionalization of power" in Germany and Europe, away from hard elements of power, under which Germany has been willing to pool sovereignty, especially with smaller European states. See Katzenstein, "Tamed Power."

47 Gutjahr, "Stability."

48 On these debates, see Langdon, "Security Debate."

49 Kahn, *Emerging*, 13; Brzezinski, *Fragile*, 108–9.

50 Pyle, *The Japanese Question*, 20. Prime Minister Shigeru Yoshida shaped the doctrine during negotiations with u.s. Secretary of State John Foster Dulles. The three main tenets of the doctrine were economic rehabilitation based on politico-economic co-operation with the United States; a security policy based on lightly armed defensive forces and avoidance of involvement in international disputes; and a long-term security policy through providing base facilities to the u.s. armed forces. Dower, *Empire*, 373–400.

51 From the period following the Meiji Restoration (1874–90) till 1945, the Japanese elite pursued a "rich nation, strong army" policy, which brought great destruction to the nation, but "after 1945, their successors reinvented national security through a program of commercial techno-nationalism, a program called 'rich nation, strong technology." Samuels, "Rich Nation, Strong Army," 319.

52 For these conceptions, see Pyle, *The Japanese Question*, 32–9.

53 Opposition parties criticized this over-reliance on the u.s. nuclear guarantee. They feared that Japan would inadvertently participate in the u.s. global nuclear strategy. Kendell, *Politics*, 44.

54 Ibid., 45.

55 Murata, "Japan"; Okimoto, "Japan's Non-Nuclear Policy"; Quester, "Japan."

56 Yeager, "Japan," 27.

57 "Japanese Defense Policy," *Survival*, 18 no. 1 (1971): 2–8.

58 Endicott, *Japan's Nuclear Option*, 42–3.

59 *New York Times*, 15 Oct., A9.

60 Pempel, "Japan's Nuclear Allergy."

61 Mochizyki, "Japan's Search," 157.

62 Ibid.

63 For the initial Japanese wavering on the permanent extension of the treaty, see Smith, "Japan," 24.

64 George, "Japan's Participation."

65 "Thinking the Unthinkable," 38.

66 "Japan May 'Go Nuclear,' Paper Says," *Japan Times*, 11 Aug. 1993, 4.

67 Sam Jameson, "Official Says Japan Will Need Nuclear Arms if N. Korea Threatens," *Los Angeles Times*, 29 July 1993, A4.

68 Japan, however, has stepped up its efforts to acquire an anti-missile defence system. "An American Shield for Asia," *Economist*, 20 Feb. 1999, 37. Less than a month after the North Korean launch, Japan decided to spend $8 million on a joint TMD research program with the United States. This program is expected to last six years and will cost Japan over $250 million. *Strategic Survey 1998/99* (London: International Institute for Strategic Studies, 1999), 46.

69 For a culturalist explanation, see Berger, "From Swords to Chrysanthemum" and *Cultures*. Similarly, Peter Katzenstein and Nobuo Okawara argue that the domestic structure and the normative context of contested goals in military security constrain Japan from going nuclear. "Japan's National Security."

70 Leading Japanese scholars whom I have interviewed believe that this is an extremely potent factor for Japan's restraint. Author's interviews, Tokyo, July 1994. In August 1994, Foreign Minister Kono stated that the nuclear option would not benefit Japan at all, as it would heighten tensions with neighbouring countries and the United States. Quoted in Matake Kamiya, "Will Japan?" 9.

71 "Japan is almost a demonstration case for those who argue that economic interdependence raises the costs and reduces the incentives of the resort to force." Buzan, "Japan's Future."

72 Okita, "Natural Resource Dependency"; Dougherty, "Nuclear Proliferation."

73 Mochizyki, "Japan's Search," 153.

74 Cited in Harrison, "Japan," 8.

75 Kishida, "Japan's Non-nuclear Policy," 16. According to Shinichi Ogawa of Tokyo's National Institute for Defense Studies, Japan's neighbours will treat a Japanese nuclear capability as offensive, even if Japan declares its defensive intentions. Interview with the author, Tokyo, 19 July 1994.

76 Harrison, "Japan," 3–4. For South Korean concerns, see Kim, "Japanese Ambitions."

77 For the importance of the U.S. relationship, see Kendell, *Politics*, 8.

78 *Far Eastern Economic Review*, 9 Oct. 1997, 24–5, 26 June 1997, 16–17. The Diet passed the defence guidelines bill in April 1999, allowing Japan for the first time to co-operate with the United States in defending itself against a direct attack and against military provocations in surrounding areas. *Financial Times*, 30 April 1999, 1.

79 Ha and Guinasso, "Japan's Rearmament Dilemma."

80 Curtis, "Japanese Security Policies."

81 Emmerson and Humphreys, *Will Japan Rearm?*, 88.

82 Yatsuhiro, "Why Japan," 101 and 104. Moreover, 40 per cent of Japan's people live in three urban areas, and so three big warheads can destroy a major portion of the population. Author's interview with Seizabro Sato, Tokyo, 18 July 1994.

83 Wakaizumi, "Problem," 84.

84 Yamamoto, "Japan's Future," 4.

85 Wakaizumi, "Problem," 78–9.

86 For perspectives that highlight institutional norms in Japanese security policy, see Katzenstein, *Culture*; Berger, "Norms," 317–21.

87 Wakaizumi, "Problem," 77–8.

88 Kendell, *Politics*, 23.

89 Sakanaka, "Defects," 50.

90 Izumi, "Japan."

91 Passin, "Nuclear Arms," 81 and 98.

92 Garnham, "Extending Deterrence."

93 Waltz, "Emerging"; Layne, "Unipolar."

94 Le Gloannec, "Implications," 264.

95 "By the 1980s, primary products accounted for less than three tenths of West German imports, imports of finished goods having gone up sixfold since 1950 ... Economic value attaches less to territory and resources and more to production processes, and more visibly to the order that permits those processes to be transferred." Treverton, *America*, 162.

96 Ibid., 165.

97 Ullman, *Securing*, 33.

98 Roger Cohen, "A Bigger Military Role for Germany," *International Herald Tribune*, 15 June 1999, 1. Over 4,200 German soldiers participated in the Kosovo operations. The air war, which lasted eleven weeks, was the first time German troops were engaged in combat since World war II. CNN *Webpage*, 13 July 1999, 1.

99 For a survey of German leaders on the possible scenarios under which Germany could acquire nuclear weapons, see Yost, "The U.S. and Nuclear Deterrence."

100 On the choices that Japan faces in the twenty-first century, see Pempel, "Japan's Changing Political Economy."

101 Nakamura and Dando, "Japan's Military Research."

102 Japanese public opinion polls in the 1980s placed China behind the United States as the most possible countries likely to attack Japan. See polls conducted by the *Asahi Shimbun*, quoted in *Japan Quarterly*, 29 no. 2 (1982):197–9.

103 Buzan, "Japan's Future," 572.

104 Moltz, "Missile Proliferation."

105 Kristof, "Rise of China." However, despite its high rate of economic growth, China's military capability, especially in technology, is not superior or equal to the American or Russian. China's small nuclear force consists of 150 warheads, deliverable by less sophisticated aircraft and missiles. Godwin and Schulz, "Arming."

CHAPTER FOUR

1 For the alliance dilemma, see Glenn H. Snyder, "The Security Dilemma."

2 Edwards, "Canada's Nuclear Industry," 123.

3 Richter, "Canadian Defence Policy," 6.

4 Munro and Inglis, "The Atomic Conference," 94–7.

5 Quoted in Legault and Fortmann, *Diplomacy*, 78.

6 Quoted in ibid., 79.

7 Ritcher, "Canadian Defence Policy," 9; see also Legault and Fortmann, *Diplomacy*, 78.

8 Edwards, "Canada's Nuclear Industry," 125–6.

9 Langille, *Changing the Guard*, 13.

10 McLin, *Canada's Changing Defence Policy*, 13.

11 Ibid., 130–3.

12 Regehr, "Canada," 107–8; McLin, *Canada's Changing Defence Policy*, 123.

13 Regehr, "Canada," 108.

14 Middlemiss and Sokolsky, *Canadian Defence*, 26–7. Notably, during this time, Canada was a permanent member of the UN Atomic Energy Commission and a member of the Commission for Conventional Armaments, the Disarmament Commission, and the Eighteen-Nation Disarmament Committee. It was the only non-great power to hold so many memberships. McLin, *Canada's Changing Defence Policy*, 147–8.

15 McLin, *Canada's Changing Defence Policy*, 136. To questions at the Progressive Conservative Party convention as to why Canada was dragging its feet on acquiring nuclear weapons, Green responded that acquiring nuclear warheads was not like buying "a better field gun or a better

rifle" and that "if Canada obtained nuclear warheads, there was no reason why 15 or 20 more nations should not do the same." "Green Hints A-Arms Objection," *Montreal Star*, 18 March 1961, 1.

16 Warnock, *Partner*, 185.

17 McLin, *Canada's Changing Defence Policy*, 143–4.

18 At a meeting with Harkness in October 1960, Diefenbaker argued that although Canada should acquire nuclear weapons, it need not do so immediately, as it would embarrass Green's efforts in disarmament. See "Harkness Papers," *Ottawa Citizen*, 23 Oct. 1977, 77.

19 Warnock, *Partner*, 175.

20 Ibid., 197.

21 Middlemiss and Sokolsky, *Canadian Defence*, 27. Regehr, "Canada," 109; Warnock, *Partner*, 196.

22 Gordon, "The Liberal Leadership," 201. For Pearson's role in the nuclear decisions, see Lentner, "Foreign Policy."

23 Gordon, "The Liberal Leadership," 200.

24 Warnock, *Partner*, 192.

25 Clearwater, *Canadian Nuclear Weapons*, 31. Although Canadian and U.S. negotiators established a framework through which the prime minister and the American president would consult each other prior to the use of the weapons, Pearson signed a memorandum agreeing to the latter's releasing the weapons in exceptional circumstances when such consultations were not feasible because of time limitations. Ibid., 44.

26 Thordarson, *Trudeau*, 75.

27 Regehr, "Canada," 110.

28 Middlemiss and Sokolsky, *Canadian Defence*, 31–4.

29 Paul Buteux, "NATO," 163. Through this act, the Trudeau government "sought to enhance its nuclear free-image by formally dissociating the Canadian armed forces from roles that involved nuclear weapons." Keating, *Canada*, 163.

30 Keating, *Canada*, 175; Langille, *Changing*, 38 and 59.

31 Middlemiss and Sokolsky, *Canadian Defence*, 119–20.

32 Barrett and Ross, "Air-Launched."

33 "Government Response to the Recommendations of the Standing Committee on Foreign Affairs and International Trade on Canada's Nuclear Disarmament and Nonproliferation Policy," Ottawa: April 1999.

34 *Gazette* (Montreal), 26 April 1999, A13.

35 Tucker, *Canadian Foreign Policy*, 7.

36 Warnock, *Partner*, 138.

37 Eayrs, "Canada," 77.

38 Buteux, "NATO," 157.

39 Barrett, "Canada," 341.

40 Munton, "Going Fission," 521.

41 Ross, "Arms Control," 252.

42 Ibid., 262 and 264–5.

43 Eayrs, "Canada," 82. John E. Mueller, "Incentives."

44 Ross, "Arms Control," 267. According to critics, Canada has often pursued "narrower, self-interested policies" in its export of the reactors. It has been argued that Canada has "frequently stretched its own environmental laws to the limit in waiving restrictions on these exports to countries with questionable environmental safety records and capabilities." Bratt, "CANDU," 1.

45 Burns, "Australia," 144. Although there was no indication that Britain transferred any weapons technology to Australia, it is reasonable to assume that a serious request from Canberra would have been heard positively in London.

46 It was estimated that Australia held about 21 per cent of the non-Communist world's known recoverable uranium reserves. Camilleri, "Nuclear Controversy," 40.

47 Reynolds, "Rethinking."

48 Baxter's Memorandum to Defense Committee on Plutonium Production in Australia, Defence Committee, *Nuclear Weapons for the Australian Forces*, Series No. A571/662, Item No. 1958/677, Australian Archives, Canberra, 16 Jan. 1958.

49 *Canberra Times*, 14 Aug. 1975.

50 This project was subsequently cancelled.

51 Gelber, "Australia."

52 Ibid., 113–14.

53 For a discussion of these efforts, see Walsh, "Surprise."

54 File No. 680/10, Part I, Series No. A1838/269, *Australian Nuclear Capability* (Canberra: National Archives.)

55 Minutes of Defence Committee Meetings of 8 Nov. 1956, Series No. A 571/162, Item No. 1958/677, Defence Committee, *Nuclear Weapons for the Australian Forces.*

56 Cited in *History of Australian Policy towards the Acquisition of Nuclear Weapons Capability*, Series A 1209/80, Item 65/6470 (Canberra: Australian National Archives).

57 *Australian Nuclear Capability.*

58 Walsh, "Surprise," 5–7.

59 Australian Archives, A5818/2, Robert Menzies to the Cabinet, Nuclear Tests Conference: Control Posts in Australia, Submission No. 1156, V6, P/3, cited in Walsh, "Surprise," 8.

60 Leaver, "Hayden's 'Mailed Fist,'" 40.

61 Bellany, *Australia*, 61–86; "The Strategic Basis Papers," *National Times*, 30 March, 5 April 1984, 23–30.

62 Burns, "Australia," 146–7.

63 Defence Department, Joint Planning Committee Study, JPC Report 8/ 1968, *An Independent Australian Nuclear Capability – Strategic Considerations* (Canberra: Department of Foreign Affairs, Historical Division).

64 *Draft Cabinet Submission on the Treaty for the Non-Proliferation of Nuclear Weapons*, File No. 919/10/5, 5 April 1968, Canberra: Department of Foreign Affairs, Historical Division.

65 Geoffrey Hutton, "Nuclear Pact's Odd Man Out," *Age*, 13 Feb. 1970, 7.

66 For these developments, see Walsh, "Surprise," 13.

67 Pugh, *ANZUS*, 36.

68 Cited in ibid., 151.

69 Alley, "Evolution," 40–1.

70 According to Foreign Minister Bill Hayden, Hawke's moves were driven largely by domestic political concerns. With Ronald Reagan's nuclear rhetoric gaining full steam in the United States, peace and disarmament became hot issues in Australian politics, especially that nation's support for the U.S. nuclear efforts through joint facilities on its own territory. These included the naval communication station at North West Cape, the Joint Defence Space Research project at Pine Gap near Alice Springs, and the Nurrungar defence space communication centre near Woomera. It was feared that if a war broke out between the superpowers, Australia would be one of the first targets of a Soviet missile attack. The Labor Party feared that its popular support would decline if it did not pre-empt the demands of left-leaning groups for Australia's declaring neutrality. The Nuclear Disarmament Party especially appeared to gain votes from traditional Labor groups. Hayden, *Hayden*, 392.

71 For these policies, see Paul, "Politics," 165.

72 The ministers agreed with him at that time, but no subsequent action was taken. Hayden, *Hayden*, 422–3. See also Leaver, "Hayden's 'Mailed Fist,'" 40–3.

73 The treaty has been called a very weak instrument, as it allows transit of nuclear weapons and continuation of nuclear bases in the region. Paul, "Nuclear-Free Zone."

74 Pugh, *ANZUS*, 1. The legislation followed a bitter dispute with the United States over the visit in February 1985 of the nuclear-capable destroyer USS *Buchanan* and the new Labor government's adamant opposition to such visits unless the United States disclosed whether nuclear weapons were on board or not. For New Zealand's initiatives, see Paul, "Politics."

75 Pugh, *ANZUS*, 3 and 38.

76 See Snyder, "Australia's Pursuit."

77 In this respect, ANZUS is weaker than NATO, as members do not inevitably view an attack on another member as an attack on themselves. See, for the provisions of the treaty, Alley, "Evolution."

78 Walsh, "Surprise,"14.

79 Frank Cranston, "Nuclear Arms against Our Best Interests," *Canberra Times*, 11 Aug. 1975, 3.

80 Gelber, "Australia," 114–15; Bellany, *Australia*, 81.

81 Submission for Cabinet, "Nuclear Non Proliferation Treaty," by Paul Hasluck, Minister for External Affairs and Allen Fairhall, Minister for Defence, No. 25, 22 March 1968, National Archives, Canberra.

82 Bellany, *Australia*, 81.

83 Comments on A.H. Tange's Memorandum by E.H. Bunting, Acting Secretary, Prime Minister's Department, 7 Feb. 1958. Tange, secretary in the Department of External Affairs, had argued that Australia would need nuclear weapons because of the possibility of the United States and United Kingdom failing Australia. Series No. A5954, Item No. 1400, National Archives, Canberra.

84 Bellany, *Australia*, 81 and 96.

85 Cited in Pugh, *ANZUS*; Joint Committee on Foreign Affairs and Defence, *The Australian Defence Force: Its Structure and Capabilities* (Canberra, 1984), xiv; *Disarmament and Arms Control in the Nuclear Age* (Canberra, 1986), 654.

86 Chakravorty, *Australia's Military Alliances*, 129–31.

87 He also mentioned the advantages of having few nuclear states. Additionally, a major war in South East Asia could not be fought with nuclear weapons. British and U.S. alliance support was also implicit in his assessments. Bellany, *Australia*, 81.

88 Ibid., 82–6.

89 Gelber, "Australia," 114–15.

90 *Report on the Canberra Commission on the Elimination of Nuclear Weapons* (Canberra: Department of Foreign Affairs and Trade, 1996).

CHAPTER FIVE

1 For instance, Beaton had argued that neutral states could not rely on the nuclear weapons of friendly countries, as it would be tantamount to abandoning neutrality. Beaton, *Must the Bomb Spread?*, 62.

2 Karsh, *Neutrality*, 174.

3 Ibid., 180–1.

4 Steve Coll, "Neutral Sweden Quietly Keeps Nuclear Option Open," *Washington Post*, 25 Nov. 1994, 1 and A-42. There is disagreement as to whether the laboratory-type experiments were meant for producing a weapons capability. According to the director of this program, Swedish research activities had been confined to materials relative to nuclear accidents, radio biology, and radio ecology. The Agesta reactor was decommissioned in 1974, and its fuel has been stored under IAEA safeguards.

The FOA was interested in nuclear weapons physics, not in acquiring the technology for purposes of protecting Sweden against advertent or inadvertent nuclear detonations, and in gaining expertise in pursuing arms control. Tor Larson, interview with the author, Stockholm, 4 July 1995. See also FOA *Statement* (Stockholm, 16 Jan. 1995).

5 Abrahamson, "Governments." In 1998, Sweden operated twelve nuclear reactors, wuich generated over 45 per cent of its electricity. IAEA *Bulletin*, 41 no. 1 (1999): 50.

6 Logue, "Sweden," 89; Agrell, "Behind the Submarine Crisis."

7 Wallin, "Sweden," in Karp, ed., *Security*, 361.

8 Logue, "Sweden," 71.

9 This was especially the case after the Swedish proposal of May 1948 for a Scandinavian defence pact involving Norway and Denmark did not materialize. See Haskel, *The Scandinavian Option*, on why the proposal failed.

10 Thunborg, *Evolution*, 48 and 51.

11 Agrell, "The Bomb," 157; Hagelin, "Margins."

12 For the Swedish energy program, see Jasper, *Nuclear Politics*.

13 For these developments, see Wallin, "Sweden," 360–5.

14 Agrell, "The Bomb," 154 and 159.

15 Karsh, *Neutrality*, 175.

16 Garris, "Sweden's Debate," 191.

17 Nils Gilden, correspondence with the author, Stockholm, 15 Aug. 1995.

18 Birnbaum, "The Swedish Experience," 68.

19 Logue, "Legacy." 55; Prawitz, "Sweden," 62.

20 Jasper, *Nuclear Politics*, 67; Karsh, *Neutrality*, 177.

21 Prawitz, "Sweden," 62.

22 Karsh, *Neutrality*, 177–8.

23 Wallin, "Sweden," 365–6.

24 Karsh, *Neutrality*, 178.

25 Quoted in Garris, "Sweden's Debate," 192.

26 Lars Wallin, interview with the author, Stockholm, 4 July 1995. The Swedish strategists doubted that a small country could achieve a nuclear deterrent capability without inviting the possibility of a pre-emptive strike and without diverting large sums from conventional defence. Goran Franzen, interview with the author, Stockholm, 5 July 1995.

27 During the 1970s, Sweden launched a massive civilian energy program. It was an active promoter of nuclear reactors, and nuclear energy contributed about 50 per cent of its energy. But by the end of the decade, its approach began to change. Opposition to nuclear energy culminated in the 1980 referendum, which called for phasing out of reactors by 2010. Sahr, *Politics*, 1 and 20; Jasper, *Nuclear Politics*, 218. Yet growing demand for energy and Sweden's economic difficulties in the 1990s, may preclude meeting of the target by 2010.

28 On this, see Ingebritsen, "Redefining National Security."

29 Cole, "Atomic Bombast," 1. See also Cole, *Sweden.*

30 Karsh, *Neutrality,* 181–3.

31 Cited in Wallin, "Sweden," 377.

32 Prawitz, "Sweden," 65.

33 Kruzel, "Sweden's Security Dilemma," 73. See also Prawitz, "Why."

34 Prawitz, "Sweden," 64.

35 Hagelin, "Margins," 211; Goran Franzen, interview with the author, 5 July 1995.

36 Roberts, *Nations,* 77 and 92.

37 Logue, "Sweden," 72.

38 Ibid., 89. The Swedes also championed the idea of a Nordic identity based on mutual co-operation, peaceful internal and external behaviour, creation and maintenance of egalitarian societies, solidarity with the developing world, hospitality to refugees and immigrants, and strong support for environmentalism. However, with the end of the Cold War, Sweden joined the European Union, thereby weakening the concept of a Nordic identity. Mouritzen, "The Nordic Model."

39 Wallin, "Sweden," 379. The NPT and the Partial Test Ban Treaty (PTBT) played a limited role in the Swedish case. The NPT especially formalized the Swedish non-nuclear position. It facilitated and quickened a decision against nuclear acquisition, even though Sweden was moving in that direction by the time the treaty came into being. Andren, "Sweden's Security Policy," 139.

40 Quoted in Wallin, "Sweden," 377.

41 Cole, "Atomic Bombast," 8–9.

42 Quester, "Sweden," 56.

43 Schwab, "Switzerland's," 901.

44 For the Swiss energy program, see Pellaud, *Geschichte.* In 1998, Switzerland operated five nuclear reactors, producing over 40 per cent of the country's electricity. *IAEA Bulletin,* 41 no. 1 (March 1999): 50.

45 Jim McGee, "Swiss Bankers Sustained Nazis, U.S. Report Says," *Washington Post,* 8 May 1997, A1.

46 Milivojevic, "The Swiss Armed Forces," 6–7.

47 de Weck and Maurer, "Swiss," 69; Zumstein, "Swiss."

48 Carrel, "Switzerland."

49 Milivojevic, "The Swiss Armed Forces," 12.

50 Pellaud, *Geschichte,* 233. Also Pellaud, interview with the author, Vienna, Dec. 1994.

51 "Why the Swiss Military Wanted the Atomic Bomb," *Tagesanzeiger,* 4 April 1995, 1–3.

52 Cited in Schwab, "Switzerland's," 902–3.

53 Winkler, *Kernenergy,* 153.

54 Theodor H. Winkler, interview with the author, Bern, 9 July 1995.
55 Cited in Schwab, "Switzerland's," 904.
56 Winkler, *Kernenergy*, 160–1.
57 "Why the Swiss Military."
58 Beaton and Maddox, *The Spread*, 162–3.
59 Michel, *La prolifération*, 44.
60 For these developments, see "Why the Swiss Military."
61 Schwab, "Switzerland's," 907.
62 "Why the Swiss Military," 3.
63 Schwab, "Switzerland's," 903–4. A majority of the electorate believed that if acquiring nuclear arms was the only way to stay independent, Switzerland should do so. Gustav Daniker, correspondence with the author, Zurich, 14 Aug. 1995.
64 "Why the Swiss Military," 1 and 3.
65 Schwab, "Switzerland's," 912.
66 Ibid., 913; Michael, *La prolifération*, 88.
67 Winkler, *Kernenergy*, 187.
68 Tanner, "Switzerland," 139. As all other industrialized nations were signing and ratifying the treaty, Switzerland feared that if it did not do so, it "would look like a proliferator." Alec Jean Baer, interview with the author, Bern, 10 July 1995.
69 de Weck and Maurer, "Swiss," 75.
70 Mumenthaler, "Civil Defense," 52; de Weck and Maurer, "Swiss," 70.
71 Winkler, *Kernenergy*, 189.
72 Ibid., 167; Winkler, interview with the author.

CHAPTER SIX

1 By the late 1980s, both countries had developed technical capabilities for the complete nuclear fuel cycle. While Brazil had achieved enrichment capabilities through the centrifuge process, Argentina had developed it through the gaseous-diffusion method. Argentina also had acquired plutonium-reprocessing and heavy-water production capabilities.
2 However, difficulties in gaining access to technology and materials from nuclear supplier states may have indirectly influenced their choices. But this factor alone cannot be attributed to the change in the civilian regimes' views on nuclear weapons. Suppliers had been pressing these countries since the 1970s, but policies changed only in the 1990s. Argentine foreign officials confirmed that there was no direct U.S. pressure on the Menem government to transform nuclear policy. Author's interviews, Buenos Aires, Feb. 1996.
3 According to Dan Benison, president of the Argentine nuclear regulatory authority, the NPT had no effect on the Argentine decision. Buenos

Aires had already signed a broad comprehensive safeguard agreement with ABACC and the IAEA before joining the NPT. Signing the NPT was a symbolic act, part of a larger process of denuclearization undertaken by the Argentine and Brazilian governments. Interview with the author, Buenos Aires, 20 Feb. 1996.

4 Solingen, "Political Economy."

5 Redick, Carasales, and Wrobel, "Nuclear Rapprochement," 110.

6 During the 1960s Brazil improved its defence capabilities vis-à-vis Argentina, while formally maintaining cordial relations, especially in the economic realm. Expanding its ties with the United States and neighbouring countries, such as Bolivia and Paraguay, was part of this strategy. Hilton, "The Argentine Factor," 36. Much of the hostility involved "posturing" and "grandstanding," in the absence of any overt conflict. Castrioto de Azambuja, "Nuclear Non-Proliferation," 126.

7 Cited in Hilton, "The Argentine Factor," 34.

8 Myers, "Brazil," 60.

9 Ibid., 62.

10 According to a Brazilian journalist who specializes in nuclear matters, the civilian leaders also wanted to rein in the military. Without a bilateral approach, Brazil's nationalistic military would have vigorously opposed surrender of the nuclear option. Tania Malheiros, interview with the author, Rio de Janeiro, 23 Feb. 1996.

11 Feu Alvim, "Common System," 1.

12 For a text of the declaration, see *Arms Control Today*, 24 no. 2 (1994): 11.

13 For the text of this agreement, see *International Atomic Energy Agency Document*, INFCIRC/395, (Vienna, 26 Nov. 1991).

14 *ABACC News* (Jan.–April 1996): 2.

15 In 1996 alone, the two countries sent 541 accounting reports, and the agency's inspectors were fully satisfied with their compliance with their non-proliferation pledges. *ABACC Annual Report 1996* (Rio de Janeiro, 1997).

16 Goldemberg and Feiveson, "Denuclearization," 11. The agreement also fulfils the safeguards requirements of the OPANAL, the administering agency for the Treaty of Tlateloco.

17 Argentina is estimated to possess over 23,000 tonnes of high-quality uranium concentrate. Redick, "Regional Restraint."

18 Argentina had a "brilliant past" to live up to. In the 1950s, nuclear energy seemed to be the new "coinage for the future discourse of global power politics." Gamba-Stonehouse, "Argentina and Brazil," 233.

19 Adler, *Power*, 281.

20 Milenky, "Argentina," 28 and 47. Peronist ideology saw acquisition of high technology as crucial to national power, pride, and defence. Raul Pelaez, interview with the author, Buenos Aires, 19 Feb. 1996.

21 Gamba-Stonehouse, "Argentina and Brazil," 234.

22 Selcher, "Brazilian–Argentine Relations," 28.

23 Milenky, "Arms Production," 269.

24 Poneman, "Nuclear Proliferation."

25 IAEA Bulletin, 41 no. 1 (1999): 50.

26 Albright, "Bomb Potential," 17.

27 Redick, Carasales, and Wrobel, "Nuclear Rapprochement," 108–9.

28 Edward Schumacher, "Argentina Claims Nuclear Capacity," New York Times, 19 Nov. 1983, 1 and 4.

29 Sanchez-Gijon, "Argentina," 384.

30 Ibid.

31 While announcing that Argentina had acquired enrichment capability, Madero repeated his previous statements that it had no intention of developing nuclear weapons. Schumacher, "Argentina," 1.

32 Selcher, "Brazilian–Argentine Relations," 30; Abraham, "Pakistan–India," 11. Defeat in the war finished the military's notions of national and regional power. Pelaez, interview with the author.

33 Selcher, "Brazilian–Argentine Relations," 32.

34 Hilton, "The Argentine Factor," 57. See also Gamba-Stonehouse, "Argentina and Brazil," 248–9.

35 Solingen, "Macropolitical Consensus"; Adler, Power, 317.

36 IAEA Bulletin, 41 no. 1 (1999): 50.

37 Myers, "Brazil: Reluctant Pursuit," 891. See also Barletta, "Military."

38 Brazil's achievements in this realm included the Sonda series of sounding rockets, developed with American assistance. In 1979, it set up the Brazilian Complete Space Mission (MECB) to design and develop indigenous satellites. The Brazilian Commission for Space Activities (COBAE) was headed by the chief of the armed forces, suggesting a military direction. The military was interested in matching the Argentine Condor missile program, and by the mid-1980s Brazilian firms Orbita and Avibras were developing ballistic missiles based on the Sonda rocket technology. Bowen, "Brazil's Accession."

39 Schneider, Brazil, 91.

40 Grabendorff, "Brazil," 324 and 335; Rosenbaum and Cooper, "Brazil," 80–1. Also a concern was that adherence to the NPT would prevent peaceful nuclear explosions (PNEs). Goldemberg and Feiveson, "Denuclearizations," 12.

41 Gall, "Atoms"; Wonder, "Nuclear Commerce."

42 Gall, "Atoms," 158.

43 Redick, Carasales, and Wrobel, "Nuclear Rapprochement," 108.

44 Albright, "Bomb Potential," 18.

45 Interview with the author, Brasilia, 22 Feb. 1996.

46 Grabendorff, "Brazil," 336–9.

47 James Brooke, "Brazil Uncovers Plan by Military to Build Atom Bomb and Stops It," *New York Times*, 9 Oct. 1990, A1 and A4.

48 *Agencia Estado*, 13 July 1998, cited in *Nonproliferation Review*, 6 no. 2 (1999): 165.

49 During its nearly 500 years, "Brazil has experienced few major military conflicts, and in the last 130 has suffered virtually no foreign aggression." Fujita, "Brazilian Policy," 577.

50 Quoted in Grabendorff, "Brazil," 348–9

51 Ibid., 352–3; see also Katzman, "Translating." On Brazil's economic strategy, see Frieden, *Debt*, chap. 4.

52 On 29 October 1962, Brazil introduced at the United Nations a draft resolution on creating a nuclear free-zone in Latin America. After the military regime came into power in 1964, it began to lose interest in the proposal. Even when it formally signed the Tlateloco Treaty in 1967, it added a note re-emphasizing its right to conduct PNEs. Narayanan, "Brazil's Policy." See also Redick, Carasales, and Wrobel, "Nuclear Rapprochement," 111.

53 Gardendorff, "Brazil," 351.

54 Selcher, "Brazilian–Argentine Relations," 30–1.

55 Jose dos Santos, interview with the author. The Brazilian navy is continuing its nuclear-powered submarine program. IAEA inspectors monitor nuclear activities under this program. Brazil sees the submarines as essential to patrolling its 9,000 kilometres of coastline. Moreover, the IAEA considers propulsion a peaceful nuclear activity. Laercio Vinhas, interview with the author, Rio de Janeiro, 23 Feb. 1997.

56 According to Holsti, the region stands as an anomaly for its near-absence of interstate warfare. *The State*, 154.

57 Perruci, "Latin America," 200; Castrioto de Azambuja, "Nuclear Non-Proliferation," 127. The Mercosur South American common market, created in March 1991, linked Argentina, Brazil, Paraguay, and Uruguay.

CHAPTER SEVEN

1 South Africa had had a fairly extensive nuclear energy program. In 1949 it set up the South African Atomic Energy Board, later renamed the Atomic Energy Corporation (AEC). It mined uranium early on and opened the first uranium plant in 1952 at Krugersdrop. The nuclear reactor SAFARI I (20 mW) opened at Pelindaba in 1965. Two French-supplied 900-mW reactors – Koeberg I and Koeberg II – became operational in 1984 and 1985, respectively. These three reactors have been under IAEA safeguards.

2 On South Africa's enrichment program, see Stumpf, "South Africa's," 65.

3 *Star* (Johannesburg), 19 March 1993, 3; *Weekly Mail*, 23–27 Dec. 1992, 3.

4 Davis and Donnelly, "South Africa's Nuclear Status," 1.

5 Reiss, *Bridled Ambition*, 9.

6 Albright, "South Africa," 40–2. The ultra-secret program employed about 1,000 personnel and cost an estimated U.S.$250 million concealed in the budgets of agencies dealing with atomic energy development and the military. *New York Times*, 25 March 1993, A1 and A12.

7 South Africa in 1974 began construction of a nuclear test site in the Kalahari desert, and by 1977 it had built three test shafts and was ready for a nuclear test. In July 1977, a Soviet spy satellite spotted the site and warned Western states of an imminent nuclear test. The U.S. and other Western governments warned Pretoria of severe repercussions, and in response it closed the site. Reiss, *Bridled Ambition*, 10.

8 Stumpf, "South Africa's," 71; Waldo Stumpf, interview with the author, Pelindaba, 1 Dec. 1994. The gun-type designs followed the U.S. Hiroshima-style weapon, and each weighed a ton. Reiss, *Bridled Ambition*, 12.

9 According to Stumpf, the leadership viewed nuclear weapons as a "political asset" intended to take away the security threat posed by neighbours. Stumpf, interview with the author.

10 For this strategy, see Albright, "South Africa," 38; Stumpf, "South Africa's," 69; Marie Muller, "South Africa."

11 Howlett and Simpson, "Nuclearisation," 158.

12 Ibid., 154. South Africa's obsession with the Soviet threat was exaggerated. Soviet activity in Southern Africa was confined to providing material support to the Angolan government and to Joshua N'Komo's Matabele warriors in the former Rhodesia. There appeared to be no reason for the Soviets to send troops directly to Southern Africa. Fischer, "Reversing," 277–8.

13 Howlett and Simpson, "Nuclearisation," 155–6. See also Flournoy and Campbell, "South Africa's Bomb," 395.

14 For the democratic transition, see Sisk, *Democratization*.

15 Albright, "South Africa," 46.

16 The white regime also was reportedly anxious to deny nuclear capability to the incoming Black rulers. Yet it is not clear that the ANC would have changed its anti-nuclear policy once it gained power. In fact, the ANC, barring some fringe groups, unequivocally opposed reintroduction of nuclear weapons. As testimony to its non-nuclear credentials, the ANC-led government strongly supported the OAU-sponsored treaty to declare Africa a nuclear-free zone. Albright, "South Africa," 47. One analyst believes that De Klerk realized that once it came to power the ANC would reveal the program, making his National Party look bad. Garth Shelton, interview with the author, Johannesburg, 28 Nov. 1994.

17 Reiss, *Bridled Ambition*, 17–19.

18 Fear of public inspections and political turmoil were two of the stated reasons for this delay of almost two years. The announcement was the result of press leaks, following the IAEA inspection team's discovery of activities related to nuclear weapons and the ANC's efforts to uncover the bomb program. Albright, "South Africa," 38–9. According to Stumpf, the announcement was delayed partly because of fear that the world media would not pay adequate attention to the decision because of the continuing crisis over Iraqi nuclear weapons. The leadership was also uncertain about the internal reaction. There was fear that white political parties would revolt against the regime over the nuclear decision. Stumpf, interview with the author.

19 See the *New York Times*, 25 March 1993, A1 and A12; Fischer, "Reversing," 280; Stumpf, "South Africa's," 72; Sole, "South Africa."

20 South Africa gave up its nuclear weapons before joining the NPT in July 1991. Adherence to the NPT was a logical conclusion to the process of nuclear forbearance initiated by the government. However, the NPT provided a formal mechanism for South Africa to denuclearize and claim non-nuclear status. Howlett and Simpson, "Nuclearisation," 168.

21 Villiers, Jardine, and Reiss, "Why." Only small sections within the ANC have expressed interest in keeping the nuclear option open. To scientist Isaac Amuah (Nelson Mandela's son-in-law), the decision to abandon nuclear weapons was made in haste and without the participation of the ANC. "It does the nation a great disservice in deciding unilaterally to destroy a strategic asset in which a fortune has been invested." Although he does not favour massive investment, he insists that a "policy for maintenance of an open nuclear weapons option must be pursued." Amuah, "Nuclear Policy"; Amuah, interview with the author, Pretoria, 30 Nov. 1995.

22 The treaty on an African nuclear-free zone was concluded in June 1995 in Pelindaba, near Pretoria, the place where South Africa had built its nuclear weapons secretly. The treaty prohibits parties from developing, manufacturing, or stockpiling nuclear explosive devices. It also prohibits them from testing nuclear devices on their territories and assisting other countries in their pursuit of nuclear weapons. Fischer, "Pelindaba."

23 Rauf and Johnson, "After the NPT's," 29.

24 James Perlez, "Sunflower Seeds Replace Ukraine's Old Missile Sites," *New York Times*, 5 June 1996, A10. These missiles included 130 SS-19 ICBMS (six warheads each), forty-six SS24 ICBMS (ten warheads), and forty strategic bombers. At the time of independence, Ukraine also was the home of 2,500 tactical warheads. For these estimates, see Potter, "Politics," 8.

25 From a strictly legal interpretation of the NPT, Ukraine could have been deemed a de facto nuclear state that had acquired nuclear arms prior to 1 January 1967 as part of the Soviet Union. In the words of former Ukrainian minister for environmental protection Yury Kostenko, Ukraine had been a "legal successor to the former USSR with respect to all its property rights and legal responsibilities" and therefore could be called a nuclear state similar to Russia. "Ukraine Weighs Future of Nuclear Arms," *Current Digest of the Post-Soviet Press*, 45 no. 17 (26 May 1993): 16.

26 Mearsheimer, "Case for." To Mearsheimer, Ukraine needs a nuclear capability to prevent possible Russian aggression because it cannot deter Russia with conventional capability, while countries such as the United States will not come to its rescue in the event of a Russian assault. For counter-arguments, see Miller, "Case against."

27 Garnett, "Ukraine's Decision," 10. See also Martel, "Why."

28 Author's interviews, Kiev, July 1995.

29 Sherr, "Russia–Ukraine Rapprochement?"

30 Garnett, "Ukraine's Decision," 7.

31 Ibid. According to one estimate presented to a Ukrainian parliamentary study group, developing the complete maintenance cycle for Ukraine's nuclear potential would have cost $40 billion. "Ukraine Weighs Future Nuclear Arms," *Current Digest*, 16. Although it was possible to figure out the codes required for nuclear launch, the maintenance costs of weapons that were fast degrading were exorbitant. Control over the missiles remained in the hands of the Kremlin. Although the Ukrainian president could override an order from Moscow to launch the missiles, he had no ability to fire them by himself. Carney, "A Nuclear Nation."

32 In an interview with two Russian journalists in January 1993, Boris Tarasyuk, Ukraine's deputy minister of foreign affairs and chairman of the National Committee on Disarmament Issues, stated that non-nuclear status was equivalent to a pass allowing Ukraine to join the international community and a condition for its participation in international economic and scientific-technical relations. In response to a question of whether Ukraine, by giving up nuclear weapons, would become a "second-rate state," Tarasyuk said that the stature of a country today depended not on its possession of nuclear weapons but on its scientific and technological progress on the path to the post-industrial society. "Ukraine's Nuclear Arms: The Underlying Issues," *Current Digest of the Post-Soviet Press*, 45, no. 2 (10 Feb. 1993): 13.

33 Garnett, "Ukraine's Decision," 8. Also Author's interviews, Kiev, July 1995.

34 "Will Ukraine Be a Nuclear Power?" *Current Digest of the Post-Soviet Press* 45 no. 23 (7 July 1993): 14. At that time, the deputies decided not to ratify the treaties and preferred to call Ukraine a "temporary nuclear power."

35 Potter, "Politics," 46.

36 Baker, "Non-Proliferation," 37. During the war in Kosovo in March 1999, the Ukrainian parliament voted to ask the government to repeal the country's non-nuclear status and rearm in protest against NATO's offensive against Yugoslavia. This was more of a symbolic protest than a policy change. Clover, "Ukraine Caught between West and Slav Brethren," *Financial Times*, 8–9 March 1999, 3.

37 *Washington Post*, 27 June 1975, A32.

38 In its report, a U.S. House International Relations Subcommittee, investigating South Korean influence-buying in the United States, discussed Korea's nuclear weapons activities as reported by a top-ranking official there. The report mentioned the activities of the Weapons Exploitation Committee, directly under the president's office, and its efforts to acquire materials from various sources for developing nuclear weapons. Plans to buy a plutonium-reprocessing facility from France and a fuel-reprocessing facility from Belgium were viewed by the U.S. government as evidence of this interest in nuclear weapons. Robert Gillette, "How the U.S. Stopped Korea's A-Bomb Plans," *San Francisco Chronicle*, 28 Nov. 1978, D4.

39 Hayes, "The Republic of Korea," 52.

40 Reiss, *Without the Bomb*, 92–3.

41 Ibid., 94–5.

42 "South Korea Planned Nuclear Weapons," *Jane's Defense Weekly*, 19 no. 9 (27 Feb. 1993): 6.

43 Hayes, "American Nuclear Hegemony," 357; Spector, *Nuclear Ambitions*, 122–3.

44 This revelation came from Su-jong Suh, chief analyst for the Democratic Liberal Party, who was also chief secretary to the head of the Agency for National Security Planning between 1987 and 1993. According to Suh, government-hired weapon specialists were forced to end operations at Daeduk, a scientific centre housing experimental reactors and a uranium-processing plant, following U.S. pressure. "Seoul Planned Nuclear Weapons until 1991," *Jane's Defence Weekly* (2 April 1994): 1

45 Park, "South Korea's Nuclear Option," 111.

46 Ibid., 97–117.

47 *IAEA Bulletin*, 41 no. 1 (1999): 50.

48 Overholt, "Nuclear Proliferation," 146.

49 Ibid., 146.

50 The sudden increase in the North's desire for nuclear weapons arose from its hope of preventing reunification with the South on the model of Germany. On its concerns, see Harrison, "Breaking," 85; see also Lanteigne, "Shadow Dancing."

51 It is possible that Seoul is still convinced that a U.S. nuclear umbrella is maintained through the Pacific submarine fleet, as Washington has not

ruled out a nuclear response to a North Korean attack. The U.S. air force also has aircraft-based gravity bombs that it can send to Korea from Pacific bases or aircraft carriers. Harrison, "Breaking," 91–2.

52 Seoul's approach to the nuclear question vacillated between "carrots" and "sticks," reflecting the competing images of North Korea in the South. Kim, "South Korean Perspectives."

53 For the declaration, see Kim, "South Korea's," 253; Lee, "Nuclear Proliferation," 10.

54 On the agreement, see Hughes, "North Korean"; Mazarr, *North Korea*. In May 1999, the Japanese government decided to release its contribution of $1 billion for construction of the reactors. *Financial Times*, 5 May 1999, 8.

55 For such an analysis, see Hayes, "American Nuclear Hegemony."

56 Kim, "South Korea's," 251. According to Kim, South Korea's "diplomatic subordination" is amplified by its vulnerability to U.S. trade pressures, and this "vicious circle" appears far too structural for South Korea to escape. Ibid., 252.

57 For these pressures, see Weinstein and Momoi et al., "The Nuclear Dimension," 110–13; Gillette, "How the U.S."

58 According to one scholar, even if South Korea had obtained nuclear weapons it would not have been able to survive as a nation-state without U.S. support. Young-Koo Cha, interview with the author, Seoul, 26 July 1994.

59 See Engelhardt, "Rewarding."

60 Overholt, "Nuclear Proliferation," 149.

61 In South Korean military thinking, however, U.S. nuclear weapons carry key deterrent and political functions in terms of deepening the U.S. commitment. Nuclear land mines could function as anti-tank weapons at choke points, and tactical weapons could destroy the North Korean underground command and control centres. Weinstein and Momoi et al., "The Nuclear Dimension," 110–11.

CHAPTER EIGHT

1 These tests were conducted in two batches. On 11 May, three devices – with yields of 12 kilotonnes, 43 kilotonnes, and 0.2 kilotonne – were tested. On 13 May, two small devices of 0.6 kilotonne and 0.2 kilotonnes were tested in the Pokhran test sites in Rajasthan. *New York Times*, 18 May 1998, A1 and A8. The tests proved that India had acquired nuclear warheads of different sizes and yields that could be fitted into a variety of delivery systems.

2 Albright "Shots."

3 On this calculation of the Indian elite, see Cohen, "Nuclear Weapons."

4 For an elaboration of these arguments, see Paul, "Systemic Bases." See also Nayar, "India," 231–3.

5 In 1954 Nehru proposed a standstill agreement to halt nuclear explosions following the U.S. atmospheric tests in the Bikini Atolls. A test ban of this nature could have been the precursor to more substantial agreements on ending production and stockpiling of nuclear weapons. Speech by Jawaharlal Nehru, Lok Sabha, New Delhi, 2 April 1954, reprinted in *India and Disarmament: An Anthology of Selected Writings and Speeches* (New Delhi: Ministry of External Affairs, 1988), 36.

6 On India's disarmament efforts under Nehru, see Jain, *India*.

7 On the early developments in the Indian atomic energy program, see Abraham, *Making*; Perkovich, *India's Nuclear Bomb*.

8 On Shastri's proposal for guarantees to all non-nuclear states, see *Hindustan Times*, 5 Dec. 1964, 1. Subrahmanyam, "India's Nuclear Policy," 27. According to a former chairman of the Indian Atomic Energy Commission, Raja Ramanna, Shastri's successor, Indira Gandhi, also sent her emissary, L.K. Jha, to the United States seeking a nuclear umbrella, but the request was turned down. *Hindu*, 19 July 1998, 9.

9 Bhatia, *India's Nuclear Bomb*, 54–69. For the early nuclear debate, see also Kapur, *India's Nuclear Option*; Poulose, ed., *Perspectives*.

10 The intention was to produce 2,700 mW of nuclear power by 1980 and to launch an Indian-made satellite by 1974. The proposals did not contain any specific reference to nuclear weapons, but the plan for establishing a fast-breeder reactor for reprocessing plutonium and a facility for producing heavy water implied a desire for nuclear capabilities. For the proposals, see *Hindu*, 25 May 1970, 1.

11 Subrahmanyam, "India's Nuclear Policy," 30.

12 Questions persist as to why the test was delayed by ten years, since it was first considered by Shastri in 1964 in the wake of the Chinese test. Technological and material constraints played a large role in the delay. Despite the claim by Homi Bhabha in 1964 that India could produce a nuclear weapon in eighteen months, the Indian scientists lacked the required plutonium. They also needed the Poornima fast breeder reactor in Trombay to carry out theoretical calculations for a nuclear test. Once it was commissioned in 1972, preparations for the test took another two years to complete. Bhatia believes that in 1966 Gandhi was in favour of a test and that her agreement to fund the reactor in 1968 is evidence to this effect. Her initial scepticism over the PNE evaporated one year after she took office. Bhatia, *India's Nuclear Bomb*, 147.

13 According to Subrahmanyam, Gandhi "developed cold feet," as she was afraid that she would be toppled by "foreign hands" if she continued with the tests. "India's Nuclear Policy," 33.

14 By 1999 India had deployed the Pritvi missiles. The Agni was yet to be deployed. Information is limited about when and where or how many

missiles will be deployed. *Times of India*, 12 April 1999, 1 and 7 May 1999, 1. For the foreseeable future, India is likely to rely heavily on aircraft such as SU-30s, MIG-23s, Jaguars, and Mirages to carry nuclear weapons. Its testing of small-yield devices suggests that it is readying different types of weapons for various kinds of delivery systems. Rajiv Nayan, "Delivery Systems Seen as Aiding Nuclear Deterrence," *India Abroad*, 26 June 1998, 2.

15 The Soviet intervention unleashed high levels of superpower activism in the Indian Ocean region as well. India's nuclear policy has also been influenced by superpower military activities in the Indian Ocean, although this may well be a secondary factor.

16 According to one analysis, Pakistan was twenty years behind India in 1971–72, but by the early 1980s it was only five years behind. Kant, "Should India?"

17 Sidhu, "Enhancing," 16–18. In a television interview, the Indian defence minister, George Fernandes, bluntly said: "China is India's potential threat number one." *India Today International*, 18 May 1998, 12.

18 Even while transferring nuclear and missile technology to Pakistan, China has been able to create the impression that it is not an enemy of India. According to one Indian analyst, "China can continue to be friendly with India, but at the same time lock India in a nuclear stand-off with Pakistan. It can also treat both Pakistan and India in the same category as regional powers, not in the same class as China, which is a global player." K. Subrahmanyam, "Understanding China: Sun Tzu and Shakti," *Times of India*, 5 June 1998, 7. For the evolution of China's conceptions of world order, based on realpolitik considerations, see Chan, "Chinese Perspectives."

19 At a meeting, foreign ministers of the permanent five members of the UN Security Council called on India and Pakistan to stop all further tests, adhere to the CTBT, participate in the Fissile Materials Cutoff Treaty (FMCT), and not weaponize or deploy nuclear weapons or missiles. *Text on India, Pakistan Statement*, 4 June 1998 (http://search.washingtonpost.com/wp-srv/WAPO/19980604/v000368-060498-idx.html). On U.S. sanctions, see Foran, "Indo-US Relations."

20 K. Subrahmanyam, "Politics of Shakti: New Wine in an Old Bomb," *Times of India*, 26 May 1998, 10. For Gandhi's proposal, see "A World Free of Nuclear Weapons," United Nations General Assembly, Third Special Session on Disarmament, New York, 9 June 1988, reprinted in *India and Disarmament*, 280–94.

21 For the Indian objections to the treaty, see Ghose, "Negotiating"; see also "India's Security Concerns Extend beyond South [Asia]," *Times of India*, 6 June 1998, 13.

22 Amitabh Mattoo, "Enough Scientific Reasons Seen for Conducting Tests," *India Abroad*, 15 May 1998, 10.

23 For such an argument, see Lavoy, "Nuclear Myths."

24 Mattoo, "India's," 45–6.

25 *Washington Post*, 18 May 1998, A13. Another opinion poll conducted by *India Today* weekly found that 87 per cent of those polled supported the nuclear testing, while 12 per cent opposed it; 86 per cent were in favour of weaponization, with 13 per cent opposing it. *India Today International*, 25 May 1998, 15.

26 "Tests Fail to Boost BJP's Poll Fortunes," *Hindu*, 7 June 1998, 9.

27 Rao's government was incensed by the indefinite extension of the NPT, which allowed the NWSS to keep their weapons in perpetuity. Atul Aneja, "NPT Extension Forced Indian Decision," *Hindu*, 20 May 1998, 14.

28 Raj Chengappa, "The Bombmakers," *India Today Webpage*, 22 June 1998 (http://www.india-today.com/itoday/22061998/cover.html).

29 Quoted in *India Abroad*, 22 May 1998, 10.

30 Sundarji, "India's," 176–81. For an analysis of the robustness and feasibility of nuclear deterrence in South Asia, see Hagerty, *Consequences*.

31 Subrahmanyam, "Nuclear Force Design." However, successful operation of such a deterrent strategy has been constrained by the failure of India and Pakistan to develop "feasible measures for nuclear restraint" and "a realistic debate about reasonable limits on regional nuclear forces and strategies," by their "unwillingness to accept arms control as a vital element of national security policy," and by their "inability to transform" bilateral strategic dialogue from "tacit to explicit bargaining." Rajamohan and Lavoy, "Avoiding." To another analyst, Indian's posture of seeking a minimum nuclear deterrent lacks credibility in the face of China's overwhelming second-strike capability, as India cannot harm Chinese nuclear weapons without using earth-penetrating or silo-destroying nuclear warheads. Poulose, "India's Deterrence Dilemma." See also Poulose, "India's Deterrence Doctrine"; Bajpai, "Fallacy."

32 Prakash Nanda, "Vajpayee Propounds Nuclear Doctrine," *Times of India*, 5 Aug. 1998, 1. Some Indian analysts have proposed the creation of a deterrent capability that includes 300-odd atomic weapons, thermonuclear devices, and atomic-demolition munitions. Karnad, "Thermonuclear."

33 *Hindu*, 18 Aug. 1999, 1.

34 Walker, "India's Nuclear Labyrinth."

35 On India's great-power aspirations, see Nayar, "India."

36 The key territorial dispute with Pakistan involves Kashmir and that with China, the disputed border regions in the northeast and northwest. For the Kashmir conflict, see Thomas, ed., *Perspectives*; Ganguly, *Crisis*.

37 *New York Times*, 29 May 1998, 1. The father of Pakistan's nuclear program, A.Q. Khan, stated in an interview that the yield of one of the devices was 30–35 kilotonnes, while the others were small

tactical weapons of low yield. *News Pakistan*, 30 May 1998
(http://www.jang-group/thenews/may98-daily/30–05–98/main/main2.html).
The sixth test, on 30 May, was also a small device that could be
mounted on a missile; *Bulletin of the Atomic Scientists*, 54 no. 4 (1998):
25. By the end of 1998, Pakistan was estimated to possess enough weapons-grade uranium to manufacture up to thirty nuclear weapons. For
these estimates, made by the Washington-based Institute for Science and
International Security, see *India Abroad*, 12 June 1998, 10.

38 Bhutto, *Myth*, 153. In response to debates in India following the 1964
Chinese nuclear test, Bhutto stated: "If India makes the atom bomb, the
people of Pakistan will eat grass but will also have the atom bomb."
Dawn (Karachi), 21 Nov. 1965, 1.

39 Moshaver, *Nuclear Weapons*, 60.

40 Weissman and Krosney, *The Islamic Bomb*, 44–6.

41 Khalilzad, "Pakistan," 244.

42 Pakistan's past efforts to capture Kashmir through military offensives
were failures, barring the 1947–48 encounter, when it gained one-third
of Kashmir. Nuclear capability became especially attractive because
Pakistani leaders feared that Indian nuclear superiority would prevent
New Delhi from making any territorial concessions. Cheema, "Pakistan's
Quest," 6.

43 Weissman and Krosney, *The Islamic Bomb*, 47.

44 For these, see Kapur, *Pakistan's Nuclear Development*, 20.

45 A.Q. Khan's interview with the Pakistani daily *Nawai Waqt*, 10 Feb.
1984, reprinted in *Public Opinion Trends Analysis and News Service*
(New Delhi, 17 Feb. 1984). For Khan's rise from a scientific position
with a Urenco facility in the Netherlands to head Pakistan's uranium-
enrichment plant at Kahuta, see Weissman and Krosney, *The Islamic
Bomb*, 174–94.

46 Beg, "Nuclear Programme," 20. By 1990, Pakistan was believed to have
built one or two weapons. According to one estimate, by 1992 Pakistan
had acquired weapons-grade enriched uranium for six to ten nuclear
weapons, and by 1995 it could have produced enriched uranium sufficient to manufacture twenty to twenty-five nuclear weapons. Albright et
al., *World Inventory*, 163 and 167.

47 For u.s. efforts in this regard, see Paul, "Influence."

48 John Kifner, "Complex Pressure, Dominated by Islam Led to Testing,"
New York Times, 1 June 1998, A6.

49 According to one report, "beginning in 1990, Pakistan is believed to
have built between 7 and 12 nuclear warheads – based on the Chinese
design, assisted by Chinese scientists and Chinese technology. That technology included Chinese magnets for producing weapons-grade enriched
uranium, a furnace for shaping the uranium into a nuclear bomb core,

and high-tech diagnostic equipment for nuclear weapons tests." Tim Weiner, "US and China helped Pakistan Build the Bomb ..." *New York Times*, 1 June 1998, A6.

50 For Pakistani views on this subject, see Jan, ed., *Pakistan's Security*.

51 Quoted in Joeck, "Maintaining," 21.

52 Hersh, "On the Nuclear Edge." Officials involved in the crisis and scholars who have studied the subject have challenged Hersh's account. Devin Haggerty argues that India and Pakistan were deterred from war in 1990 by each side's knowledge about the other's nuclear capability and that therefore it was unlikely that any military hostilities could have escalated to the nuclear level. The fear of pre-emptive attacks makes war even more unlikely among new nuclear nations such as India and Pakistan. "Nuclear Deterrence."

53 Ahmed, "Pakistan's Nuclear Weapons Program," 194.

54 Since 1988, Pakistan's Inter-Service Intelligence Agency (ISI) has been training and supplying arms and assistance to the Kashmiri insurgents. Following the nuclear testing, Pakistan attempted to gain international attention for Kashmir by linking nuclear testing with the dispute. John Kifner, "Through Nuclear Crisis, Pakistan Publicizes Kashmir Struggle," *New York Times*, 3 June 1998, 8.

55 See John Lancaster, "Kashmir Crisis Defused on the Brink of War," *Washington Post*, 26 July 1999, A1.

56 Diamond, "Indian, Pakistani Missile Activities ... ," 24.

57 "Saber Rattling and Sober Response Greet Ghauri Test Fire," *India Abroad*, 17 April 1998, 12.

58 Malik, *Quranic Concept*, 58–60.

59 Interview of General Beg by Mushahid Hussain, "Pakistan Responding to Change," *Janes Defence Weekly*, 12 no. 15 (14 Oct. 1989): 779. For an analysis of the Pakistani nuclear program and its strategic bases, see Pande, "Pakistan's Nuclear Strategy." For Pakistan's offensive-defence doctrine in previous conflicts, see Stephen P. Cohen, *The Pakistan Army*, 145. For Pakistani intervention strategies, see Roy, "Intervention."

60 Amit Baruah, "Pakistan Rejects Offer of No First Use Pact," *Hindu*, 19 July 1998, 1.

61 Many Pakistani strategists have presented this "equalizer" role of nuclear weapons in terms of narrowing the political, economic, and conventional military weaknesses of Pakistan vis-à-vis India as the chief rationale for maintaining the weapons capability. Beg, "Pakistan's Nuclear Programmme," 167; Saleem, "Nuclear Deterrence," 27.

62 For a history of the Israeli nuclear program, see Avner Cohen, *Israel and the Bomb*.

63 Barnaby, "Capping," 96.

64 The Kennedy administration convinced Israel to allow annual American inspection of the facility, which continued until 1966. These inspections were severely limited in scope, as the inspectors had only restricted access and scant information and could not detect any military-related activities. Jabber, *Israel*, 33–4.

65 Insight Team, "Revealed: The Secrets of Israel's Nuclear Arsenal," *Sunday Times*, 5 Oct. 1986, 1 and 4–5.

66 Barnaby, "Capping," 96–7.

67 Evron, *Israel's Nuclear Dilemma*, 10; Weissman and Krosney, *The Islamic Bomb*, 127.

68 Miller, "Israel," 63–4.

69 Barnaby, "Capping," 98–9.

70 Steinberg, "Future," 3.

71 Nuclear ambiguity also serves to maintain Israel's close relations with the United States and other Western countries. If Israel openly declares its nuclear capability, it might lose a bargaining chip with the United States for new and sophisticated conventional weapons. Pry, *Israel's Nuclear Arsenal*, 33.

72 Barnaby, "Capping," 94.

73 For proposals for mutual deterrence, see Rosen, "A Stable System"; Feldman, *Israeli Nuclear Deterrence*.

74 Avner Cohen, "The Nuclear Issue," 54.

75 According to one Israeli strategist, nuclear weapons were not relevant in either the War of Attrition (1969–70) or the 1973 war. Evron, *Israel's Nuclear Dilemma*, 17. For the limitations of the Israeli deterrent strategy, see Freedman, "Israel's Nuclear Policy."

76 On the Egyptian constraints, see Bhatia, *Nuclear Rivals*, chap. 4; Gregory, "Egypt's Nuclear Program."

77 Egypt was constrained by other factors in formulating a limited-aims strategy. Its small amount of conventional capability, the possibility of superpower intervention, and the political objective of a post-war negotiated settlement all affected its assessment. For its strategic calculations, see Paul, *Asymmetric Conflicts*, 130–4. On 8 October 1973, at the height of the war, when Egyptian and Syrian forces were making military headway, the Israelis reportedly went on a nuclear alert on the assumption that the Soviet spy satellites would notice it and warn the Egyptians to limit the offensive or face a nuclear strike. This would also encourage the United States to refurbish Israel's fast-depleting conventional weaponry. Hersh, *The Samson Option*, 225–40.

78 President Sadat reportedly told Israeli Minister of Defence Ezer Weizman in 1977 that the Israeli nuclear capability substantially influenced the decision to make peace with Israel. Quoted in Karsh and Navias, "Israeli Nuclear Weapons," 86.

79 These wars occurred in 1948, 1956, 1967, 1969–70, 1973, and 1982.
80 On protracted conflicts and tendencies to nuclear acquisition see Khan, "Nuclear Proliferation."

CHAPTER NINE

1 My theoretical argument with respect to these cases could be falsified if Japan and Germany opted for nuclear weapons without such an enduring rivalry emerging or chose not to acquire nuclear weapons even when they developed enduring rivalries with nuclear states while simultaneously losing their alliance relationships.

2 Failure to explain how units respond to the systemic environment is a weakness especially of structural realism. James, "Neorealism."

3 On co-ordinated policies designed to avoid arms races and on co-operative policies that can communicate benign motives, see Glaser, "Realists," 122–3.

4 The structural accounts of international politics do not accord the agents – i.e., individual states – much choice in their security strategies, because structure determines or constraints what agents can do. But in the realm of nuclear weapons, many agents seem to have made conscious choices to overcome structural constraints. For the agent–structure debate, see Buzan, Jones, and Little, *Logic*, 102–6.

5 Morgenthau, *Politics*, 30. Aron also argues that "in the last analysis" states "seek to be powerful – that is capable of imposing their will on their neighbours and rivals in order to influence the fate of humanity, the future of civilization." Aron, *Peace*, 73. Carr goes a step further when he argues that "military power, being an essential element in the life of the state becomes not only an instrument, but an end in itself." Carr, *The Twenty Years' Crisis*, 111.

6 Greico, *Cooperation*, 10.

7 On some such approaches, see Brito, Intriligator, and Wick, eds., *Strategies*.

8 On the limits of sanctions, see Paul, "Strengthening." On multilateral security approaches, see Job, "Matters."

9 According to one analysis, the increasing level of globalization and integration of formerly closed economies into the Western-led world economic system provides an opportunity for sanctions to work against nuclear fence-sitters. Solingen, "Domestic Sources." Analysts such as Huntington argue that the "hold down efforts of the West may slow the weapons buildup of other societies, but they will not stop it." *Clash*, 190.

10 Some have claimed that Taiwan and South Korea gave up their nuclear ambitions under the threat of U.S. economic sanctions. It is not clear

that, in the absence of credible U.S. security guarantees, economic sanctions would have made any difference in these cases. These cases show that in situations of extreme security threats, economic carrots and sticks are no substitutes for effective security assurances.

11 On the limitations of currently fashionable non-proliferation approaches, see Betts, "Paranoids."

12 In some instances, alliance guarantees could cause an opponent to acquire nuclear weapons. They could also prohibit delegitimization of nuclear weapons. Sagan, "Why?" 86.

13 For a discussion of this possibility, see Paul, "The NPT."

Bibliography

Abraham, Itty. *The Making of the Indian Atomic Bomb*. London: Zed Books 1998.

– "Pakistan–India and Argentina–Brazil: Stepping Back from the Nuclear Threshold." Occasional Papers, No. 15. Washington, DC: Stimson Center, Oct. 1993.

Abrahamson, Dean. "Governments Fall as Consensus Gives Way to Debate." *Bulletin of the Atomic Scientists* 35, no. 9 (1979): 30–7.

Adler, Emanuel. *The Power of Ideology: The Quest for Technological Autonomy in Argentina and Brazil*. Berkeley: University of California Press 1987.

Agrell, Wilhelm. "Behind the Submarine Crisis: Evolution of the Swedish Defence Doctrine and Soviet War Planning." *Cooperation and Conflict* 21, no. 4 (1986): 197–217.

– "The Bomb that Never Was: The Rise and Fall of the Swedish Nuclear Weapons Programme." In Nils Peter Gleditsch and Olav Njølstad, eds., *Arms Races: Technological and Political Dynamics*, 154–74. London: Sage Publications 1990.

Ahmed, Samina. "Pakistan's Nuclear Weapons Program: Turning Points and Nuclear Choices." *International Security*, 23, no. 4 (1999): 178–204.

Ahonen, Pertti. "Franz-Josef Strauss and the German Nuclear Question, 1956–1962." *Journal of Strategic Studies* 18, no. 2 (1995): 25–51.

Albright, David. "Bomb Potential for South America." *Bulletin of the Atomic Scientists* 45, no. 4 (1989): 16–20.

– "South Africa and the Affordable Bomb." *Bulletin of the Atomic Scientists* 50, no. 4 (1994): 37–47.

– "The Shots Heard Round the World." *Bulletin of the Atomic Scientists* 54, no. 4 (1998): 21–5.

Albright, David, et al. *World Inventory of Plutonium and Highly Enriched Uranium*. Oxford: Oxford University Press 1992.

Alley, Roderic. "The Evolution of ANZUS." In Jacob Bercovitch Houndmills, ed., *ANZUS in Crisis*, 25–51. Hampshire: Macmillan 1988.

Amuah, Isaac. "Nuclear Policy in South Africa: Past, Present, and the Future." Paper Presented at the African National Conference Seminar, "The Nuclear Debate: Policy for a Democratic South Africa," Cape Town, 11–13 Feb. 1994.

Andren, Nils. "Sweden's Security Policy." *Cooperation and Conflict* 7, no. 2 (1972): 127–53.

– "Sweden's Security Policy." In Johan Jorgen Holst, ed., *Five Roads to Nordic Security*, 238–40. Oslo: Universitetsforlaget 1973.

Aron, Raymond. *Peace and War: A Theory of International Relations*. New York: Praeger Publishers 1968.

Art, Robert J. "Why Western Europe Needs the United States and NATO." *Political Science Quarterly* 111, no. 1 (1996): 1–39.

Axelrod, Robert. *The Evolution of Cooperation*. New York: Basic Books 1984.

Bajpai, Kanti. "The Fallacy of an Indian Deterrent." In Amitabh Mattoo, ed., *India's Nuclear Deterrent: Pokhran II and Beyond*, 150–88. New Delhi: Har-Anand Publishers 1999.

Baker, John C. "Non-Proliferation Incentives for Russia and Ukraine." Adelphi Paper, No. 309. London: International Institute of Strategic Studies 1977.

Baldwin, David A. *Paradoxes of Power*. New York: Basil Blackwell 1989.

Barletta. Michael. "The Military Nuclear Program in Brazil." Working Paper. Stanford: Center for International Security and Arms Control 1997.

Barnaby, Frank. "Capping Israel's Nuclear Volcano." In Efraim Karsh, ed., *Between War and Peace: Dilemmas of Israeli Security*, 93–111. London: Frank Cass 1996.

Barrett, John. "Canada." In Regina Cowen Karp, ed., *Security with Nuclear Weapons? Different Perspectives on National Security*, 340–59. Oxford: Oxford University Press 1991.

Barrett, John, and Ross, Douglas. "The Air-Launched Cruise Missile and Canadian Arms Control Policy." *Canadian Public Policy* 11, no. 4 (1985): 711–30.

Beaton, Leonard. *Must the Bomb Spread?* Middlesex: Penguin Books 1966.

Beaton, Leonard, and Maddox, John. *The Spread of Nuclear Weapons*. London: Chatto and Windus 1962.

Beg, General Mirza Aslam. "Nuclear Programme and Political Ramblings." *Defence Journal* 19, no. 11–12 (1993): 19–21.

– "Pakistan's Nuclear Programme: A National Security Perspective." In Jørn Gjelstad and Olav Njølstad, eds., *Nuclear Rivalry and International Order*, 158–72. London: Sage Publications 1996.

Bellany, Ian. *Australia in the Nuclear Age*. Sydney: Sydney University Press 1972.

Berger, Thomas U. *Cultures of Anti-Militarism: National Security in Germany and Japan*. Baltimore: Johns Hopkins University Press 1998.

- "From Swords to Chrysanthemum: Japan's Culture of Anti–militarism." *International Security* 17, no. 4 (1993): 119–50.
- "Norms, Identity, and National Security in Germany and Japan." In Peter Katzenstein, ed., *The Culture of National Security: Norms and Identity in World Politics*, 317–56. New York: Columbia University Press 1996.

Bertram, Christopher. "European Security and the German Problem." *International Security* 4, no. 3 (1979): 105–16.

Betts, Richard K. "Paranoids, Pygmies, Pariahs and Nonproliferation Revisited." *Security Studies* 2, no. 3–4 (1993): 100–23.

Bhatia, Shyam. *India's Nuclear Bomb*. Sahibabad: Vikas 1979.
- *Nuclear Rivals in the Middle East*. New York: Routledge 1988.

Bhutto, Zulfikar Ali. *The Myth of Independence*. London: Oxford University Press 1969.

Bielfeldt, Carola. "Detente, Military Security and Arms Control: Policy Inconsistencies in the FRG." *Bulletin of Peace Proposals* 10, no. 1 (1979): 122–7.

Birnbaum, Karl. "The Swedish Experience." In Alastair Buchan, ed., *A World of Nuclear Powers?*, 68–75. Englewood Cliffs, NJ: Prentice-Hall 1966.

Blackaby, Frank, Goldblat, Jozef, and Lodgaard, Sverre. "No First Use of Nuclear Weapons." *Bulletin of Peace Proposals* 15, no. 4 (1984): 321–32.

Blacker, Coit D., and Duffy, Gloria. *International Arms Control: Issues and Agreements*. Stanford: Stanford University Press 1984.

Boutwell, Jeffrey. *The German Nuclear Dilemma*. Ithaca, NY: Cornell University Press 1990.
- "Politics and the Peace Movement in West Germany." *International Security* 7, no. 4 (1983): 72–92.

Bowen, Wyn Q. "Brazil's Accession to the MTCR." *The Non-Proliferation Review* 3, no. 3 (1996): 86–91.

Bracken, Paul. *The Command and Control of Nuclear Forces*. New Haven, Conn.: Yale University Press 1983.

Bratt, Duane. "CANDU or Candon't: Competing Values Behind Canada's Nuclear Sales." *Nonproliferation Review* 5, no. 3 (1998): 1–16.

Brawley, Mark R. *Liberal Leadership: Great Powers and Their Challengers in Peace and War*. Ithaca, NY: Cornell University Press 1993.

Brecher, Michael. *Crises in World Politics: Theory and Reality*. Oxford: Pergamon Press 1993.

Brecher, Michael, and Wilkenfeld, Jonathan. *Crisis in the Twentieth Century*. New York: Pergamon 1989.

Brito, Dagobert L., Intriligator, Michael D., and Wick, Adele E., eds. *Strategies for Managing Nuclear Proliferation*. Lexington: Lexington Books 1993.

Brodie, Bernard. "War in the Atomic Age." In Brodie and Dunn, *The Absolute Weapon*.

Brodie, Bernard, and Dunn, Frederick S. *The Absolute Weapon: Atomic Power and World Order*. New York: Harcourt, Brace and Company 1946.

Brown, Seyom. *The Causes and Prevention of War.* New York: St Martin's Press 1987.

Brzezinski, Zbigniew. *The Fragile Blossom: Crisis and Change in Japan.* New York: Harper & Row 1972.

Bundy, McGeorge. *Danger and Survival.* New York: Random House 1988.

Burns, A.L. "Australia and the Nuclear Balance." In H.G. Gelber, ed., *Problems of Australian Defence,* 144–65. Melbourne: Oxford University Press 1970.

Buteux, Paul. "NATO and the Evolution of Canadian Defense and Foreign Policy." In David B. Dewitt and David Leyton-Brown, eds., *Canada's International Security Policy,* 153–70. Scarborough, Ont.: Prentice Hall 1995.

Buzan, Barry. "Japan's Future: Old History versus New Roles." *International Affairs* 64, no. 4 (1988): 557–73.

– *People, States and Fear: The National Security Problem in International Relations.* Chapel Hill: University of North Carolina Press 1983.

Buzan, Barry, Jones, Charles, and Little, Richard. *The Logic of Anarchy: Neorealism to Structural Realism.* New York: Columbia University Press 1993.

Calleo, David. *The German Problem Reconsidered: Germany and the World Order, 1870 to the Present.* Cambridge: Cambridge University Press 1978.

Camilleri, Joseph. "Nuclear Controversy in Australia: The Uranium Campaign." *Bulletin of the Atomic Scientists* 35, no. 4 (1979): 40–4.

Carney, James. "A Nuclear Nation in Trouble." *Time,* 19 April 1993, 38–43.

Carr, E.H. *The Twenty Years' Crisis – 1919–1939.* New York: Harper Torchbooks 1939.

Carrel, Laurent F. "Switzerland." In Richard E. Bissel and Curt Gasteyger, eds., *The Missing Link,* 78–95. Durham, NC: Duke University Press 1990.

Castrioto de Azambuja, Marcos. "Nuclear Non-Proliferation and Confidence Building in Southern Cone." *Disarmament* 16, no. 2 (1993): 123–33.

Chakravorty, B. *Australia's Military Alliances.* New Delhi: Sterling Publishers 1977.

Chan, Steve. "Chinese Perspectives on World Order." In T.V. Paul and John A. Hall, eds., *International Order and the Future of World Politics,* 197–212. Cambridge: Cambridge University Press 1999.

Checkel, Jeffrey T. "The Constructivist Turn in International Relations Theory." *World Politics* 50, no. 2 (1988): 324–48.

Cheema, Pervaiz Iqbal. "Pakistan's Quest for Nuclear Technology." ANU Working Paper 19 Canberra, 1980.

Clearwater, John. *Canadian Nuclear Weapons.* Toronto: Dundurn Press 1998.

Cohen, Avner. *Israel and the Bomb.* New York: Columbia University Press, 1998.

– "The Nuclear Issue in the Middle East in a New World Order." In Efrain Inbar and Shmuel Sandler, eds., *Middle Eastern Security: Prospects for an Arms Control Regime,* 49–69. London: Frank Cass 1995.

Cohen, Stephen P. "Nuclear Weapons and Conflict in South Asia." Paper Presented to the Harvard/MIT Transnational Security Project Seminar, Cambridge, Mass., 23 Nov. 1998.

– *The Pakistan Army.* Berkeley: University of California Press 1984.

Cole, Paul M. "Atomic Bombast: Nuclear Weapon Decisionmaking in Sweden 1945–1972." Occasional Paper, No. 26, The Henry L. Stimson Center, Washington, DC, April 1996.

– *Sweden without the Bomb.* Santa Monica: Rand Corporation 1994.

Curtis, Gerald. "Japanese Security Policies and the United States." *Foreign Affairs* 59, no. 4 (1981): 852–74.

Daalder, Ivo H., Kosminsky, Jay, and Garnham, David. "Correspondence: Extending Deterrence with ... What?" *International Security* 10, no. 4 (1986): 201–7.

Davis, Zachary S. "The Realist Nuclear Regime." *Security Studies* 2, no. 3–4 (1993): 79–99.

Davis, Zachary S., and Donnelly, Warren H. "South Africa's Nuclear Status." CRS Issue Brief. Washington, D.C.: Congressional Research Service, 31 March 1993.

Den Uyl, Douglas J. *The Virtue of Prudence.* New York: Peter Lang 1991.

Desch, Michael C. "Culture Clash: Assessing the Influence of Ideas in Security Studies." *International Security* 23, no. 1 (1998): 141–70.

de Villiers, J.W., Jardine, Roger, and Reiss, Mitchell. "Why South Africa Gave Up the Bomb." *Foreign Affairs* 72, no. 5 (1993): 98–109.

de Weck, Herve, and Maurer, Pierre. "Swiss National Defense Policy Revisited." In Marko Milivojevic and Pierre Maurer, eds., *Swiss Neutrality and Security,* 65–80. New York: Berg 1990.

Deutsch, Karl. *Arms Control and the Atlantic Alliance: Europe Faces Coming Policy Decisions.* John Wiley & Sons: New York 1967.

Deutsch, Karl, et al. *Political Community and the North Atlantic Area.* Princeton, NJ: Princeton University Press 1957.

Dogan, Mattei, and Kazancigil, Ali. "Introduction: Strategies in Comparative Research." In Dogan and Kazancigil, eds., *Comparing Nations, Concepts, Strategies and Substance,* 1–13. Oxford: Basil Blackwell 1994.

Dougherty, James E. "Nuclear Proliferation in Asia." *Orbis* 19, no. 3 (1975): 925–57.

Dower, John W. *Empire and Aftermath: Yoshida Shigeru and the Japanese Experience, 1878–1954.* Cambridge, Mass.: Harvard University Press 1979.

Dunn, Frederick S. "The Common Problem." In Bernard Brodie, ed., *The Absolute Weapon,* 3–17. New York: Harcourt, Brace 1946.

Eayrs, James. "Canada, NATO, and Nuclear Weapons." *Survival* 3, no. 2 (1961): 76–83.

Edwards, Gordon. "Canada's Nuclear Industry and the Myth of the Peaceful Atom." In Ernie Regehr and Simon Rosenblum, eds., *Canada and the Nuclear Arms Race,* 122–70. Toronto: James Lorimer 1983.

Emmerson, John K., and Humphreys, Leonard A. *Will Japan Rearm? A Study in Attitudes.* Washington, DC: American Enterprise Institute for Public Policy Research 1973.

Enders, Thomas, et al. "The New Germany and Nuclear Weapons." In Patrick J. Garrity and Steven A. Maaranen, eds., *Nuclear Weapons in a Changing World*, 127–43. New York: Plenum Press 1992.

Endicott, John E. *Japan's Nuclear Option: Political, Technical and Strategic Factors.* New York: Praeger 1975.

Engelhardt, Michael J. "Rewarding Non-Proliferation: The South and North Korean Cases." *Nonproliferation Review* 3, no. 3 (1996): 31–7.

Evron, Yair. *Israel's Nuclear Dilemma.* Ithaca, NY: Cornell University Press 1994.

Feaver, Peter D., "Command and Control in Emerging Nuclear Nations." *International Security* 17, no. 3 (1992–93): 160–87.

Feldman, Shai. *Israeli Nuclear Deterrence: A Strategy for the 1980s.* New York: Columbia University Press 1982.

Feu Alvim, Carlos. "Common System for Accounting and Control of Nuclear Materials between Brazil and Argentina." Paper presented at International Law Conference, Rio de Janeiro, Sept. 1993.

Fischer, David. "The Pelindaba Treaty: Africa Joins the Nuclear Free World." *Arms Control Today* 25, no. 10 (1995–96): 9–20.

– "Reversing Nuclear Proliferation: South Africa." *Security Dialogue* 24, no. 3 (1993): 273–86.

Flournoy, Michele A., and Campbell, Kurt M. "South Africa's Bomb: A Military Option?" *Orbis* 32, no. 3 (1988): 385–401.

Foran, Virginia I. "Indo–US Relations after the 1998 Test: Sanctions versus Incentives." In Gary K. Bertsch, Seema Gahlaut, and Anupam Srivastava, eds., *Engaging India*, 40–76. New York: Routledge 1999.

Frankel, Benjamin. "The Brooding Shadow: Systemic Incentives and Nuclear Weapons Proliferation." *Security Studies* 2, no. 3–4 (1993): 37–78.

Freedman, Lawrence. "Great Powers, Vital Interests, and Nuclear Weapons." *Survival* 36, no. 4 (1994–95): 35–52.

– "Israel's Nuclear Policy." *Survival* 17, no. 3 (1975): 114–20.

Frieden, Jeffrey A. *Debt, Development and Democracy.* Princeton, NJ: Princeton University Press 1991.

Fujita, Edmundo Sussumu. 'The Brazilian Policy of Sustainable Defence." *International Affairs* 7, no. 3 (1998): 577–85.

Gaddis, John Lewis. "Nuclear Weapons, the End of the Cold War, and the Future of the International System." In Patrick J. Garrity and Steven A. Maaranen, eds., *Nuclear Weapons in the Changing World*, 15–31. New York: Plenum Press 1992.

Gall, Norman. "Atoms for Brazil, Dangers for All." *Foreign Policy* no. 22 (1976): 155–201.

Gamba-Stonehouse, Virginia. "Argentina and Brazil." In Regina Cowen Karp, ed., *Security with Nuclear Weapons? Different Perspectives on National Security*, 229–56. Oxford: Oxford University Press 1991.

Ganguly, Sumit. *The Crisis in Kashmir*. Washington, DC: Woodrow Wilson Center Press 1997.

Garnett, Sherman W. "Ukraine's Decision to Join the NPT." *Arms Control Today* 25, no. 1 (1995): 7–12.

Garnham, David. "Extending Deterrence with German Nuclear Weapons." *International Security* 10, no. 1 (1985): 96–110.

Garris, Jerome H. "Sweden and the Spread of Nuclear Weapons: A Study in Restraint." PhD dissertation, University of California, Los Angeles, 1972.

– "Sweden's Debate on Proliferation of Nuclear Weapons." *Cooperation and Conflict* 8, no. 3–4 (1973): 189–207.

Geipel, Gary L. "The Nature and Limits of German Power." In Geipel, ed., *Germany in a New Era*, 19–48. Indianapolis: Hudson Institute 1993.

Gelber, Harry G. "Australia and Nuclear Weapons." In Johan Jørgen Holst, ed., *Security, Order and the Bomb*, 107–8. Oslo: Universitetsforlaget 1972.

George, Alexander. "Case Studies and Theory Development: The Method of Structured, Focused Comparison." In Paul G. Lauren, ed., *Diplomacy: New Approaches in History, Theory and Policy*, 43–68. New York: Free Press 1979.

George, Aurelia. "Japan's Participation in U.N. Peacekeeping Operations." *Asian Survey* 33, no. 6 (1993): 560–75.

Ghose, Arundhati. "Negotiating the CTBT: India's Security Concerns and Nuclear Disarmament," *Journal of International Affairs* 5, no. 1 (1997): 239–61.

Gilpin, Robert. *U.S. Power and the Multinational Corporation: The Political Economy of Foreign Direct Investment*. New York: Basic Books 1975.

Glaser, Charles L. "Realists as Optimists: Cooperation as Self-help." *Security Studies* 5, no. 3 (1996): 50–90.

Gochman, Charles S., and Maoz, Zeev. "Militarized Interstate Disputes, 1816–1976." *Journal of Conflict Resolution* 28, no. 4 (1984): 585–615.

Godwin, Paul, and Schulz, John J. "Arming the Dragon for the 21st Century: China's Defense Modernization Program." *Arms Control Today* 23, no. 10 (1993): 3–8.

Goertz, Gary, and Diehl Paul. "Enduring Rivalries: Theoretical Constraints and Empirical Patterns." *International Studies Quarterly* 37, no. 2 (1993): 147–71.

Goldemberg, Jose, and Feiveson, Harold A. "Denuclearization in Argentina and Brazil." *Arms Control Today* 24, no. 2 (1994): 10–14.

Goldman, Joe. "Argentina, Brazil Open to Inspections." *Bulletin of the Atomic Scientists* 47, no. 4 (1991): 9–10.

Goldstein, Avery. "Discounting the Free-ride: Alliances and Security in the Post-War World." *International Organization* 49, no. 1 (1995): 39–71.

Gompert, David, Watman, Kenneth, and Wilkening, Dean. "Nuclear First Use Revisited." *Survival* 37, no. 3 (1995): 27–44.

Gordon, Walter. "The Liberal Leadership and Nuclear Weapons." In Ernie Regehr and Simon Rosenblum, eds., *Canada and the Nuclear Arms Race*, 199–203. Toronto: James Lorimer 1983.

Grabendorff, Wolf. "Brazil." In Harald Muller, ed., *A European Non-Proliferation Policy: Prospects and Problems*, 323–65. Oxford: Clarendon Press 1987.

Gregory, Barbara M. "Egypt's Nuclear Program: Assessing Supplier-Based and Other Developmental Constraints." *Nonproliferation Review* 3, no. 1 (1995): 20–7.

Grieco, Joseph M. "Anarchy and the Limits of Cooperation: A Realist Critique of the Neo Liberal Institutionalism." *International Organization* 42, no. 3 (1988): 485–507.

– *Cooperation among Nations*. Ithaca, NY: Cornell University Press 1990.

Gutjahr, Lothar. "Stability, Integration and Global Responsibility: Germany's Changing Perspectives on National Interests." *Review of International Studies* 21, no. 3 (1995): 301–17.

Ha, Joseph M., and Guinasso, John. "Japan's Rearmament Dilemma: The Paradox of Recovery." *Pacific Affairs* 53, no. 2 (1980): 245–68.

Haas, Ernst B. "Why Collaborate? Issue Linkage and International Regimes." *World Politics* 32, no. 3 (1980): 357–405.

Hagelin, Bjorn. "The Margins of Security: Politics and Economics in Sweden." *Policy Sciences*, no. 9 (1978): 207–28.

Hagerty, Devin T. *The Consequences of Nuclear Proliferation: Lessons from South Asia*. Cambridge, Mass.: MIT Press 1998.

– "Nuclear Deterrence in South Asia: The 1990 Indo–Pakistani Crisis." *International Security* 20, no. 3 (1995–96): 79–114.

Hall, John A. *International Orders*. Cambridge: Polity Press, 1996.

Hall, John A., and Paul T.V., "Preconditions for Prudence: A Sociological Synthesis of Realism and Liberalism." In T.V. Paul and John A. Hall, eds., *International Order and the Future of World Politics*, 67–77. Cambridge: Cambridge University Press 1999.

Harknett, Richard J. "State Preferences, Systemic Constraints, and the Absolute Weapon." In T.V. Paul, Richard J. Harknett, and James J. Wirtz, eds., *The Absolute Weapon Revisited: Nuclear Arms and the International Order*, 47–72. Ann Arbor: University of Michigan Press 1998.

Harrison, Selig S. "Breaking the Nuclear Impasse: Paths to Cooperative Security in Korea." In *Evolving Multilateral Security Regimes in Northeast Asia*, 83–99. Seoul: Institute of Foreign Affairs and National Security 1994.

– "Japan and Nuclear Weapons." In Harrison, ed., *Japan's Nuclear Future: The Plutonium Debate and East Asian Security*, 3–44. Washington, DC: Carnegie Endowment for International Peace 1996.

Harvey, Frank P., and James, Patrick. "Nuclear Crisis as a Multi-Stage Threat Game: Toward an Agenda for Comparative Research." In Harvey and Ben D. Mor, eds., *In Conflict in World Politics*, 142–61. Houndmills, England: Macmillan 1998.

Haskel, Barbara G. *The Scandinavian Option*. Oslo: Universitetsfolaget. 1976.

Hayden, Bill. *Hayden: An Autobiography*. Sydney: Angus & Robertson 1996.

Hayes, Peter. "American Nuclear Hegemony in Korea." *Journal of Peace Research* 25, no. 4 (1988): 351–64.

– "The Republic of Korea and the Nuclear Issue." In Andrew Mack, ed., *Asian Flashpoint: Security and the Korean Peninsula*, 51–83. Canberra: Allen and Unwin 1993.

Hersh, Seymour M. "On the Nuclear Edge." *New Yorker* no. 29 (1993): 56–73.

– *The Samson Option: Israel's Nuclear Ambition and American Foreign Policy*. New York: Random House 1991.

Herz, John H. *International Politics in the Atomic Age*. New York: Columbia University Press 1967.

Hilton, Stanley E. "The Argentine Factor in Twentieth-Century Brazilian Foreign Policy Strategy." *Political Science Quarterly* 100, no. 1 (1985): 27–51.

Hoffmann, Stanley. "Nuclear Proliferation and World Politics." In Alaistar Buchan, ed., *A World of Nuclear Powers?* 89–121. Englewood Cliffs, NJ: Prentice Hall 1966.

Holst, Johan Jorgen. Ed. *Security, Order, and the Bomb*. Oslo: Universitetsforlaget 1972.

Holsti, K.J. *Peace and War: Armed Conflicts and International Order 1648–1989*. Cambridge: Cambridge University Press 1991.

– *The State, War, and the State of War*. Cambridge: Cambridge University Press 1996.

Howlett, Darryl, and Simpson, John. "Nuclearisation and Denuclearisation in South Africa." *Survival* 35, no. 3 (1993): 154–73.

Hughes, Christopher W. "The North Korean Nuclear Crisis and Japanese Security." *Survival* 38, no. 2 (1996): 79–103.

Huldt, Bo and Lejins, Atis, eds. *European Neutrals and the Soviet Union*. Swedish Institute of International Affairs, Utrikespolitiska Institutet, Conference Papers 6, 1985.

Huntington, Samuel P. *The Clash of Civilizations and the Remaking of World Order*. New York: Simon and Schuster 1996.

Ikenberry, G. John, and Kupchan, Charles A "Socialization and Hegemonic Power." *International Organization* 44, no. 3 (1990): 283–316.

Ingebritsen, Christine. "Redefining National Security: Scandinavia Comes Out of the Cold." *Journal of Strategic Studies* 20, no. 3 (1997): 27–44.

Izumi, Hajime. "Japan and the Nuclear Issue." Paper Presented at the Conference on Security and Nuclear Issues in Northeast Asia, East–West Center, Honolulu: University of Hawaii, 18–19 July 1994.

Jabber, Paul. *Israel and Nuclear Weapons*. London: Chatto & Windus 1971.

Jain, Jagdish P. *India and Disarmament: Nehru Era*, Vol. I. New Delhi: Radiant Publishers 1974.

James, Patrick. "Neorealism as a Research Enterprise." *International Political Science Review* 14, no.2 (1993): 123–48.

Jan, Tarik, ed. *Pakistan's Security and the Nuclear Option*. Islamabad: Institute of Policy Studies 1995.

"Japanese Defense Policy." *Survival* 18, no. 1 (1971): 2–8.

Jasper, James M. *Nuclear Politics: Energy and the State in the United States, Sweden and France*. Princeton, NJ: Princeton University Press 1990.

Jepperson, Ronald L., Wendt, Alexander, and Katzenstein, Peter J. "Norms, Identity, and Culture in National Security." In Peter Katzenstein, ed., *The Culture of National Security: Norms and Identity in World Politics*, 33–75. New York: Columbia University Press 1996.

Jervis, Robert. "Cooperation under the Security Dilemma." *World Politics* 30, no. 1 (1978): 167–214.

– "Security Regimes." In Stephen D. Krasner, ed., *International Regimes*, 173–94. Ithaca, NY: Cornell University Press 1983.

Job, Brian L. "Matters of Multilateralism: Implications for Regional Conflict Management." In David A. Lake and Patrick M. Morgan, eds., *Regional Orders*, 165–91. University Park: Pennsylvania State University Press 1997.

Joeck, Neil. "Maintaining Nuclear Stability in South Asia." Adelphi Paper, No. 312. Oxford: Oxford University Press for the International Institute for Strategic Studies 1997.

Joffe, Josef. "Europe's American Pacifier." *Foreign Policy* no. 14 (1984): 64–82.

Kahn, Herman. *The Emerging Japanese Superstate*. Englewood Cliffs, NJ: Prentice-Hall 1970.

Kamiya, Matake. "Will Japan Go Nuclear? Myth and Reality." *Asia-Pacific Review* 2, no. 2 (1995): 5–19.

Kant, Krishan. "Should India Go Nuclear?" *IDSA Journal* 14, no. 3 (1982): 307–28.

Kapur, Ashok. *India's Nuclear Option: Atomic Diplomacy and Decisionmaking*. New York: Praeger 1976.

– *Pakistan's Nuclear Development*. London: Croom Helm 1987.

Karnad, Bharat. "A Thermonuclear Deterrent." In Amitabh Mattoo, ed., *India's Nuclear Deterrent: Pokhran II and Beyond*, 108–49. New Delhi: Har-Anand 1999.

Karsh, Efraim. *Neutrality and Small States*. London: Routledge 1988.

Karsh, Efraim, and Navias, Martin. "Israeli Nuclear Weapons and Middle East Peace." In Karsh, ed., *Between War and Peace: Dilemmas of Israeli Security*, 75–92. London: Frank Cass 1996.

Katzenstein, Peter J. *Cultural Norms and National Security: Police and Military in Post-War Japan*. Ithaca, NY, Cornell University Press 1996.

– "Tamed Power: United Germany in an Integrating Europe." Paper Presented at American Political Science Association Conference, San Francisco, 29 Aug.–1 Sept., 1996.

Katzenstein, Peter J., and Okawara, Nobuo. "Japan's National Security: Structures, Norms and Policies." *International Security* 17, no. 4 (1993): 84–119.

Katzenstein, Peter J., ed. *The Culture of National Security: Norms and Identity in World Politics*. New York: Columbia University Press 1996.

Katzman, Martin. "Translating Brazil's Economic Potential International Influence." In Wayne A. Selcher, ed., *Brazil in the International System: The Rise of a Middle Power*, 99–122. Boulder, Col.: Westview Press 1986.

Kaufman, Robert G. "E.H. Carr, Winston Churchill, Reinhold Niebuhr, and Us: The Case for Principled, Prudential, Democratic Realism." *Security Studies* 5, no. 2 (1995): 314–53.

Keating, Tom. *Canada and World Order: The Multilateralist Tradition in Canadian Foreign Policy*. Toronto: McClelland and Stewart 1993.

Kelleher, Catherine M. *Germany and the Politics of Nuclear Weapons*. New York: Columbia University Press 1975.

– "The Issue of German Nuclear Armament." *Proceedings of the Academy of Political Science* 29, no. 2 (1968): 95–107.

– "The New Germany: An Overview." In Paul B. Stares, ed., *The New Germany and the New Europe*, 11–54. Washington, DC: Brookings Institution 1992.

Kendell, Joseph P. Jr. *The Politics of Defense in Japan: Managing Internal and External Pressures*. Armonk, NY: M.E. Sharpe 1993.

Keohane, Robert O. *After Hegemony: Cooperation and Discord in the World Political Economy*. Princeton, NJ: Princeton University Press 1984.

Keohane, Robert O., ed., *Neorealism and Its Critics*. New York: Columbia University Press 1986.

Keohane, Robert O., and Nye, Joseph S. *Power and Interdependence*. 2nd ed. New York: Harper Collins 1989.

Khalilzad, Zalmay. "Pakistan and the Bomb." *Survival* 21, no. 6 (1979): 244–50.

Khan, Saira. "Nuclear Proliferation in Protracted Conflict Regions: A Comparative Study of South Asia and the Middle East." PhD dissertation. McGill University, April 1999.

Kim, Taehyun. "South Korean Perspectives on the North Korean Nuclear Question." *Mershon International Studies Review* 40, no. 2 (1996): 255–61.

Kim, Taewoo. "Japanese Ambitions, U.S. Constraints, and South Korea's Nuclear Future." In Selig Harrison, ed., *Japan's Nuclear Future: The Plutonium Debate and East Asian Security*, 87–109. Washington, DC: Carnegie Endowment for International Peace 1996.

– "South Korea's Nuclear Dilemmas." *Korea and World Affairs* 16 (summer 1992): 250–93.

Kishida, Junnosuke. "Japan's Non-Nuclear Policy." *Survival* 15, no. 1 (1973): 15–20.

Kitamura, Motoya. "Japan's Plutonium Program: A Proliferation Threat?" *Nonproliferation Review* 3, no. 2 (1996): 1–15.

Knopf, Jeffrey W. *Domestic Society and International Cooperation: The Impact of Protest on US Arms Control Policy.* Cambridge: Cambridge University Press 1998.

Knorr, Klaus. *Military Power and Potential.* Lexington, Ky.: D.C. Heath, 1970.

Kohli, Atul, et al. "The Role of Theory in Comparative Politics: A Symposium." *World Politics* 48, no. 1 (1995): 1–49.

Krasner, Stephen, ed. *International Regimes.* Ithaca, NY: Cornell University Press 1983.

Kratochwil, Friedrich V. *Rules, Norms, and Decisions.* Cambridge: Cambridge University Press 1989.

Kristof, Nicholas D. "The Rise of China." *Foreign Affairs* 72, no. 5 (1993): 59–74.

Kruzel, Joseph. "Sweden's Security Dilemma: Balancing Domestic Realities with Obligations of Neutrality." In Bengt Sundelius, ed., *The Committed Neutral: Swedish Foreign Policy,* 67–93. Boulder, Col.: Westview, 1989.

Kuntzel, Mathias. *Bonn and the Bomb: German Politics and the Nuclear Option.* London: Pluto Press 1995.

Labs, Eric J. "Beyond Victory: Offensive Realism and Its Expansion of War Aims." *Security Studies* 6, no. 4 (1997): 1–49.

Lake, David A. "Regional Security Complexes: A Systems Approach." In Lake and Patrick Morgan, eds., *Regional Orders: Building Security in a New World,* 45–67. University Park, Penn.: Pennsylvania State University Press 1997.

Lake, David, and Morgan, Patrick. "The New Regionalism in Security Affairs." In Lake and Morgan, eds., *Regional Orders: Building Security in a New World,* 3–19. University Park, Penn.: Pennsylvania State University Press 1997.

Langdon, Frank. "The Security Debate in Japan." *Pacific Affairs* 58, no. 3 (1985): 397–410.

Langille, Howard Peter. *Changing the Guard: Canada's Defence in a World in Transition.* Toronto: University of Toronto Press 1990.

Lanteigne, Marc "Shadow Dancing: Seeking Cooperation on the North Korean Problem." *Pacific Focus* 14, no. 1 (1999): 49–77.

Lavoy, Peter R. "Nuclear Myths and the Causes of Nuclear Proliferation." *Security Studies* 2, no. 3/4 (1993): 192–212.

Layne, Christopher. "The Unipolar Illusion: Why New Great Powers Will Arise." *International Security* 17, no. 4 (1993): 5–51.

Leaver, Richard. "Hayden's 'Mailed Fist': What Was His Real Concern?" *Current Affairs Bulletin* 72, no. 6 (1996): 40–3.

Lee, Seo-Hang. "Nuclear Proliferation in Northeast Asia: A South Korean Perspective." Paper Presented at the UNIDIR Conference on Nuclear Policies in Northeast Asia, Seoul, 25–7 May 1994.

Lefever, Ernest W. *Nuclear Arms in the Third World: U.S. Policy Dilemma.* Washington, DC: Brookings Institution 1979.

Legault, Albert, and Fortmann, Michel. *A Diplomacy of Hope: Canada and Disarmament, 1945–1988.* Montreal: McGill-Queen's University Press 1992.

Le Gloannec, Anne-Marie. "The Implications of German Unification for Western Europe." In Paul B. Stares, ed., *The New Germany and the New Europe*, 251–78. Washington, DC: Brookings Institution 1992.

Legro, Jeffrey. *Cooperation under Fire.* Ithaca, NY: Cornell University Press 1995.

Lentner, Howard H. "Foreign Policy Decision Making: The Case of Canada and Nuclear Weapons." *World Politics* 29, no. 1 (1976): 29–66.

Levy, Jack S. "Learning and Foreign Policy: Sweeping a Conceptual Minefield." *International Organization* 48, no. 2 (1994): 279–312.

Linnenkamp, Hilmar. "The Security Policy of the New Germany." In Paul B. Stares, ed., *The New Germany and the New Europe*, 93–125. Washington, DC: Brookings Institution 1992.

Logue, John. "The Legacy of Swedish Neutrality." In Bengt Sundelus, ed., *The Committed Neutral: Swedish Foreign Policy*, 35–65. Boulder, Col.: Westview Press 1989.

– "Sweden." In S. Victor Papacosma and Mark R. Rubin, eds., *Europe's Neutral and Non-aligned States*, 71–102. Wilmington, Del.: Scholarly Resources 1989.

Lynn-Jones, Sean M. "Offense–Defense Theory and Its Critics." *Security Studies* 4, no. 4 (1995): 660–91.

McLin, Jon B. *Canada's Changing Defense Policy, 1957–1963: The Problems of a Middle Power in Alliance.* Baltimore: Johns Hopkins University Press 1967.

Malcolmson, Robert W. *Beyond Nuclear Thinking.* Montreal: McGill-Queen's University Press 1990.

Malik, Brigadier S.K. *The Quranic Concept of War.* Lahore: Wajidalis 1979.

Mandelbaum, Michael. *The Nuclear Future.* Ithaca, NY: Cornell University Press 1983.

Martel, William C. "Why Ukraine Gave up Nuclear Weapons: Non-Proliferation Incentives and Disincentives." In Barry R. Schneider and William L. Dowdy, eds., *Pulling Back from the Nuclear Brink*, 88–104. London: Frank Cass 1998.

Martin, Lisa. "International Institutions and State Strategies." In T.V. Paul and John A. Hall, eds., *International Order and the Future of World Politics*, 78–98. Cambridge: Cambridge University Press 1999.

Mastanduno, Michael. "A Realist View: Three Images of the Coming International Order." In T.V. Paul and John A. Hall, eds., *International Order and the Future of World Politics*, 19–40. Cambridge: Cambridge University Press 1999.

Mattoo, Amitabh. "India's Nuclear Status Quo." *Survival* 38, no. 3 (1996): 41–57.

Mattox, Gale A. "West German Perspectives on Nuclear Armament and Arms Control." *Annals of the American Academy of Political and Social Sciences* no. 469 (1983): 104–16.

Mazarr, Michael J. *North Korea and the Bomb*. Houndmills, England: Macmillan 1995.

Mearsheimer, John J. "Back to the Future: Instability in Europe after the Cold War." *International Security* 15, no. 1 (1990): 5–54.

– "The Case for a Ukrainian Nuclear Deterrent." *Foreign Affairs* 72, no. 3 (1993): 50–66.

Mendershausen, Horst. "Will West Germany Go Nuclear?" *Orbis* 16, no. 2 (1972): 411–34.

Meyer, Stephen M. *The Dynamics of Nuclear Proliferation*. Chicago: University of Chicago Press 1984.

Michel, Nicholas. *La prolifération nucléaire*. Fribourge: Éditions Universitaires 1990.

Middlemiss, D.W., and Sokolsky, J.J. *Canadian Defence: Decisions and Determinants*. Toronto: Harcourt, Brace. Jovanovitch 1989.

Milenky, Edward S. "Argentina." In Edward Kolodziej and Robert Harkavy, eds., *Security Policies of Developing Countries*, 27–51. Lexington, Mass.: Lexington Books 1982.

– "Arms Production and National Security in Argentina." *Journal of Interamerican Studies and World Affairs* 22, no. 3 (1980): 267–88.

Milivojevic, Marko. "The Swiss Armed Forces." In Marko Milivojevic and Pierre Maurer, eds., *Swiss Neutrality and Security*, 3–48. New York: Berg 1990.

Miller, Marvin M. "Israel." In Eric Arnett, ed., *Nuclear Weapons after the Comprehensive Test Ban*, 62–7. Oxford: Oxford University Press 1996.

Miller, Steven E. "The Case against a Ukrainian Nuclear Deterrent." *Foreign Affairs* 72, no. 3 (1993): 67–80.

Milner, Helen. "The Assumption of Anarchy in International Relations Theory." *Review of International Studies* 17, no. 1 (1991): 67–85.

Mlyn, Eric. *The State, Society, and Limited Nuclear War*. Albany: SUNY Press 1995.

Mochizyki, Mike. "Japan's Search for Strategy." *International Security* 8, no. 3 (1983–84): 152–79.

Moltz, James Clay. "Missile Proliferation in East Asia: Arms Control vs. TMD Responses." *Nonproliferation Review* 4, no. 3 (1997): 63–71.

Morgenthau, Hans J. *Politics among Nations* 4th ed. New York: Alfred A. Knopf 1967.

Moshaver, Ziba. *Nuclear Weapons Proliferation in the Indian Subcontinent.* Houndsmills, England: Macmillan 1991.

Mouritzen, Hans. "The Nordic Model as a Foreign Policy Instrument: Its Rise and Fall." *Journal of Peace Research* 32, no. 1 (1995): 9–21.

Mueller, John E. "The Escalating Irrelevance of Nuclear Weapons." In T.V. Paul, Richard J. Harknett, and James J. Wirtz, eds., *The Absolute Weapon Revisited: Nuclear Arms and the International Order,* 73–98. Ann Arbor: University of Michigan Press 1998.

– "Incentives for Restraint: Canada as a Nonnuclear Power." *Orbis* 11, no. 3 (1967): 864–84.

Mueller, Karl. "Strategy, Asymmetric Deterrence, and Accommodation." PhD dissertation, Princeton University, 1991.

Muller, Harald. "The Role of Hegemonies and Alliances." In Regina Cowen Karp, ed., *Security without Nuclear Weapons? Different Perspectives on Nuclear Security,* 226–49. Oxford: Oxford University Press 1992.

Muller, Marie. "South Africa Crisscrosses the Nuclear Threshold." In W. Gutteridge, ed., *South Africa's Defense and Security into the 21st Century,* 29–48. Aldershot: Dartmouth 1996.

Mumenthaler, Hans. "Civil Defense: Means for Disaster Relief." In Marko Milivojevic and Pierre Maurer, eds., *Swiss Neutrality and Security,* 49–64. New York: Berg, 1990.

Munro, J.A. and Inglis, A.I. "The Atomic Conference 1945 and the Pearson Memoirs." *International Journal* 29, no. 1 (1973–74): 90–109.

Munton, Don. "Going Fission: Tales and Truths about Canada's Nuclear Weapons." *International Journal* 51, no. 3 (1996): 506–28.

Murata, Kiyoaki. "Japan and Nuclear Non-Proliferation." *Survival* 9, no. 8 (1967): 267–68.

Myers, David J. "Brazil." In Eduard Kolodzjiej and Robert Harkavy, eds., *Security Policies of Developing Countries,* 53–72. Lexington, Ky.: Lexington Books 1982.

– "Brazil: Reluctant Pursuit of the Nuclear Option." *Orbis* 27, no. 4 (1984): 881–911.

Nakamura, Hisashi, and Dando Malcolm. "Japan's Military Research and Development: A High Technology Deterrent." *Pacific Review* 6, no. 2 (1993): 177–90.

Narayanan, R. "Brazil's Policy towards Nuclear Disarmament." *Institute for Defence Studies and Analysis Journal* 3, no. 2 (1970): 178–91.

NATO *Facts and Figures.* Brussels: NATO Information Service 1969.

Nayar, Baldev Raj. "India as a Limited Challenger." In T.V. Paul and John A. Hall, eds., *International Order and the Future of World Politics,* 213–33. Cambridge: Cambridge University Press 1999.

– "International Regimes, Power and International Aviation." *International Organization* 49, no. 1 (1995): 139–70.

Nye, Joseph S. *Bound to Lead: The Changing Nature of American Power.* New York: Basic Books 1990.

– "Nuclear Learning and U.S.–Soviet Security Regimes." *International Organization* 41, no. 3 (1987): 371–402.

Okimoto, Daniel I. "Japan's Non-Nuclear Policy: The Problem of the NPT." *Asian Survey* 15, no. 4 (1974): 313–27.

– "Peace and Security in Statistics." *Japan Quarterly* 29, no. 2 (1982): 197–9.

Okita, Saburo. "Natural Resource Dependency and Japanese Foreign Policy." *Foreign Affairs* 52, no. 4 (1974): 714–24.

Olson, Mancur, and Zeckhauser, Richard. "An Economic Theory of Alliances." *Review of Economics and Statistics* 48 (Aug. 1966): 266–79.

Overholt, William H. "Nuclear Proliferation in Eastern Asia." In Overholt, ed., *Asia's Nuclear Future*, 133–59. Boulder, Col.: Westview Press 1977.

Pande, Savita. "Pakistan's Nuclear Strategy." In *Asian Strategic Review, 1993–1994*, 324–47. New Delhi: Institute for Defence Studies and Analysis 1994.

Park, Tong Whan. "South Korea's Nuclear Option: The Interplay of Domestic and International Politics." In Tong Whan Park, ed., *The U.S. and the Two Koreas: A New Triangle*, 97–117. Boulder, Col.: Lynne Reinner 1998.

Passin, Herbert. "Nuclear Arms and Japan." In William Overholt, ed., *Asia's Nuclear Future*, 67–131. Boulder, Col.: Westview Press 1977.

Paul, T.V. *Asymmetric Conflicts: War Initiation by Weaker Powers.* Cambridge: Cambridge University Press 1994.

– "Great Equalizers or Agents of Chaos? Weapons of Mass Destruction and the Emerging International Order." In T.V. Paul and John A. Hall, eds., *International Order and the Future of World Politics*, 373–91. Cambridge: Cambridge University Press 1999.

– "Influence through Arms Transfers: The U.S.–Pakistani Relationship." *Asian Survey* 32, no. 12 (1992): 1078–92.

– "The NPT and Power Transitions in the International System." In Raju G.C. Thomas, ed., *The Nuclear Non-Proliferation Regime: Prospects for the 21st Century*, 56–74. Houndmills, England: Macmillan 1998.

– "Nuclear-Free zone in the South Pacific: Rhetoric or Reality?" *Round Table* no. 299 (July 1986): 252–62.

– "Nuclear Taboo and War Initiation in Regional Conflicts." *Journal of Conflict Resolution* 39, no. 4 (1995): 696–717.

– "The Politics of Unilateral Nuclear-Free Zones: The Case of the South Pacific." In Bennett Ramberg, ed., *Arms Control without Negotiation*, 159–74. Boulder, Col.: Lynne Rienner 1993.

– "Power, Influence and Nuclear Weapons: A Reassessment." In T.V. Paul, Richard J. Harknett, and James J. Wirtz, eds., *The Absolute Weapon Revisited: Nuclear Arms and the International Order*, 19–46. Ann Arbor: University of Michigan Press 1998.

– "Strengthening the Nonproliferation Regime: The Role of Coercive Sanctions." *International Journal* 51, no. 3 (1996): 440–65.

– The Systemic Bases of India's Challenge to the Global Nuclear Order." *Nonproliferation Review* 6, no. 1 (1998): 1–11.

Pellaud, Bruno. *Geschichte der Kerntechnik in der Schweiz.* Zurich: Olynthvs 1992.

Pempel, T.J. "Japan's Nuclear Allergy." *Current History* 68, no. 404 (1975): 169–73.

– "Unsteady Anticipation: Reflections on the Future of Japan's Changing Political Economy." In T.V. Paul and John A. Hall, eds., *International Order and the Future of World Politics*, 178–96. Cambridge: Cambridge University Press, 1999.

Perekovich, George. *India's Nuclear Bomb: Exploding Illusions of the Nuclear Age, 1948–1998.* Berkeley: University of California Press 1999.

Perruci, Gamaliel. "Latin America and International Security in the Post Cold War Order." *Security Dialogue* 25, no. 2 (1994): 199–209.

Poneman, Daniel. "Nuclear Proliferation: Prospects for Argentina." *Orbis* 27, no. 4 (1984): 853–80.

Potter, William C. *Nuclear Power and Non-proliferation: An Interdisciplinary Perspective.* Cambridge, Mass.: Oelgeschlager, Gunn and Hain Publishers 1982.

– "The Politics of Nuclear Renunciation: The Cases of Belarus, Kazakhstan, and Ukraine." Occasional Paper No. 22, The Henry L. Stimson Center, Washington, DC, April 1995.

Poulose, T.T. "India's Deterrence Dilemma." *Hindustan Times*, 23 Oct. 1997.

– "India's Deterrence Doctrine: A Nehruvian Critique." *Nonproliferation Review* 6, no. 1 (1998): 77–84.

– *Nuclear Proliferation and the Third World.* New Delhi: ABC Publishing House 1982.

Poulose, T.T., ed. *Perspectives of India's Nuclear Policy.* New Delhi: Young Asia 1978.

Powell, Robert. *Nuclear Deterrence Theory: The Search for Credibility.* Cambridge: Cambridge University Press 1990.

Prawitz, Jan. "Sweden – A Non-Nuclear Weapon State." In Johan Jørgen Holst, ed., *Security, Order and the Bomb*, 61–71. Oslo: Universitetsforlaget 1972.

– "Why Sweden Ended Pursuit of Nuclear Weapons?" In Kathleen C. Bailey, ed., *Weapons of Mass Destruction: Costs Versus Benefits*, 45–62. New Delhi: Manohar Publishers 1994.

Price, Richard. "A Genealogy of the Chemical Weapons Taboo." *International Organization* 49, no. 1 (1995): 73–103.

Pry, Peter. *Israel's Nuclear Arsenal.* Boulder, Col.: Westview Press 1984.

Public Papers of the Presidents of the United States: Dwight D. Eisenhower, 1953. Washington, DC: United States Government Printing Office 1960.

Public Papers of the Presidents of the United States: John F. Kennedy, 1963. Washington, DC: United States Government Printing Office 1964.

Pugh, Michael C. *The ANZUS Crisis: Nuclear Visiting and Deterrence.* Cambridge: Cambridge University Press 1989.

Pyle, Kenneth B. *The Japanese Question: Power and Purpose in a New Era.* Washington, DC: AEI Press 1992.

Quester, George H. "Japan and the Nuclear Non-Proliferation Treaty." *Asian Survey* 10, no. 9 (1970): 765–78.

– "Sweden and the Nuclear Non-Proliferation Treaty." *Cooperation and Conflict* 5, no. 1 (1970): 52–64.

Rajamohan, C., and Lavoy, Peter R. "Avoiding Nuclear War." In Michael Krepon and Amit Serak, eds., *Crisis Prevention, Confidence Building and Reconciliation in South Asia,* 25–52. New York: St Martin's Press 1995.

Rauf, Tariq, and Johnson, Rebecca. "After the NPT's Indefinite Extension: The Future of the Global Nonproliferation Regime." *Nonproliferation Review* 3, no. 1 (1995): 28–41.

Redick, John. "Regional Restraint: U.S. Nuclear Policy and Latin America." *Orbis* 22, no. 1 (1978): 161–201.

Redick, John R., Carasales, Julio C., and Wrobel, Paulo S. "Nuclear Rapprochement: Argentina, Brazil, and the Non-Proliferation Regime." *Washington Quarterly* 18, no. 1 (1994): 107–22.

Regehr, Ernie. "Canada and the U.S. Nuclear Arsenal." In Ernie Regehr and Simon Rosenblum, eds., *Canada and the Nuclear Arms Race,* 101–21. Toronto: James Lorimer 1983.

Reiss, Mitchell. *Bridled Ambition.* Washington, DC: Woodrow Wilson Center Press 1995.

– *Without the Bomb: The Politics of Nuclear Nonproliferation.* New York: Columbia University Press 1988.

Reynolds, Wayne. "Rethinking the Joint Project: Australia's Bid for Nuclear Weapons 1945–1960." *Historical Journal.* 41, no. 3 (1998): 853–73.

Richter, Andrew. "Canadian Defence Policy in a Changing Global Environment, 1945–1952." Paper Presented at the Canadian Political Science Association Annual Conference, Montreal, 4–6 June 1995.

Risse-Kappen, Thomas. "Deja vu: Deployment of Nuclear Weapons in West Germany: Historical Controversies." *Bulletin of Peace Proposals* 14, no. 4 (1983): 327–56.

Roberts, Adam. *Nations in Arms: Theory and Practice of Territorial Defence.* New York: Praeger 1976.

Rose, Gideon. "Neoclassical Realism and Theories of Foreign Policy." *World Politics* 51, no. 1 (1998): 144–72.

Rosecrance, Richard. "International Theory Revisited." *International Organization* 35, no. 4 (1981): 691–713.

– *The Rise of the Trading State: Commerce and Conquest in the Modern World.* New York: Basic Books 1986.

Rosen, Stephen J. "A Stable System of Mutual Nuclear Deterrence in the Arab–Israeli Conflict." *American Political Science Review* 71, no. 4 (1977): 1367–83.

Rosenau, James. "A Desirable but Improbable Future for IR Theory." In Steve Smith and Marysia Zalewski, eds., *International Theory: Positivism and Beyond*, 309–17. Cambridge: Cambridge University Press 1996.

Rosenbaum, H. Jon, and Cooper, Glen A. "Brazil and the Nuclear Non-Proliferation Treaty." *International Affairs*. 46, no. 1 (1970): 74–90.

Ross, Douglas A. "Arms Control and Disarmament and the Canadian Approach to Global Order." In David B. Dewitt and David Leyton-Brown, eds., *Canada's International Security Policy*, 251–86. Scarborough, Ont.: Prentice Hall 1995.

Roy, A. Bikash. "Intervention across Bisecting Borders." *Journal of Peace Research* 34, no. 3 (1997): 303–14.

Ruggie, John G. "International Responses to Technology: Concepts and Trends." *International Organization* 29, no. 3 (1975): 557–83.

Sabia, Daniel R. "Prudence." American Political Science Association Convention Paper, Washington, DC, Aug. 1997.

Sagan, Scott D. "Why Do States Build Nuclear Weapons? Three Models in Search of a Bomb." *International Security* 21, no. 3 (1996–97): 54–86.

Sahr, Robert C. *The Politics of Energy Policy Change in Sweden*. Ann Arbor: University of Michigan Press 1985.

Sakanaka, Tomohisa. "Defects in Japan's Defense Policy." *Japan Echo* 5, no. 4 (1978): 49–59.

Saleem, Lieutenant-Colonel Muhammad Ashraf. "Nuclear Deterrence: A Subcontinental Logic." *Defence Journal* 19, no. 11–12 (1993): 23–8.

Samuels, Richard J. *"Rich Nation, Strong Army": National Security and Technological Transformation of Japan*. Ithaca, NY: Cornell University Press 1994.

Sanchez-Gijon, Antonio. "Argentina." In Harald Mueller, ed., *A European Non-Proliferation Policy: Prospects and Problems*, 367–99. Oxford: Clarendon Press 1987.

Sato, Seizaburo. "Reassessing Japan's International Role." *Korea Herald*, 17 Sept. 1996, 6.

Schelling, Thomas C. "The Role of Nuclear Weapons." In L.B. Ederington and M.J. Mazarr, eds., *Turning Point: The Gulf War and U.S. Military Strategy*, 105–15. Boulder, Col.: Westview Press 1994.

– *The Strategy of Conflict*. 2nd ed. Cambridge, Mass.: Harvard University Press 1980.

Schmidt, Helmut. *Deterrence or Retaliation*. Edinburgh: Oliver and Boyd 1962.

– *A Grand Strategy for the West*. New Haven, Conn.: Yale University Press 1985.

Schneider, Ronald M. *Brazil: Foreign Policy of a Future World Power*. Boulder, Col.: Westview Press 1976.

Schwab, George. "Switzerland's Tactical Nuclear Weapons Policy." *Orbis* 13, no. 3 (1969): 900–14.

Schwartz, David N. *NATO's Nuclear Dilemmas*. Washington, DC: Brookings Institution 1983.

Selcher, Wayne A. "Brazilian–Argentine Relations in the 1980s: From Wary Rivalry to Friendly Competition." *Journal of Interamerican Studies and World Affairs* 27, no. 2 (1985): 25–53.

Seng, Jordan. "Less Is More: Command and Control Advantages of Minor Nuclear States." *Security Studies* 6, no. 4 (1997): 50–92.

Sharp, Gene. *Making Europe Unconquerable: The Potential of Civilian-Based Deterrence and Defense*. London: Taylor and Francis 1985.

Sherr, James. "Russia–Ukraine Rapprochement?: The Black Sea Fleet Accords." *Survival* 39, no. 3 (1997): 33–50.

Sidhu, Waheguru Pal Singh. "Enhancing Indo-US Strategic Cooperation." Adelphi Paper No. 313. London: International Institute of Strategic Studies 1997.

Sisk, Timothy D. *Democratization in South Africa: The Elusive Social Contract*. Princeton, NJ: Princeton University Press 1995.

Smith, Charles. "Japan: Unclear Signals: Nuclear Weapons' Policy Shrouded in Ambiguities." *Far Eastern Economic Review* 156, no. 30 (1993): 24.

Snyder, Craig A. "Australia's Pursuit of Regional Security into the 21st Century." *Journal of Strategic Studies* 21, no. 4 (1998): 1–17.

Snyder, Glenn H. "The Security Dilemma in Alliance Politics." *World Politics* 36, no .4 (1984): 461–95.

Snyder, Jack. *Myths of Empire: Domestic Politics and International Ambition*. Ithaca, NY: Cornell University Press 1984.

Sole, Donald B. "South Africa and the Non-Proliferation Treaty." *American Review* 13 (1993): 2–7.

Solingen, Etel. "The Domestic Sources of Nuclear Postures." Policy Paper No. 8. San Diego: Institute on Global Conflict and Cooperation 1994.

– "Macropolitical Consensus and Lateral Autonomy in Industrial Policy: The Nuclear Sector in Brazil and Argentina." *International Organization* 47, no. 2 (1993): 263–98.

– "The Political Economy of Nuclear Restraint." *International Security* 19, no. 2 (1994): 126–69.

Spector, Leonard S. *Nuclear Ambitions*. Boulder, Col.: Westview Press 1990.

Speier, Hans. *German Rearmament and Atomic War: The Views of German Military and Political Leaders*. Evanston, Ill.: Row, Peterson and Company 1957.

Stein, Arthur. *Why Nations Cooperate: Circumstance and Choice in International Relations*. Ithaca, NY: Cornell University Press 1990.

Steinberg, Gerald M. "The Future of Nuclear Weapons: Israeli Perspectives." Paper Presented at the Ninth Amaldi Conference, Geneva, 21–23 Nov. 1996.

Strange, Susan. "Cave! hic dragones: A Critique of Regime Analysis." In Stephen Krasner, ed., *International Regimes*, 337–54. Ithaca, NY: Cornell University Press 1983.

Stumpf, Waldo. "South Africa's Nuclear Weapons Programme." In Kathleen C. Bailey, ed., *Weapons of Mass Destruction: Costs Versus Benefits*, 63–81. New Delhi: Manohar Publishers 1994.

Subrahmanyam, K. *India and the Nuclear Challenge*. New Delhi: Lancer 1986.

– "India's Nuclear Policy – 1964–98: A Personal Recollection." In Jasjit Singh, ed., *Nuclear India*, 26–53. New Delhi: Institute for Defence Studies and Analysis 1998.

– "Nuclear Force Design and Minimum Deterrence Strategy for India." In Bharat Karnad, ed., *Future Imperiled: India's Security in the 1990s and Beyond*, 176–95. New Delhi: Viking 1994.

Sundarji, General K. "India's Weapons Policy." In Jørn Gjelstad and Olav Njølstad, eds., *Nuclear Rivalry and International Order*, 173–95. London: Sage Publications 1996.

Tannenwald, Nina. "The Nuclear Taboo." *International Organization* 53, no. 3 (1999): 433–68.

Tanner, Fred. "Switzerland and Arms Control: Constraints and Opportunities." In Marko Milivojevic and Pierre Maurer, eds., *Swiss Neutrality and Security*, 137–61. New York: Berg 1990.

Thayer, Bradley A. "The Causes of Nuclear Proliferation and the Utility of the Non-Proliferation Regime." In Raju G.C. Thomas, ed., *The Nuclear Non-Proliferation Regime: Prospects for the 21st Century*, 75–129. Houndsmills, England: Macmillan 1998.

Thomas, Raju G.C., ed. *Perspectives on Kashmir: The Roots of Conflict in South Asia*. Boulder, Col.: Westview Press 1992.

Thompson, William R. "The Regional Subsystem: A Conceptual Explication and a Propositional Inventory." *International Studies Quarterly* 17, no. 1 (1973): 89–117.

Thordarson, Bruce. *Trudeau and Foreign Policy: A Study in Decision-Making*. Toronto: Oxford University Press 1972.

Thunborg, Anders. *Evolution of Doctrines and Economics of Defense*. Oskarshamn: Swedish Institute AB Primo, 1973.

Treverton, Gregory F. *America, Germany, and the Future of Europe*. Princeton, NJ: Princeton University Press 1992.

Tucker, Michael. *Canadian Foreign Policy: Contemporary Issues and Themes*. Toronto: McGraw Hill Ryerson 1980.

Ulam, Adam. *Expansion and Coexistence: The History of the Soviet Foreign Policy*. New York: Praeger 1974.

Ullman, Richard H. *Securing Europe*. Princeton, NJ: Princeton University Press 1991.

Vasquez, John. *The War Puzzle*. Cambridge: Cambridge University Press 1993.

Wakaizumi, Kei. "The Problem of Japan." In Alastair Buchan, ed., *A World of Nuclear Powers?* 76–87. Englewood Cliffs, NJ: Prentice-Hall 1966.

Walker, William. "India's Nuclear Labyrinth." *Nonproliferation Review* 4, no. 1 (1996): 61–77.

Wallin, Lars B. "Sweden." In Richard Bissel and Curt Gasteygar, eds., *The Missing Link*, 9–41. Durham, NC: Duke University Press 1990.

– "Sweden." In Regina Cowen Karp, eds., *Security with Nuclear Weapons? Different Perspectives on National Security*, 360–81. Oxford: Oxford University Press, 1991.

Walsh, Jim. "Surprise Down Under: The Secret History of Australia's Nuclear Ambitions." *Nonproliferation Review* 5, no. 1 (1997): 1–20.

Walt, Stephen M. *The Origins of Alliances*. Ithaca, NY: Cornell University Press 1987.

Waltz, Kenneth. "The Emerging Structure of International Politics." *International Security* 8, no. 2 (1993): 44–79.

– "More May be Better." In Scott D. Sagan and Waltz, eds., *The Spread of Nuclear Weapons: A Debate*, 1–46. New York: W.W. Norton 1995.

– *Theory of International Politics*. New York: Random House 1979.

Warnock, John W. *Partner to Behemoth*. Toronto: New Press. 1970.

Weinstein, Franklin B., and Momoi, Makoton, et al. "The Nuclear Dimension." In Weinstein and Fuji Kamiya, eds., *The Security of Korea*, 107–49. Boulder, Col.: Westview Press 1980.

Weissman, Steve, and Krosney, Herbert. *The Islamic Bomb: The Nuclear Threat to Israel and the Middle East*. New York: Times Books 1981.

Wendt, Alexander. "Anarchy Is What States Make of it: The Social Construction of Power Politics." *International Organization* 46, no. 2 (1994): 391–425.

Winkler, Theodor. *Kernenergy and Aussenpolitik* (Nuclear Energy and Foreign Policy). Berlin: Berlin Verlag 1987.

Wirtz, James J. "Beyond Bipolarity: Prospects for Nuclear Stability after the Cold War." In T.V. Paul, Richard J. Harknett, and Wirtz, eds., *The Absolute Weapon Revisited: Nuclear Arms and the Emerging International Order*, 137–65. Ann Arbor: University of Michigan Press 1998.

Wonder, Edward. "Nuclear Commerce and Nuclear Proliferation: Germany and Brazil, 1975." *Orbis* 21, no. 2 (1977): 277–307.

Yamamoto, Atsumasa. "Japan's Future Defense Capability." IIPS Policy Paper No. 126E, Institute of International Policy Studies, Tokyo, June 1994.

Yatsuhiro, Nakagawa. "Why Japan Should Let Nuclear Arms In." *Japan Echo* 7, no. 4 (1980): 99–110.

Yeager, Joseph A. "Japan." In Joseph Yaeager, ed., *Non-Proliferation and U.S. Foreign Policy*, 9–46. Washington, DC: Brookings Institution 1980.

Yost, David. "The U.S. and Nuclear Deterrence in Europe." Adelphi Paper, no. 326, 1999.

Young, Oran. "The Effectiveness of International Institutions: Hard Cases and Critical Variables." In James N. Rosenau and Ernst-Otto Czempel, eds., *Governance without Government*, 160–94. Cambridge: Cambridge University Press 1992.

Zacher, Mark W., and Sutton, Brent A. *Governing Global Networks*. Cambridge: Cambridge University Press 1996.

Zakaria, Fareed. "Realism and Domestic Politics." *International Security* 17, no. 1 (1992): 177–98.

Zumstein, Jorg. "Swiss Security Policy and National Defence." In Bo Huldt and Alis Lejins, eds., *Neutrals in Europe: Switzerland*, 31–7. Stockholm: Swedish Institute of International Affairs 1988.

Index